Lord (Peter) Temple-Morris is a Labour peer. He was elected as the Conservative MP for Leominster in 1974 and sat as a Conservative MP until 1998 when he crossed the floor. He served on numerous Foreign Affairs Committees and was one of the main creators and first British co-chairman of the British–Irish Inter-Parliamentary Body which supplied the Parliamentary input into the Northern Ireland peace process. He remained an MP until 2001. Educated at Malvern and St Catharine's College, Cambridge, he was part of the so-called 'Cambridge Mafia' and was Chairman of the Cambridge University Conservative Association in 1961. He was a practising barrister and, from 1989, a solicitor. He is married to Taheré, née Khozeimeh Alam, who was born in Iran. They have four grown-up children and five grandchildren.

'Peter Temple-Morris has produced a brilliant political memoir, which is insightful, informative and eminently readable. Peter's career is significant not just in British politics, but also in Ireland. He was a key player in the work to deliver a lasting peace in Northern Ireland. This book gives a gripping account of the huge effort of democratic politicians of every persuasion in Ireland and Britain to consign the violence that inflicted so much misery on Northern Ireland to the dustbin of history. Peter was an insider in the Irish peace process and he played an honourable and brave role in ensuring the triumph of constitutional politics over violence. Anyone with an interest in the work of reconciliation, peace-building and conflict resolution should read this book.'

– Bertie Ahern, Irish Prime Minister 1997–2008

'A candid, thoughtful reflection of his own personal journey set against a backdrop of major world events and players. His principled and brave decision to join Labour, his tireless commitment to achieving peace for the people of Northern Ireland, and his genuinely internationalist out-look make this a thoroughly engaging and absorbing memoir.'

– Tony Blair, British Prime Minister 1997–2007

'A frank and very personal account of a political defection. A fascinating procession of politicians move across the pages. Overseas there is a par-ticularly strong account of Iran under and after the Shah. A very good read – just a pity we Tories let him get away.'

– Norman (Lord) Fowler

'*Across the Floor* is the well-written memoir of a committed one nation politician who has been both a Tory and then a Labour MP and peer. His fascinating account of his defection from Conservative to Labour is required reading for anyone thinking of crossing the floor. A convinced internationalist he paints colourful pen portraits of key figures in the Irish peace process, gives a dramatic personal account of the Iranian Revolution, and describes how he hosted Gorbachev's crucial visit to Britain in 1984. I highly recommend this book.'

– Giles (Lord) Radice

ACROSS THE FLOOR

A LIFE IN DISSENTING POLITICS

PETER TEMPLE-MORRIS

I.B. TAURIS
LONDON · NEW YORK

Published in 2015 by I.B. Tauris & Co. Ltd
London • New York
www.ibtauris.com

ISBN: 978 1 78453 450 9
eISBN: 978 0 85773 979 7

A full CIP record for this book is available from the British Library
A full CIP record is available from the Library of Congress

Library of Congress Catalog Card Number: available

Typeset by Out of House Publishing
Printed and bound by CPI Group (UK) Ltd, Croydon, CR0 4YY

MIX
Paper from
responsible sources
FSC   FSC® C013604
www.fsc.org

Harold Macmillan was often asked what was the most difficult thing about being prime minister. His reply is often quoted and attributed to various occasions. The author first heard it from Harold Macmillan himself at a reception held for him by the Cambridge University Conservative Association at Trinity Hall, Cambridge, in November 1960. It was in answer to a question from Nick Budgen, put in an ordinary conversation with a small group: 'Events, dear boy, events', came the famous reply.

This book is dedicated to my dear wife, Taheré, her parents, Amir Hussein and Fatemeh, and her brothers, Amir Parviz and Amir Dariouch, and sister, Ziba, and wider family, who lost so much in the Iranian Revolution.

CONTENTS

LIST OF ILLUSTRATIONS

All images are from the author's personal collection.
1. Cambridge Mafia.
2. Prime Minister Harold Macmillan at Cambridge, 1960.
3. Cambridge Mafia and Bow Group.
4. The young candidate for Newport, Monmouthshire, at Llandudno Conference, 1962 with the Earl of Home, foreign secretary and later prime minister.
5. With wife Taheré after the count when first elected as MP for Leominster, February 1974.
6. The new Hereford-Worcester MPs take their seats, February 1974.
7. Mrs Thatcher's visit to Leominster, 1980.
8. Mrs Thatcher at the Rankin Club, Leominster, 1980.
9. Parliamentary Regatta for St Margaret's, Westminster 1986.
10. Record Early Day Motion for the BBC World Service, 1993.
11. Geoffrey Howe with Leominster farmers, 1975.
12. Michael Heseltine at Leominster, 1989.
13. The old Iran at the court of the Shah.
14. HM the Shah at home.
15. Gorbachev's arrival at London Heathrow, December 1984.

ACKNOWLEDGEMENTS

I have received considerable help and guidance from friends who have taken the time and trouble to read the earlier drafts and to comment. First and foremost must come the Radices, both Giles and Lizanne. They provided me with a double expertise, being a writer and a literary agent respectively. They read the book in turn and gave guidance on presentation, sequence and all the other essentials that an author needs to know. In addition Giles gave the whole book a grammatical going-over which I regret to have to admit was needed.

My other readers all played a valuable part. Professor Jeremy Black of Exeter University kindly read and commented on the whole book. Former District Commissioner Christopher Jarrett of Scotland Yard went through the legal chapter, with particular reference to the Flying Squad, of which he was a former member, and made valuable suggestions. My wife, Taheré, applied her expertise to a close scrutiny of the Iran section, not to mention the references to her family. As for the Irish chapters, Mike Burns, ever the journalist, advised and corrected, and then did the same thing for the book as a whole.

I much needed advice on how to begin the marketing process from old friends and this I got from two outstanding Lobby figures of my time, namely Philip Webster of *The Times* and George Jones of the *Telegraph*. It is good that the complex relationship between the Lobby and us, the members, can continue to be close, well after the events that brought us all together in the first place.

Last but not least come all at my publishers, I.B.Tauris. Iradj Bagherzade is an old friend and a wise counsellor. His help with the book and his willingness to take it on are much appreciated. Jo Godfrey of I.B.Tauris, my editor and mentor, has been invaluable. With tact and professionalism she has contributed much to making this book what it is. For the final editing process I am grateful to Jenny Slater of OOH Publishing and most particularly to Christopher Feeney, my copy-editor, for his considerable attention to detail and obvious political and literary knowledge.

The final salute must go to all the personalities that feature in these pages. I hope readers will enjoy them.

PREFACE

One minute and almost exactly thirty seconds after Tony Blair, as prime minister, stood up in the Commons to make his statement on the Luxembourg summit on Monday, 24 November 1997, I stood at the Bar of a full House of Commons, about to cross the floor. All had been immaculately arranged beforehand, but this was the moment. I bowed and walked slowly forward to the gangway before the front benches, and then turned left to the government side rather than right to the Conservative opposition, to which I had hitherto belonged. I took my prearranged seat three rows up between Dale Campbell-Savours and Harry Barnes. On the government side the whole place erupted, with members waving order papers, shaking my hand and clapping me on the back. The Prime Minister was brought completely to a halt. The only hitch at that stage was the Speaker, Betty Boothroyd, who was furious at the interruption as she had not been warned of what was about to happen when the statement began. Fortunately it soon settled down and Tony Blair got going again.

A full House of Commons is a formidable place at any time, but to go through this physical realisation of a defection that had been simmering for years is, to put it mildly, difficult. That you feel as if you are in a goldfish bowl is an understatement. I particularly remember Dale saying to me: 'You will remember this day, Peter, for the rest of your life. It is the day you crossed the floor of this house.' Indeed I do.

INTRODUCTION

This is not an autobiography, although it is autobiographical in that it is an eclectic mix of interesting events that happen in a political life. It is about politics and the life of politicians. But it includes much else, including the drama of the Iranian Revolution, the tension of the Irish peace process and many anecdotes about personalities and foreign places.

The most dramatic part of the book is Part V, 'The anatomy of a defection': the disillusion and frustration of the lead-up to and the ups and downs of my defection itself, a saga that took virtually a year to complete.

The reasons for the defection are set out both at the time and, perhaps more interestingly, some seventeen years later. 'The problem for the defector is that the party you join is as susceptible to change as the one that you left.' You move for what you want and in the longer term you take what you get and you live in hope!

Part IV on Ireland is politically the most significant part of the book. Ireland, which recurs during the defection sequence, was, together with Europe, a main reason for my disillusion with the Conservative Party, and the attraction to Labour, leading to defection. The British–Irish Inter-Parliamentary Body, which I took a leading part in creating, played a significant role in establishing the necessary confidence at parliamentary level that facilitated the success of the two governments in achieving an agreed solution.

A major revelation on the peace process and its near-demise is contained in Chapter 11. By 1995 I was known and trusted by all parties on the Irish side of the process, including Sinn Féin. In July 1995 at the Forum for Peace and Reconciliation at Dublin Castle I was asked separately to see all these parties and given the same message. This included a very serious private meeting with Gerry Adams and Martin McGuinness. As co-chairman of the Inter-Parliamentary Body, I was the only Conservative MP with a permanent seat on the Forum, the British government joining the Unionists in declining to be represented. I was asked to deliver to John Major the plain fact that, unless he and his government progressed the IRA ceasefire, violence would resume. The Irish and Sinn Féin would not be able to contain the situation for much longer. The message was duly delivered and ignored by Major. Without Unionist support he had no parliamentary majority and must have gambled that he could hold the situation until the General Election provided an answer. This was not to be. As soon as the Clinton visit was over in the autumn and Senator Mitchell had reported to the government in early 1996, with no active response from the British government, the Canary Wharf bomb went off in February 1996. Violence had resumed and the peace process was perilously near complete failure. The only hope was the probability that Tony Blair would win the 1997 General Election.

Drama is not limited to Ireland. Mrs Thatcher's fall from power, seen from the Heseltine campaign, has plenty. Similarly the Iranian Revolution, and the personal account of a very considerable event seen from the perspective of the author and his Iranian wife, Taheré, shows how a turn of fate, and human error, can permanently change the lives of so many people.

But enough of drama. Amusement and interest is here too. Mrs Thatcher and her way with her backbenchers in private meetings is a case in point. The comparison of the Conservative and Labour parties within and outside Parliament is something few have had the experience to deliver. On the foreign side there is a 1961 visit to the Soviet Union as a student and comparisons with today. This combines with much about Mr Gorbachev, whose famous 1984 visit to the UK I hosted as chairman of the Inter-Parliamentary Union. Parliamentary activity abroad includes Rhodesian independence, war in Namibia and later preparations for South African independence. What stands out above all is the usefulness of parliamentary diplomacy and the potential of the British Group of the Inter-Parliamentary Union, not only in itself, but in working constructively with the government of the day.

Personalities abound and not least in South Wales, thanks to the influence of my father, Sir Owen Temple-Morris QC, himself a Conservative MP before he became a judge. Many of the friendships recorded, from the outset of the story, are with members of the Labour Party, from experiencing the skills of George Thomas during the 1959 General Election in Cardiff to friendship with the late John Smith, with whom I was joint vice-chairman of the GB–USSR Association. Finally, we go back to the Conservative side where it all began in Cambridge, with one of the most talented political generations that university produced, later known as the Cambridge mafia. Thanks to Ken Clarke we are still represented in the Commons, but now many of us have the good fortune to be still around and in the Lords. This book fittingly begins with us all at Cambridge, together then as now, in those halcyon days of our youth.

Note

Throughout the book I have tried to refer to people as they were at the time I am writing about. Hence Mrs Thatcher and not Lady Thatcher. Titles acquired later are only referred to if they involve a change of name.

Part I
THE BEGINNING

One
THE CAMBRIDGE MAFIA

He knows nothing; and he thinks he knows everything. That points clearly to a political career.

George Bernard Shaw, *Major Barbara*, Act 3, 1905

In October 1958, when I went up to Cambridge, I formally joined the Conservative Party at the Societies' Fair in the Guildhall. My membership card for the Cambridge University Conservative Association (CUCA) was signed by the late Leon Brittan, then a committee member. More of him later.

In the 1960s the Conservative Party was still a generally relaxed, paternalistic sort of family. Back in South Wales, where my father had been Conservative MP for Cardiff East for some years before becoming a judge, it seemed for me a very natural and welcoming place to be. I never considered going elsewhere and anyway why bother? I was more than happy with the likes of Harold Macmillan, 'Rab' Butler, Iain Macleod, the Earl of Home, Edward Heath, Reginald Maudling, Edward Boyle and the rest. Against this background we got serious about politics, in an undergraduate way, but our Cambridge life in no way stopped there. For me, college life, dining clubs, pretty girls, regular trips to London to eat my Bar dinners at the Inner Temple, the camaraderie of friends and the lovely atmosphere of Cambridge made up undergraduate life. We were still able to enjoy it all, as a wider preparation for the future, and did not have to worry about what precise degree was necessary to get a particular

3

job. I well remember a post-exam party in 1960 when virtually everyone there, except me, was about to go down, and most still had no idea what they wanted to do. I did, in that I was going to the Bar, but I was the exception and not the rule. At that time the fact that we had a Cambridge degree was sufficient to give us some choice in employment. Obviously it helped if one knew what one wanted and went for it, but this was not so overwhelmingly important as it is today.

I was very lucky. I went up to Cambridge with one of the most politically talented groups of Conservative undergraduates of recent history. Leon Brittan was one year ahead of most of us when we arrived and beginning his second year. He proceeded, taking first-class honours along the way, to emerge after four years as one of the outstanding undergraduates of his generation. He was intellectually gifted, ambitious and personable. He came from a Jewish family, being the son of a London doctor, and on occasion did suffer from anti-Semitism with, for example, constituency selection committees. He seemed happiest in cosmopolitan urban seats, and was a very effective candidate in North Kensington. At the time we thought that Hampstead, or somewhere like it, would be a good seat for him to enter Parliament, but the opportunity there did not occur at the right time. However, he did the rounds, and eventually struck oil in Yorkshire, a fine county, becoming MP for Cleveland and Whitby; later after boundary changes he went to Richmond in the same county. He had a home in Yorkshire and was President of the Richmond Conservative Association, where he was succeeded as MP by William Hague.

Taking the Michaelmas term of 1960 as a marker, about half of the CUCA Committee of the then chairman, Norman Fowler, became MPs and many made it into Cabinet and government. Some like me later changed party, but this only added to the variety of the group. From the first Norman Fowler was the confident and debonair figure he has remained throughout his political life. He was educated at King Edward VI School, Chelmsford, a first-class grammar school, and from there he went into national service and was commissioned into the Essex Regiment. It was interesting how those like him, who went through that experience, came out far more rounded as personalities and much better able to make the best of Cambridge. As for Norman, in contrast to those mentioned earlier, who had little idea what they wanted to do with their lives, he knew precisely where he was going and got there. It was politics via journalism; and after some vacation jobs on local newspapers, he was accepted as a trainee at *The Times* when he came down to London in 1961. He had read law as an extra option, but found it unnecessary to complete this by reading for the Bar.

After Norman Fowler, I became chairman in the Lent term of 1961 and after me, John Gummer in the summer. I met John during my first term in 1958 when I arrived at Selwyn College to deliver some CUCA literature to the college representative, who turned out to be him. I got to the staircase where I was told he was, wheeling my somewhat precarious bicycle, and down came this fresh-faced, perennially youthful figure: engaging, bright and friendly. From there on our CUCA careers ran together, and after his chairmanship of CUCA, he went on in a fourth year to become a successful President of the Union. Once he got under way there was no stopping him. He contested Greenwich in the 1964 and 1966 elections and was elected MP for Lewisham West in 1970, with Eye, later Suffolk Coastal, to come from 1979. His youthful looks never left him, and later on could be claimed as an advantage. Earlier they were a mixed blessing, as he was promoted early into various offices of state and party. Becoming vice-chairman of the party in charge of youth under Heath in 1972, he sported a beard, until with office under Mrs Thatcher the beard went, to the relief of some of his friends. In 1983 came his promotion as chairman of the Conservative Party, to constitute an answer to the new young Labour leader, Neil Kinnock. It was again a mixed blessing, as his youthful looks in that particular job turned out not to be an advantage. Perhaps this set him back a little, and two years later he returned to government at his former Minister of State rank. After four years he deservedly entered the Cabinet as Minister of Agriculture. One of my affectionate personal memories of him at Cambridge was his preference, when living out of college, to seek refuge by lodging with various priests in their High Church vicarages. I visited him frequently and remember my first experience of the smell of incense, which seemed to be all-pervading. Coming from an Anglican background in the Church in Wales this was something new, with the slightly forbidden element of a Catholic experience! Sure enough in later life John went over to the Roman Catholic Church.

The following year featured the prominence of Michael Howard and Ken Clarke, good-natured but serious rivals then, as they have been throughout their political lives. They were both outstandingly able examples of the very successful grammar school system, and they chased each other up the CUCA and Union ladders throughout their time at Cambridge. They were both very different. Michael Howard was the son of Jewish immigrants from Romania who made good in Llanelli, South Wales. A product of Llanelli Grammar School, he went up to Peterhouse, Cambridge, holding out against some school pressure that he should go to the University of Wales at Cardiff. Had he done so, goodness knows what his politics would have been as he would have been a leading player wherever he landed. As it turned out, he first came to see me at St Catharine's over some CUCA business, and then as now he displayed a natural charm which has never left him. His perceived swing to the right in Conservative politics does its best to conceal an attractive personality, and he has always been excellent company to his friends. He rapidly adapted to Cambridge, and for my part I used, as secretary of CUCA, the one bit of patronage I ever had as far as he was concerned, being one year ahead of him, and made him the assistant secretary. Many years later this caused great amusement in the Commons, as related later in Michael's profile (p. 290).

Ken Clarke was something else. An alumnus of Nottingham High School, he always remained just what he always was. Whereas Michael Howard was an agreeable dinner guest at our London home in Redington Road, Hampstead, Ken was the Nottingham man, always stayed there, lived there with his wife Gillian and still does. He chose to practise at the Birmingham Bar, rather than joining the rest of us in London. He got elected in 1970 for the Nottinghamshire seat of Rushcliffe, conveniently adjacent to his home town, and became a whip in 1972, which established him as an aspirant for the future. In typical style he has always been his own man, and looked after his family while the party was in opposition by resuming practice at the Bar on the Midlands Circuit, whilst at the same time occupying a junior Shadow position for the Department of Trade. This meant high demands on his time as he juggled his parliamentary and legal careers. When it came to the 1979 election, and the change in government, the spoils obviously went to those who served most in opposition. Ken was barely one of them and only just scraped into government as Transport Under-Secretary, it is said thanks to the support of his Cambridge friend Norman Fowler, Minister and then Secretary of State for Transport. Once in, and a Minister now able to concentrate on one job, he excelled. Again he did not change. He was as happy in high circles as he was having his chicken curries at his local Indian restaurant. He has been a great help to the Cameron Cabinet.

Norman Lamont arrived on the scene in 1961, which was the year I went down. I never had the chance to get to know him at Cambridge, but later on we became, and remain, good friends. Again he was destined for great things from the outset and never disappointed. Chairman of CUCA and President of the Union, he proceeded via the Conservative Research Department to Rothschilds and thence into the Commons for Kingston upon Thames in 1972. Much later he had an unhappy time as Chancellor, with John Major as prime minister, when he protected Major from even more damage after Black Wednesday in 1992 and the exit from the ERM, only to be dismissed a year later. He was offered Environment, but understandably had his pride and declined, returning to the backbenches. His resignation statement to the Commons was memorable, not least for using the phrase that the Major government showed every appearance of 'being in office but not in power'. He had no particular love for John Major after this, and his feelings spilled over to Major's party chairman, Norman Fowler, a fellow member of the Cambridge mafia. Lamont on the backbenches went through a phase of being difficult, no doubt feeling rejected and unappreciated as Chancellor, which was understandable, but has now emerged once more as an active peer and a valued media commentator, as an ex-Chancellor, and a very good one, too.

In the Lent term of 1959, the President of the Union was Julian Grenfell, who conducted proceedings with some style. With a solemn pronouncement that 'this House do now adjourn at 10.37 OF THE CLOCK', he could turn a simple announcement into an occasion. Julian became a much-married man, and via television went into the World Bank in 1965 and had a very distinguished career, returning later to the House of Lords. One of his Etonian friends at King's was David Howell, who concentrated on his first-class degree and developing his connections, rather than university politics. He emerged successfully, as did others who chose this calmer path to success in the outside world. There are many other examples of this. David Owen was at Cambridge in my time for instance, and concentrated on medicine. Another David, one Cameron, much later, took his first at Oxford, enjoyed life and turned to politics via the Conservative Research Department when he came down. Each to his own.

Our number included many others, including Peter Lloyd, CUCA chairman, Michaelmas 1959, Peter Viggers, who held the chairmanship in summer 1960 at the end of his second year, and Hugh Dykes, notable pro-European and now a Lib-Dem peer. Each is referred to in the appendix, 'Cambridge profiles', but I should give special mention to Nick Budgen, MP for Wolverhampton South West, who sadly died prematurely in 1998. He was a special friend and a great character. With his blimpish side, he enjoyed playing to the gallery at Cambridge and indeed later. This lasted until he spent a long vacation in South Africa, then at the height of apartheid. His social conscience was suddenly and unexpectedly stirred, and he returned to Cambridge in the autumn of 1960 so left wing on the issue that we could hardly contain him. This alarming trait did not last, but it was splendid to observe as it progressed. We each attended the other's wedding and he went to the Birmingham Bar, where he did very well, entering the House with me in February 1974. We soon shared a room in Dean's Yard, next to the Abbey, and immediately rebellion was in the air. He had succeeded Enoch Powell, and was inspired, as he had been all those years before in South Africa, to take an independent line. I lost him to economic thoughts as he composed a great oration for the House, totally disagreeing with Conservative economic policy. We were in opposition, so nobody took much notice but the die was cast for Budgen in

Parliament. Some years later, the powers that be had the brilliant idea of taming him by putting him in the Whips' Office. What transpired was poetic, as Budgen looked more and more miserable, condemned as he was to silence and observation. He lasted about a year and then once more we had the pleasure of his company in the Smoking Room, when he would set about destroying various of our more pompous colleagues in a way that was very astute, was not harmful and was delightful to listen to. I miss him still.

Some were close to CUCA but concentrated on the Union scene, such as Julian Grenfell and Christopher Tugendhat, President of the Union, MP and European Commissioner. Others were very active in CUCA but chose something other than a political life; such as Colin Renfrew, distinguished archaeologist and later Master of Jesus College, Cambridge; Roger Graham, who made no bones about the fact that he was going to make some money having prematurely lost his father, and indeed did just that in the IT industry; Robin Pedler, a history first from Caius who went on to succeed in corporate management; and John Barnes, another history first from Caius, who enjoyed a more academic career writing various historical and biographical books and diaries including a history of the Conservative Party and the two volumes of Leo Amery's *Diaries*, a formidable work. Two others who were sons of sitting Tory MPs, namely George Clark Hutchison and Hugh Wilson, were active among us, but did not follow their fathers into the House. David Hacking was a hereditary peer who followed his father to the Lords, although sadly to lose his place later on when hereditaries were largely excluded from the Lords in 1999. Last but not least was Martin Suthers, a great friend of Ken Clarke and another Nottingham stalwart, who edited our magazine, the *Tory Reformer*. This title had taken us some agonising and reflects where we, as aspirant Conservatives, were at that time. We wanted change and to be on the side of change. Martin was very much the life and soul of CUCA. He returned to Nottingham, became a successful solicitor and entered local politics, becoming Lord Mayor of Nottingham. Over the years we have all spoken for him, in the cause of one or other of his many interests there.

It is interesting to speculate how such a collection of people were all around at the same time. My view, which seemed to be accepted when I put it to the others, is that it was the first established grammar-school generation coming up postwar which quite naturally combined with the public schoolboys. When I put it recently to one illustrious member of our fraternity, he replied: 'It was a brief period when the question of class disappeared.' I can honestly say that it was unimportant to us where anyone happened to go to school; we all got on in a common cause and had a great time together. These great grammar schools were later disrupted by the advent of the comprehensives, which unintentionally revived the gap between private and public education, which is still too visible for comfort today. As we all descended on the House of Commons we became known in the Press as the 'Cambridge mafia', which was not totally inappropriate as we have always stuck together, with regular reunions over the years. We are currently making them more regular, as the years roll by only too rapidly.

People ask whether my change of political party made any difference to my relationship with the group. The answer is, not the slightest. For example I stayed away from one of Ken Clarke's birthday parties, immediately after my final defection to Labour, only to receive an effective rebuke. In addition to our reunions we have a tradition in the Lords of giving a small dinner party for those of our number who arrive there. I arrived in 2001 with Norman Fowler in the same intake, and we were both invited to a Cambridge dinner attended by Colin Renfrew, Leon Brittan, Norman Lamont, Christopher Tugendhat, Julian Grenfell and David Hacking. It amused me to think that of those present, Julian Grenfell, David Hacking and myself had all left the Conservative Party at various stages to join Labour. At a later such dinner we were joined by Hugh Dykes, who had become a Liberal Democrat. Long may such tolerance continue.

For those interested in going into politics, being at Oxbridge was, and probably still is, an enormous advantage. Over our three years of residence we heard more than our fair share of distinguished speakers and enjoyed the privilege of meeting a great number of them. One of the most illustrious and memorable was undoubtedly Harold Macmillan as prime minister in November 1960. As honorary secretary of CUCA I had written to Number 10 on behalf of the committee, back in the summer, to invite him, and much to our surprise and delight he accepted. It turned out to be a very grand occasion under the chairmanship of Norman Fowler, with me as his vice-chairman. I was delegated to stay with Macmillan from his arrival until the meeting, while the chairman and the secretary, Robin Pedler, busied themselves with last-minute arrangements. However, the three of us all met the Prime Minister at Cambridge railway station. He arrived in a reserved compartment (the small ones of those days) with his Parliamentary Private Secretary (PPS), Knox Cunningham QC, MP, and one solitary detective. What a comparison with today's armoured cars, back-up Range Rovers, heavily armed protection squads and so on. We greeted the great man and escorted him to a waiting car. As we passed through the ticket hall, the crowd parted to let us through and warm applause broke out. Cynics today would say that this was because it was then a more deferential society, which it was, but it was more than that and involved some level of respect for the office and the man, surely no bad thing. These days, by the time our vociferous media have finished with the Prime Minister, or indeed any major politician, not much is left of them to applaud!

I then went with the PM and his PPS to the Garden House Hotel, where the manager had lent his flat for Macmillan to relax in before he went to a private dinner we were giving for him at Trinity, then to a meeting of some 2,000 undergraduates. Relaxed he certainly was. Off came his jacket, as he passed irreverent comments on current matters, plus a lot of teasing of his PPS for his then enormous Ulster majority in the Commons compared with his efforts, and comparatively meagre reward, at Stockton, which he fought, held and eventually lost in 1945. Throughout the evening he seemed to exhibit a regret that he had spent eighteen years on the backbenches before Churchill brought him into government. However, he also seemed very proud of not being associated with the appeasement brigade before the war, and of the independent line he had always tried to take. 'Eighteen years on the backbenches, Henry', he grumbled to Sir Henry Willink, as he perched on a chair after dinner that evening.

We left him at the Garden House, while Knox Cunningham and I went to the meeting hall to adjust the lectern to the exact desired height, and we returned to bring him to Trinity for the dinner in the attractive Great Court rooms of Leon Brittan. Our worry, even in those days, was a demonstration of some kind which would spoil what was developing into a successful visit, and that was in our mind as we entered Trinity through the main gate. Lo and behold, banners were on display and we all winced. We quickly detected that it had nothing to do with the PM, and all to do with Kenya, where Jomo Kenyatta was persecuting the minority Yoruba tribe, with particular reference to a promising young Kenyan named Tom Mboya. 'It's nothing to do with you, Sir', we told an impassive but relieved Macmillan, as we strode on towards Leon's rooms.

Dinner, preceding Macmillan's later speech, then began. For the first time I noticed how tense the Prime Minister was. It was magnificently concealed, but tense he certainly was. The occasion was suitably grand, and the Trinity silver was out in quantity on the table. That said, the occasion was not pompous and Macmillan was most certainly not a pompous man; grand yes, pompous no. But the formalities were followed and, for example, Sir Henry Willink, former Minister and then Master of Magdalene, a school friend and contemporary of Harold Macmillan, greeted him warmly as 'Prime Minister' and it was not until after dinner, when they were sitting together, that Christian names were used on both sides. Respect for office once more.

Macmillan hardly touched all the elaborate food that had been prepared for him. He had just the soup plus a glass of red wine, and port at the end with his chat to Sir Henry Willink. One incident made the dinner. In its early stages, the roar of a crowd went up in Great Court, right outside our first-floor window. We froze in anticipation of some awful demonstration, but no: we listened and the chant became clear: 'We want Mac. We want Mac', they chanted. We peeped through the curtains and there were identified some forty to fifty Trinity Beagles just back from their hunt. It was with some relief that this was reported to the PM, the curtains were drawn and the great man gave one of his grandest waves and smiles to the assembled admirers. It was lovely to behold and fortified him to do his bit with the big meeting he was facing.

The speech was a majestic Macmillan-style performance. Stylish, digni-fied and theatrical: lengthy reference to his Oxford days, service in World War I and the many friends of his youth he had lost in it, as a tear seemed to roll down his cheek. Whether he intended it or not, it was genuinely moving. Afterwards we took him over to Trinity Hall, Norman Fowler's college, for a reception and he was much more relaxed. He seemed liber-ated as he enjoyed the company of admiring youth. The most amusing sight for me was, when no doubt tired but very friendly, he had his arm around Nick Budgen's shoulders as he expounded to a small group of us the difficulties of high office. The famous answer to the question: 'What is the greatest difficulty about being Prime Minister?' was, if not coined for the first time, at least repeated: 'Events, dear boy, events.' Nick Budgen was shaking with suppressed mirth as Macmillan leant heavily upon him. He could not quite believe it as he himself, among us undergraduates, did a splendid turn at the time mimicking Macmillan. This was too good to be true. At some stage a group photo was taken, and I remember standing directly behind Macmillan. Just before each photo, he would adjust his profile to get the best angle and his face for the best expression. Vanity it might have been, but he did not have the image of the Edwardian gentle-man for nothing. This went beyond angles and expressions and included tucking his evening black tie inside his collar; doing up the top button of his jacket so it looked more like a morning coat; plus-fours on the grouse moor; and of course seldom wearing any tie but the Old Etonian one or that of the Brigade of Guards. It all gave him an attractive image, dated but dignified, helping to create a certain mystique all of his own.

Many of the prominent figures we met, mainly through CUCA, were surprisingly frank with us when we entertained them after meetings. I doubt whether this would apply to the same extent today. Nigel Birch MP, an ex-Treasury Minister who resigned with Chancellor Peter Thorneycroft in 1958, made no secret of his dislike for Harold Macmillan but also gave us a riveting account of the sex life of Sir Oswald Mosley, which greatly added to the breadth of our education. After another meeting I found myself sitting on a settee alone with Selwyn Lloyd, discussing the Suez Crisis, he having been Foreign Secretary at the time. I couldn't understand why the Americans turned quite so vehemently and rapidly against us. He added to my knowledge of the affair by saying that personal relations had not helped, as the most powerful figure in the then US Administration was the Secretary of State, John Foster Dulles, who was jealous of the pre and postwar reputation in foreign affairs of Anthony Eden and was all too pleased to take the opportunity to undermine him.

CUCA president 'Rab' Butler was always good to us and on call to help. However, the impressions of youth can be not too far off the verdict of history. He came across as a very nice man and a great figure, but also as the man apart and somehow too reserved in nature for a politician. He was an interesting contrast with Harold Macmillan, who had his academic side but also the common touch, which, certainly as prime minister, he could put on at will. Butler eventually settled in Cambridge as Master of Trinity when his political career had run its course in 1965.

However our hero, as Michael Howard recently reminded me, was Iain Macleod, whose sharp mind and riveting oratory had us all sitting on the edge of our seats. He was a man of outstanding ability who could have made his fortune, which he needed to do, in many walks of life. He chose politics, and always acted independently whatever the personal cost. He came to CUCA for one of our annual dinners, able as ever but not at close quarters immediately *sympathique*. He lacked the human touch, that immediate charm, that a political leader needs, though not necessarily a Chancellor. Later in his life he developed severe arthritis, so much so that he could not turn his head without turning his entire body. I got my first lesson in the power of television from this. During vacations I used to do television work, by way of panels, small interviews, voiceovers and general tasks, for what was then Television Wales and the West (TWW). One day I went into the editing room to see a recent interview with Iain Macleod being reduced for emphasis and duration. The producer turned to me and showed me the different camera shots he could choose from. 'If I use this one, I can spoil the whole interview for him, as it will show up his arthritis', he said, 'whereas if I use this one, you cannot see a trace of it.' He used the helpful shot and I learnt a good lesson.

Peter Thorneycroft staggered us at one meeting in February 1960, by making a speech of one sentence. Ever the cavalier, he got up and said: 'Europe is at sixes and sevens (the EEC and EFTA) – questions!?' It took us time to get going but it turned into a very good meeting. I had to meet him at the station and he came to us direct from a Friday sitting of the Commons. First we had to deal with a Cambridge taxi-driver, long tormented by the number of bicycles in that city. 'Tell him to put a tax on bicycles', he kept repeating. The fact that Thorneycroft had resigned as Chancellor the year before made no difference at all. I often think of him, when I hear London taxi-drivers on the subject of bicycles today. In the taxi Thorneycroft mentioned that he had listened to an excellent maiden speech in the House that afternoon. 'Jolly girl from Finchley, called Margaret Thatcher.' Later on in 1966, Peter Thorneycroft was defeated at Monmouth in the General Election by a bright young Labour barrister, Donald Anderson. Thorneycroft retired to a prominent business career, going to the Lords in 1967 and returning to the political front line as Mrs Thatcher's first appointed party chairman in 1975. He played an invaluable role in helping to see her through her years of opposition and early years of government. The affection for her that he expressed in that taxi was well placed.

Edward Heath came several times to CUCA or the Union. Sadly he was as competent as he was uninspiring. In private conversation with us undergraduates, it was the same. He seemed to lack inner confidence. He never really changed, and I remember how awkward he seemed when greeting his MPs, as leader, at the traditional summer reception in 1974. A more senior colleague, Tom Boardman, who had been one of his ministers, entered with me, and we had to carry the conversation, whilst our host seemed distracted and uneasy. As a new MP I was very put out at a time when a few words of encouragement would have had me for life. Much later on Heath mellowed considerably and his very apt sense of humour came out. Once, towards the end of his time in the Commons, I was talking to him in the Smoking Room and for the sake of my own conscience, confessed to him that I had not supported him in 1975. By then he knew enough of me to know that I was one of those whose support he really should have had. His face set in a benign but rueful expression of intense sadness and he said nothing at all. He clearly never got over it all.

Christopher Soames addressed CUCA in 1959–60 as Minister of Agriculture. He made little impression, and even to us seemed to lack an intellectual grip on his then brief. However, that was only part of the man. He had an assurance and style that came from his social position, plus of course the fact that he was Churchill's son-in-law. In the early 1950s during his second term as prime minister, Churchill had a serious heart attack and Soames was his Parliamentary Private Secretary. Sitting in Number 10 he virtually ran the country, in the name of his father-in-law, and Churchill was able to get through the period without premature resignation. In those days the press treated the matter with discretion and all went well. Soames went on to other high offices. Harold Wilson made him Ambassador in Paris in 1968, after he lost his Bedford seat, in order to ease the path for Wilson's intended application to join the EEC. With the 1970 change of government he remained in post until 1972 to see through Edward Heath's successful application. He was summoned again in 1979 to become interim Governor of Southern Rhodesia, 1979–80, during the hand-over period for the independence of Zimbabwe. A formidable public record, and all carried out in an apparently effortless and laid-back manner.

On the lighter side, a prominent and wealthy MP, Gerald Nabarro, turned up in Cambridge in a sports car, identified as his third car, a Daimler Dart, by NAB 3 on the licence plate, with a glamorous secretary in the passenger seat. Needless to say he was staying overnight and our undergraduate thoughts were allowed a certain licence.

There were many fine Union debates. The first time Sir Oswald Mosley, Conservative and then Labour MP and minister, who in the 1930s became Britain's fascist leader-in-waiting, came to Cambridge to a CUCA meeting in the Union chamber chaired by the then chairman, Peter Viggers, in the summer of 1960. Mosley retained his gentlemanly ways. This was proved when one provocative undergraduate darted forward when he was speaking and threw a jelly into his face. There was no plate, but it was still not very pleasant. It hit Mosley and carried on in small pieces to drench the secretary, sitting behind him. Dabbing his face with his handkerchief Mosley carried on speaking as if nothing had happened. He came to tea with us after the meeting, and discussed personalities and issues as the establishment figure he was and as if he had never left mainstream politics. A formidable performance by any account. He was never abandoned by many of his personal friends, although he felt obliged to live in France, where he entertained visitors in some style.

One of the more dramatic debates was between Julian Amery MP, of the Tory right, and Fenner Brockway MP, of the Labour left, on colonial affairs, an emotive subject in those days. It was hard-hitting on both sides, when Julian Amery waded into Brockway, saying 'Why take any notice of him. During the Kenya emergency no less than five Mau Mau Generals called themselves Fenner Brockway.' The place went into uproar as undergraduate consciences brought forth shouts of 'Dirty' and 'Below the belt'. Fenner Brockway appeared gentle, by comparison to the tough Amery, and won the debate on the back of this attack. As for us we could not invite Amery to either the CUCA or the Union for the next year. We then invited him to a CUCA meeting and again there was never a dull moment. Back in Trinity after his meeting, the Chairman of the Labour Club, who had rooms underneath, played the 'Red Flag' at full blast with all windows open. Undaunted, Amery stood up on a chair and sang 'Land of Hope and Glory' right through.

Julian Amery was of the old British imperialist school, and loved nothing more than the 'Great Game' of Central Asia, or wherever an equivalent could be found. I came into considerable contact with him over the Iranian Revolution of 1979 and its consequences. The hospitality of his Eaton Square home was considerable, and meetings, lunches and dinners were always highly civilised. A meeting in his library, which was his favourite room, would be gently interrupted at 12 noon precisely by his butler bringing in a bottle of Champagne. Amery regarded this as a good excuse not to drink anything heavier before he got to lunch. We travelled together to meet various of the former Shah's ministers and generals, including one rather special meeting in Paris with Dr Shahpour

Bakhtiar, a left-wing Persian aristocrat and one of the Shah's last Prime Ministers. He set up in exile in Paris, where he had studied and lived for many years. He took us to a fashionable restaurant at l'Opéra, patronised by the wealthier elements of the French left. We were in a private room with police bodyguards, headed by Bakhtiar's son, a serving French police officer. It was a fine lunch, with Amery in his element. 'Would His Excellency like to drink Burgundy or Bordeaux?', our host asked. 'They say Burgundy is the King and Bordeaux the Queen.' Amery replied, 'We will have the King!' As we were enjoying all this splendour, there was suddenly an almighty crash outside the door and then a big wallop as something directly hit it. We all froze. Threats were regularly made against Bakhtiar, and sadly he was assassinated a few years after this. I wondered for that brief moment whether my time had come. After a pause the door was pushed open, with an inert body being pulled out of the way. Then some laughter eased the situation as it was explained that a fully laden waiter had tripped and fallen full-tilt into the door, knocking himself out in the process.

In a university union, as in the Commons Chamber, the deficient are soon found out. A prime example of this was the Hon. Hugh Fraser MP, younger son of the Lord Lovat, who arrived with his then wife, The Hon. Antonia Fraser, née Pakenham, to do the annual No Confidence debate in the Union in October 1960. Central Office must have sent him to us, but I fear he was a complete disaster. This was the key debate for the party in power nationally and also the most difficult. Under pressure during it, he swept his arm back in a splendid histrionic gesture and scored a direct hit on his full glass of water, which soaked the Union Secretary, Colin Renfrew, sitting on the other side of his dispatch box. The place convulsed and we lost the debate.

The next day I was over in Trinity Hall discussing the disaster with Norman Fowler when in came the Young Turks in the form of Michael Howard and Ken Clarke, then beginning their second year at Cambridge and gathering their confidence. They were rightfully angry at the mess of the night before and we got the message loud and clear. We had to do better and the appropriate missives were sent off to Conservative Central Office.

It was a choice moment. For us it was the first appearance together of the two up-and-coming men, who competed with each other for office and political prominence at Cambridge and throughout their political lives.

Who better to end this chapter than John Gummer, who had one early difficulty in the Cambridge Union. Because of his clerical background and High Church beliefs he was an absolute natural for what we called the 'God Debate', which in those days occurred every term. He became so good at defending the Almighty, that the Almighty would not let him go. Desperately he appealed to successive presidents that he had at some stage to be released into the secular world. Eventually he succeeded, with mixed consequences. In the summer of 1960 we had a normal secular debate starring Randolph Churchill, son of Winston. He was well known to be over-committed to the delights of alcohol, and that term's president, Laurence Giovene, mounted a major effort, through friends at the Suffolk village where Churchill lived, to keep him sober during the day of the debate. Into this uncertain situation came John Gummer, who was replying to the motion. Randolph Churchill was speaking later as a guest on the other side. Before and during dinner Churchill's consumption of alcohol had been contained with some difficulty, but when we got into the committee room just before the debate, he called grandly for a bottle of whisky from the steward, and had a large part of it well inside him by the time we knew what was happening.

Into the chamber he went, literally fighting fit. In fact he could not be contained, and when Gummer began to speak second, from the other side as the undergraduate responder, up leapt Churchill and striding over to Gummer's side of the chamber ordered him to sit down and proceeded to contradict everything Gummer was trying to say. At the time it was hilarious, and we had not seen anything like it. Eventually John recovered the dispatch box and Churchill returned to his side. Next, amusingly Churchill literally ran out of fuel. It was some time before he was due to speak and by the time his turn came, and without further refreshment, he was almost asleep and consequently we had the opposite problem of getting him to speak at all. He was all over the place and Gummer was deservedly vindicated.

Those were the days and the companions of my youth. Before long we were to begin our political careers for real in the House of Commons, but first we had to get there.

Two
INTO POLITICS

The Socialists can scheme their schemes and the Liberals can dream their dreams, but we, at least, have work to do.

Iain Macleod, speech at Conservative Party conference, 1960

If Conservative backbench MPs want to get on in politics they will have to find a foothold in the narrow strip of land that lies between sycophancy and rebellion.

Kenneth Baker, Queen's Speech debate, 1979

Part 1: The party we joined

At Cambridge we were all progressive Conservatives. If we had a hero it was Iain Macleod; our magazine, under Martin Suthers, was called the *Tory Radical*, which reflected our thinking and, perhaps more important to us, how we wanted to be perceived. We were doubtful about Suez, mostly against capital punishment and wanting to identify with the social conscience of the 'one nation, image. The Conservative Party had a good feel about it, and the grandees arrived and treated us as the heirs apparent. At that time interviews to become a parliamentary candidate required two relatively informal meetings with the gentlemanly knights who were for the time being the vice-chairmen in charge of candidates; in my case firstly Sir Donald Kaberry MP, and secondly Sir Paul Bryan MP. I was fortunate to be adopted as candidate at Newport, Monmouthshire in January 1962, at the age of nearly twenty-four, and before I had taken my Bar finals, which I did in May of that year.

The main reason we in the 'Cambridge mafia' felt politically comfortable was that over the previous decade the one nation tradition had emerged as the dominant force within the party. The old prewar Conservative Party was of another world, and whilst right-wing groups such as the Monday Club remained, they were somewhat on the sidelines. We felt suitably modern and progressive, as we entered a still gentlemanly and very agreeable party. These days everyone competes for the title of 'One Nation' but it is in terms of recent history the creation of Conservatives. The legacy of Benjamin Disraeli and his writings is generally given credit for the term, although, as the historian Lord Blake pointed out, the term 'One Nation' was not actually used by Disraeli. Others have claimed that Stanley Baldwin should take the credit by his urging between the wars: 'The union of those two nations of which Disraeli spoke, two generations ago; union among our own people to make one nation of our own people at home, which, if secured, nothing else matters in the world.' I think it fair to say that the description 'One Nation' came out of Disraeli via Baldwin and others, to be claimed by a group of ambitious young Conservative MPs of the 1950 intake who established the One Nation Group and got the whole idea off the ground.

The beginnings of the group are well covered in Robert Shepherd's biography of Iain Macleod (Hutchinson, 1994) and many names are mentioned. I only repeat here those of Iain Macleod, Ted Heath, Cub Alport, Angus Maude and Enoch Powell. Their overwhelming concern was to distinguish themselves and the party from its prewar right-wing and imperialistic image and establish the social policies and conscience of the Conservative Party in the eyes of the public. They took the name of One Nation with that in mind. They met, organised and published their views. They also began to contest the internal elections to Conservative Party committees. They concentrated on committees to do with social policy, which was their particular interest to change and which, incidentally, gave them a better opportunity to get elected. This was because there was less competition than in the committees to do with foreign and colonial affairs and defence, these being very much the traditional Conservative Party interest areas.

During the 1950s, many leading members of the group became ministers, which meant leaving the group for the duration of their period of office. The group flourished nevertheless, published regularly and became part of the Conservative establishment.

Like all parties, the Conservative Party has certain issues upon which it is traditionally divided. On the domestic front capital punishment was a key conference issue over the years. For obvious reasons decolonisation was a sensitive postwar issue, and by the 1960s, South Africa and Rhodesia had become paramount. In the 1960s Southern Rhodesia, with its Unilateral Declaration of Independence under Ian Smith and others, came to a head. The effect on the Conservative Party was divisive, as between its more progressive elements and its still active 'colonial' wing. The right began to organise and the left quickly responded. The left's answer was not to turn directly to the One Nation Group but to form a new organisational entity called 'the Lollards'. I always think it unfortunate that the original Lollards were mostly burnt at the stake as heretics, which did not bode well for this new organisation. However, as is the way with the Conservative Party, names used seldom bear a direct relationship with the subject matter involved. The use of the term Lollards came from the flat in Lollards' Tower, Lambeth Palace, of one of the founders, Sir William Van Straubenzee, MP for Wokingham, 1959–87, which was the early meeting place. Many of these early and subsequent members of the group were members of One Nation, a smaller body suitable for a dining club, whereas the Lollards went far wider, including the entire centre and left of the Parliamentary Party. By the traditions of the time members kept a low profile, as factions within the party were not something to be publicised. When I took over the chairmanship of the Lollards in 1987, the full list of members was kept firmly within my possession and that of the secretary.

The problem within a political party of organising by faction is that others organise too. The Rhodesia faction that had itself provoked the formation of the Lollards translated into a group in the general right-wing interest which was called the 'Committee of 92'. As with the Lollards, the name had a territorial source, rather than numerical, in that it came from the then home of Sir Patrick Wall MP, at 92 Cheyne Walk, Chelsea. Sir Patrick was a diehard imperialist long after the concept was history, but the group he helped to create became the Praetorian Guard of Mrs Thatcher as leader and later prime minister. To match the One Nation Group there appeared the No Turning Back Group, which still exists today and in my day contained the ultras of the Conservative right. The important point here was that the party became more formally factionalised, at the same time as a strong and naturally divisive leader, Margaret Thatcher, took over. This helps to explain why the Conservative Party to this day remains unsure of its roots and vulnerable to division. Gone was the natural cama-raderie of the pre-Thatcher years where the party was a pragmatic party of government, at ease with itself, and in came the oft-asked question from the top: 'Is he one of us?' In the 1980s the late Julian Critchley MP referred somewhat crudely to the advent of the 'Garageistes'. This reflected the fact that self-made right-wing elements were steadily tak-ing over the party. Strange concepts for Conservatives became part of the parlance of the day. For example we were expected to become 'conviction politicians'. The old Conservative Party viewed 'convictions' as something very suspicious indeed. We were not expected to have them. We were the natural pragmatic party of government and should act accordingly.

After 1979, from a starting base of a Parliamentary Party where the majority were moderate centrists, and where the concept of one nation stood very high indeed, the party steadily changed at each General Election. Today 'the Nation', as its members tended to call it, may not be as influential as it once was but is very much in existence as a very agreeable club to belong to within the parliamentary Conservative Party. They have done this by moving, during the Thatcher years and afterwards, to the right in step with the party but always keeping in the centre of where the party was judged to be, and with an able and generally accept-able membership. This happened while the party as a whole was drawn inexorably to the right through the 1980s and beyond as the gentle Tory moderates left the Commons and the self-made conviction politicians replaced them. The soul of the party had changed, be it a sign of the times or a fact of life. The constituencies reflected the same change. In my own, Mrs Thatcher was not to the taste of the traditional Tory grandees and they quietly melted away to be replaced by middle-ranking retired military or the wives of their civilian equivalents. Gone was gentle paternalism and in came middle-class convictions.

As the changes nationally were reflected in the constituencies, each accelerated the progress of the other as candidates were selected in the image of their constituency parties. At Westminster the story can be told in numbers. In 1991, at the end of the 1987 Parliament, out of 376 Conservative MPs, there were on the backbenches, as distinct from in government, a total of 112 Lollards, even if some were considerably more dedicated than others. However, we still had, just, enough firepower to hold the right when it really mattered. The best example of this, which was the last great victory of the old party, occurred in the Conservative parliamentary committee elections of late 1990, just after the exit of Mrs Thatcher. The key election was for the Conservative European Committee, which had been a fundamental battleground over the years and was then entirely in the hands of the Euro-sceptics and their leader, Bill Cash MP. We decided that a major effort was required, and rather amusingly the government whips thought the same but chose for safety not to liaise with us. So they selected their champion to dethrone Cash in the form of the well-qualified Peter Hordern MP, who was both a member of the One Nation Group and the Committee of 92. They completely underestimated the reaction of the right. When they discovered that Peter Hordern was to run against Cash they immediately expelled him from the Committee of 92, and the whips' great plan came to a grinding halt. At the same time we had settled on the ex-Cabinet minister Norman Fowler MP as the best candidate, if we could persuade him to do the job. At the time he was on the backbenches, having resigned from the Cabinet to 'see more of his family' and before John Major recalled him after the election to be chairman of the party. Norman was interested, but in his position he had to think carefully whether what he might do was in the best interest of the party, and himself within it. As ever fate took a hand in the aggressive guise of one Norman Tebbit. He approached Norman Fowler in the Lobby and, in effect, tried to bully him into not standing: telling him he might stand himself, and so forth. There was no way Norman Fowler was going to put up with this, and stand he most certainly did.

The election arrived, and took place in a small committee room at the Lords end of the committee corridor, which was the normal room used by the committee for its meetings. We pulled out all the stops, and even Ted Heath and others, who had not voted in such an election in years, turned out to vote. Too late Tebbit saw what was happening and, standing up on a chair, demanded a closure on this election so that it might be held in a larger room at another time. During a party election a whip presides, who in this case was well briefed on the background and turned down Tebbit's somewhat frantic request. The election proceeded and the pro-Europeans won every office. Norman Fowler was chairman, I was vice-chairman and so on. Cash and his acolytes were completely vanquished.

After the 1992 election the number of Lollards shrank to sixty-nine, and amongst them the activists amounted to a much smaller number than that. Towards the end of 1992 we decided that something had to be done, not least because, with a few exceptions, we could not effectively recruit from amongst the new members. In their eyes we were not the Tory party of today, but rather representative of the old anti-Thatcher wets of the 1970s and 1980s. We had to somehow stay in the game, as we were no longer seen as a force able to enhance the career prospects of the new members. We had to find ways to keep the party in the centre, moderate and electable.

Our first effort was to create a centre grouping within the party which we called Mainstream. This was later successfully revived, but our first effort failed. We were very well supported at a dinner at the St Stephen's Club, with over a hundred present. Many had declined to support factions, and it reflected the desire of ordinary members to encourage a reasonably united Parliamentary Party. For better or worse we resolved to contest the important 1922 Committee elections for the officers and committee of Conservative backbenchers. However, being moderates, we were influenced towards an inclusive approach by various senior members who had little experience of internal faction fighting. This had largely come about while they occupied ministerial office, and were far above such vulgar activities. We therefore formed a balanced ticket, which included the more acceptable right-wingers together with our own people. This was a useless liberal gesture, and the Committee of 92 thanked us very much for our generosity and plumped as usual for their own, greatly helped by our support for some of them. With hindsight it was a lesson in the questionable virtue of toleration when facing the committed. The only redeeming feature of that election was that Sir George Gardiner, chairman of the 92, was unexpectedly defeated against the trend and thrown off the 1922 Executive Committee. I do not believe it was our direct doing but a reflection of the fact that his own group saw the opportunity, created by us, to get rid of him. I was told privately that the Prime Minister was delighted, but this headline result concealed the fact that overall we had failed.

The party's situation was deteriorating, and the last desperate effort to get back on an even keel was the utterly ineffectual Conservative Party leadership election of 1995. John Major resigned as party leader, but remained as prime minister, while standing for re-election. Potential opponents were told to 'put up or shut up', and it was hoped to go flat out in the first ballot against any backbench opposition showing itself, which much to the disappointment of the media the wise Norman Lamont did not. No member of the Cabinet was expected to stand in the first ballot, when suddenly the unexpected happened. In came the Welsh Secretary, John Redwood, to be greeted with hilarious space-themed headlines, such as 'The Mekon has landed', which made it difficult for him to seriously declare his earthly intentions.

As for Michael Heseltine's position, this ballot was effectively his last chance to become prime minister. For this to occur Major had to fail on the first ballot, yet Heseltine, who had brought about Mrs Thatcher's resignation, had to be seen to do absolutely nothing towards this end. Whilst I reported to him via his political secretary each sitting day, and personally on the two Sundays, it was a question of persuading all and sundry how much we supported Major. If Major fell at the first ballot, then we could inherit the centre vote and in my view Heseltine would have become prime minister.

Heseltine had to make contingency plans, but even these were left to the end of the election period. At that time an embryo campaign team was provisionally decided upon, and the night before, Michael Mates, director of the 1990 campaign, was told by Heseltine that the new team had to be new, and from across the party. Mates could not serve in that or a similar capacity. He took it well, but said half-jokingly 'Michael, you are a bastard', to which Heseltine replied, 'If, after your long association with me, you did not know that, then I have seriously underestimated you.'

Major had to get the support of two-thirds of the Parliamentary Party to survive. He barely scraped it, with 218 votes and a total of 111 MPs who did not support him. A dreadful result in the circumstances, but just enough for the media to concentrate on the 218 rather than the 111. Major stayed, Heseltine became deputy prime minister and the government resumed its journey to electoral defeat.

A general but organised retreat of the left within the party had already begun. The Lollards shrank to its 'Shepherd's Committee', who formed a lunch club meeting at the Carlton Club. In early 1995 we established the Macleod Group of Conservative MPs, of which I was the founding chairman, and which had a membership of around forty-eight. We held regular meetings, began publishing views and held lunches for luminaries. Ken Clarke was the first, and at the end of the Parliament John Major came as prime minister. I welcomed him by saying he was amongst friends and I felt he appreciated it.

In late 1995 Trevor Smith, now Lord Smith of Clifton, chairman of the Joseph Rowntree Reform Trust, came to see me to offer financial support in the interest of preserving the moderate elements within the Conservative Party. This was invaluable and enabled us to rent an office at Westminster and hire a director, Justin Powell-Tuck, one of the few left-wingers to emerge from Conservative Central Office in those days. We created a working alliance with the Tory Reform Group and held regular meetings for policy discussion. This became the Mainstream Group, mark two, and we concentrated on expansion into the more moderate and, as we saw it, civilised elements, of a party drifting inexorably to the right.

Over the years this group, which still exists, has tried to keep the Conservative Party on a reasonably moderate course with mixed results. The party has gone to the right and is all too vulnerable. If the Labour Party was a modern social democratic party, it would be all over for the Conservatives. To bring the picture into sharp focus, I refer to one Cabinet minister under Thatcher, who amuses us all by saying that he was always regarded in the old days as a mild Euro-sceptic but now, in the modern party, he is regarded as a raving Europhile.

Part 2: The life we led

The path to Westminster is tough going. Inevitably you give up much of your life, and the rest of it has to fit in. The key is ambition to get there and this kept me going in the early days at Newport, as evening after evening I was off attending a dreary function, or addressing a small audience in some ever-remote church hall. As my car came to the top of Rumney Hill on the outskirts of Cardiff, on the way to Newport, I used to pass a cinema on the right which inevitably was showing some film I wanted to see. More importantly, my girlfriends of the period would be keen on seeing it too. To this day I can still remember the feeling. 'Why on earth am I doing this?' I would ask myself.

I fought the 1964 and 1966 elections at Newport and the good side is that I enjoyed it, and met all manner of people that otherwise would not have crossed my path. The same very much goes for my political career overall, and the variety of life it represented in comparison with the some-what narrow confines of a law court. Taheré and I got married in July 1964 and I fought my first election with my wife pregnant. She was marvellous, but she married me knowing what I was going to do and throughout has been an important part of it. Newport was great in that I could fight the seat without any expectation that I could possibly win. I had a whole town seat, with suburbs, working-class terraces, industry, great people and no fewer than ten Conservative Clubs. At an election I would have to get around them in one night, which meant the daunting challenge of a half pint in each. I arrived at one club needing a break from the constant travails of the campaign, and the support of friendly Conservatives. I got on a chair to speak and to my astonishment got the worst heckling of the evening. Worse because it was unexpected. No relaxation for me, and after dealing with it, I asked the chairman what on earth was going on. 'No worry, Sir', he said, 'we've been playing skittles with the local Trades and Labour Club tonight; one of our regular fixtures.'

In 1966 Taheré and I moved to London, and I went into London chambers in the Temple. This was to get my practice near Westminster, so I could combine it with the House. My father had had a dreadful time, with a large South Wales legal practice, which he needed to earn his living, at the same time as being an MP. I did not want to repeat that experience. In 1968 I was selected for the Epping constituency, one of the largest seats in the country. We lived in Notting Hill, and night after night I was at some 'do' or other in one of the diverse parts of the constituency, which all had to be kept happy as separate entities. On the approach to Christmas it was utterly exhausting. For one thing, Taheré and I had to turn up at no fewer than four different Christmas dinner-dances, going on until late at night, and with me having to be in court in the morning. The speech had to be a bit different each time, and in my dance steps with the wives of dignitaries I had to tread very carefully indeed. At that time we had two out of our four children, but if my wife had been a career person in her own right we could not have got through it all.

As a result of boundary changes that never actually got through Parliament, I left Epping and was succeeded by, of all people, Norman Tebbit, who was elected for Epping in 1970. For my part I was then selected to fight Norwood, Lambeth, and had an exhilarating contest in June 1970, which I failed to win by some 600 votes. It was my first experience of race issues, and I was gaining support with the black population, who were comparatively recent arrivals in those days and who sympathised in many cases with the then Labour Party of Jamaica, which was a conservatively inclined party. It was a brief opportunity to engage the black population with the Conservative Party and I thought I was making good progress. Then Enoch Powell came upon the electoral scene, and ignited strong political division on racial lines. To counter this I took the then Sir Edward Boyle MP around in an open Land Rover to see many white voters, in areas where blacks also lived, ripping down Conservative posters. The neighbouring Brixton seat, where the election was fought on right-wing Powellite terms, achieved a much larger swing to the Conservatives than we managed.

Into the Commons came the first of my Cambridge contemporaries, such as Norman Fowler, Hugh Dykes and John Gummer. At the time I was upset, as I should have been with them, from Epping if not Norwood, but very soon realised that the fates had dealt me a better overall hand. I was free to be with my growing family, to earn a decent income and to compete for the safer seats as they came on the market for the next election. I was excused the awful experience of sitting for, and then losing, through no fault of mine, a marginal seat. I got on with the Bar and became chairman of the Hampstead Conservative Political Centre, which gave me a base from which to invite people to speak and organise functions. But selection committees were never far away.

My first adventure was nearly being selected for the Macclesfield by-election in 1971. I led the field at the interview stage, and so much so that the third runner, Douglas Hurd, then Political Secretary to the Prime Minister and, like me, a pro-European, helpfully dropped out of the race to give me a clear field of fire against Nick Winterton. He was making hay all over the place as an anti-European, infuriating Prime Minister Heath in the process. Before an audience of Euro-sceptic middle-class Conservatives, Nick Winterton swept the board, and there was nothing I could do to arrest the process. He entered the House, and I returned to the search for a seat. It got tough as my legal career was fortunately blossoming at the same time. The pressure of being in front of, say, the Court of Appeal by day and dashing off to some selection committee in the evening was a hard slog. I had the additional demand of my whole life being before me, when I appeared before a selection committee in a safe seat. In other words it would dictate where my family and I would live our lives. A lovely safe seat in an area I had no connection with could turn out to be a good thing, but the reality at the outset was that it was for life. A little daunting for a young married man with roots in Wales and the Border counties. Thank goodness the fates took a hand and I ended up being selected for the Leominster Division of Herefordshire, a lovely place on the Welsh Borders, with people to match. Earlier, when I had gone through the options, the two seats I most wanted were either Leominster or South Worcestershire and Leominster came up first. The reason was simple, in that I spent ten years of my youth at school at Malvern, where I was very happy and loved the whole area, which I still do.

Our lives then changed. We became immersed in the rural life and affairs of Herefordshire. My practice in London was increasing at the same time, as day after day I was in court and weekend after weekend I was in Herefordshire. Sometimes my wife would bring the car to the Royal Courts of Justice, and we would drive like mad to Herefordshire for some vital meeting, and then back to London, arriving in the small hours after driving nearly 400 miles, and back to court in the morning. It was quite mad in retrospect. Our social life in London with friends, theatre, cinema, dinner parties, weekends in nearby countryside and so on all went out of the window. It was only after leaving the Commons some thirty years later that I realised what normal life had been like, as we resumed it. That said, it was not all negative by a long shot. I had the most agreeable seat and we enjoyed our lives there, meeting many people whom I would not have met otherwise. The social life of the county was ours, if we had the time to enjoy it, which included many nice things like point to points, race meetings, parties, shooting and a host of functions of one sort or another.

So into the Commons I went. My first impression was how agreeable it was. Other members were immediately hospitable, and on virtually my first day I was greeted at lunch by Sir Derek Walker-Smith Bt., QC, MP, almost Father of the House by then, with the words: 'Peter, where is your constituency? Ah, yes, Leominster; definitely a life sentence!' I felt at home. The Smoking Room, of some fame as the haunt of Winston

Churchill and many famous men, was surprisingly egalitarian. Once you had gained admittance to the club, that was enough; you could find yourself sitting down for a drink with the illustrious, who treated you with complete normality. You would then process into dinner, and we sat down as we entered, so you could find yourself sitting next to a minister, a leading lawyer, a businessman, a retired general, a county grandee or whatever. It was with cause still referred to as the best club in London.

At this time there were very few women about so the Commons retained a male 'club' atmosphere. It was something the public school-boys took to naturally, and perhaps we were more ready than a modern generation to put up with many of the more uncomfortable, and even ridiculous, aspects of this revered but antiquated system. The hours of the House were appalling, although as a counterbalance, the social life such hours generated could be enjoyable. On top of this I had a demanding London practice at the Bar, which meant that by tradition I was excused all committee work in the mornings. I would generally turn up at 5 p.m., or a bit earlier if I could get away, and having missed Question Time and all the fun, would have to settle down to dealing with the morning mail and constituency matters. Everything would be dictated for my secretary to see to the next day, while I was in court. I was basically spoken for from Monday until at least 10 p.m. on Thursday evenings, and on Friday there would be a dash down to the constituency as soon as I could get free. My wife and I had a policy of always travelling together so that, unlike some wives, she would not be abandoned in the country all week long, and then hardly see me for functions at the weekend. We always laugh at a particular member, who, after I was selected for Leominster, advised my wife as to the lovely life she could lead in the country just like his wife, while I travailed at Westminster. We took no notice, but in any event he was divorced within two years of offering this wisdom.

The one thing I dreaded was all-night sittings. These always struck me as a particularly stupid way for grown men, many, including ministers, with very responsible jobs, to get themselves completely exhausted in a few easy weeks. I was young and managed it, with all sorts of dodges in the process. Camp-beds set up in odd places was one; a mattress in the back of my estate car in the car-park was another; grabbing a chair in the families' room was an option and was comfortable while it lasted, which was until the Division Bell went in the middle of the night. The gallop to get to the vote, and back again, before someone grabbed your nice chair resembled the Olympics at Westminster. If one went into the main library out of desperation, the sight of so many illustrious characters trying to get through the night in their own very British way, as if it was all quite normal, never ceased to amuse me. The best thing about it all was the full English breakfast that awaited us in the cafeteria in the morning. Sometimes the session went on even longer, so that the government would lose the next day's business altogether, if we were still at it when the next day's sitting was due to begin at 2.30 p.m. A clean set of clothes was then demanded, which meant thinking ahead, but this extreme did not occur very often. The radio would solemnly announce that the Commons had sat all night and the nation would think us all quite mad. The effect of all this on older and senior members and ministers could be both tragic and comic. Anthony Crosland's heart attack when he was Foreign Secretary, which led to his death, occurred after such a sitting. After another, Fred Mulley, Defence Secretary, was caught by the cameras of the press sound asleep in an all-too-comfortable armchair, while sitting next to HM the Queen, watching an air display. The 1974–9 period, when the government did not have a proper majority, was the worst for this in my time, and ministers and even the sick had to be there to vote. The period 1950–1, which was a war of attrition against a tired government, is regarded as the very worst example of what it was like to be on the receiving end of this sad, but legitimate, abuse of the system of government.

The bringing in of the wounded was a spectacle in itself. It only happened to me once when I had bad flu, and I arrived, all wrapped up and having being driven by a long-suffering wife. Even ambulances would be there. You were then inspected and counted by a government and an opposition whip. 'Oh, what a life, Peter', said Bill Benyon, the Conservative whip. The rule was that you had to be within the premises of the Palace of Westminster when the vote was taken, and you could then depart. The rules were adapted for those physically disabled, and the method of inspection could vary, as for example they could be sitting in their office. All this was far too medieval for one of Labour's million-aire Cabinet ministers of the 1970s, Harold Lever. A Manchester MP, he took no salary and provided the Labour Prime Minister of the day with sound financial and general advice. Sadly he had difficulty walking and the Whips' Offices gave him a sort of free pass to be 'nodded through' at Divisions without close inspection. This licence afforded him the oppor-tunity of enjoying the delights of the outside world, and he developed the habit of quietly venturing forth to that world, rather than sitting around miserably in his room all evening. Sadly for him the word got about, and on one momentous evening the Conservative opposition whips formed a special quasi-military detail, which successfully followed the great man on one of his evening excursions. They let him settle down for his dinner with friends at the Savoy Grill Room and then politely introduced them-selves. He took it very well by all accounts, his dinner continued but his vote was not counted.

Even if the power of the whips was in my time allowed to get too all-pervading, it did have a serious and necessary purpose to it. The Commons included, amongst other things, a pool for the selection of the government of the country, and also a party of government whose job it was to keep the elected government in office. With no separation of pow-ers, these two elements related to each other. The desire for office could have the effect of diminishing the urge for independence of thought. However, the need to keep the government in office was paramount and required some discipline if this requirement was to be met. The instru-ment, both for the talent-spotting involved in the first element and the delivery of the vote involved in the second, was that of the Whips' Office. The etiquette of possibly not supporting the party in a Commons vote was first to inform your whip. If you felt strongly, you could raise the matter in the relevant party committee to get support, and even ask to see ministers to put your case. All this was in private. Once you begin to organise support against the line and/or it gets into the public domain, a completely different ball game applies. A request to see the chief whip would be the start to this process, which could go on to the application of pressure in a number of different ways, should the issue be a major one. Tactful mention of your future prospects could start the process. Foreign trips were often an inducement, as was office accommodation and pairing opportunities. Places on a desired committee were also then within whips' patronage, as was a placing on some interminable standing committee considering a bill in which you had no conceivable interest.

During my career as a Conservative MP, I never had any real bad feeling or lasting problems with the Whips. My defection is in a different league and is covered in a separate section of this book. I was not out for office and was sufficiently independent of view and from influence, by virtue of my professional background and general situation, as not to be an easy target for any pressure. This is an important point for the future, in that backbenchers should have some qualification, role or status other than just being Members of Parliament. This is more and more lacking these days. With most of us the Whips well knew pressure would be counter-productive and were tactful in approach. In addition my constituency base was a solid one, which was a great reassurance. Relations were civilised on both sides and conducted on a basis of equality. None of the pressure points was ever exercised on me personally. On the few big occasions when I was going against the party line, I made a point, when I had finally decided, to give it to the press. On to the national news it came, and this meant that my intentions were evident and known by all, including my constituents. In the face of that there was little the Whips could do, and they had the sense not to try.

In the grand old days patronage to suit the occasion was relentlessly used. That was primarily the honours system, and it was a regular feature of the Conservative Party up to the leadership of Edward Heath from 1965. Loyal service on the backbenches was rewarded after twelve to fifteen years, if the party was in power, with a knighthood. As for the Whips, if they achieved senior status, which meant Lord Commissioner of the Treasury, then a baronetcy awaited them: a senior and convenient honour, being hereditary, but not involving any obligation to sit in the Lords. The last of these to go to a Whip was awarded in 1964 to Graeme Finlay, who lost his seat in Epping and went on to become a judge. As for ministers, the rank of viscount was the order of the day for those of Cabinet rank, with baronies going to good Ministers of State and others, like the Chairman of the 1922 Committee of Conservative MPs. Earldoms were reserved mainly for prime ministers, and the last to receive one was Harold Macmillan, by courtesy of Mrs Thatcher. When he took over the leadership, Edward Heath had little sympathy with this and did not restore hereditary titles or give knighthoods to backbenchers as such. When I arrived in February 1974, it was all too evident in the Members' Dining Room that the long-serving gentlemen members were distressed at the lack of knighthoods bestowed upon them. It was human nature, which was not Heath's strong point, and he suffered from it when he was defeated by Margaret Thatcher in 1975. Once the Conservatives got back into power in 1979, the honours lists again featured worthy Conservative backbenchers, two or three at a time. Nowadays it is a different story, as politics becomes a way of life in its own right, rather than something taken on in addition to normal responsibilities.

I did twenty-eight years in the Commons, and taking the rough with the smooth, I thoroughly enjoyed myself. It was a hectic life overall but it suited me. As a former miner and Labour MP said to me in my early days, 'It's much better than working, Peter!' Looking back, the key to enjoying the life and making something of it was for me twofold. Firstly I was always a lawyer, either in practice or with the opportunity of returning to practice. This meant I could be of independent mind when appropriate and I could not be unduly pressured by the whips which from their point of view could be counter-productive. Politics was not everything, and I had a status apart from being an MP. Secondly I did not enter the House with the one idea of getting office. Had it been offered, I would have been delighted. That said, I did not go out to get it and, perhaps naively, saw my role within the system as playing some part in monitoring, and on occasion moderating, government. For me an additional factor was that I disliked the Thatcher style of government, and some of its content, so much that I had no inclination to put myself out to please anyone for the sake of ambition.

So with the right frame of mind, the backbenches, particularly on the government side but also generally, can be a very desirable place to be. Every door is open or was; every cause can be taken up if so desired; opportunities arise to do some good; as you get more senior a nice, and reasonably safe, constituency can be very rewarding for the life it offers and for the opportunity to do some good for people and localities; back at Westminster the social life is constantly entertaining; and last but not least in my case, as foreign affairs was my strong point, I had abundant opportunity for travel and the international politics that went with it. Whatever I might say about today's Commons and the future, I am sure a lot of this still applies.

I was in the Commons from February 1974 until 2001. And during that first Blair Parliament of 1997 it all began to change. With the mass of new members overall and the considerable increase in the number of women members, change was in the air. Many able young people came into the House thinking they would have a worthwhile job to do. They had little preparation, and in many cases did not expect to win their seats. In they came, and suddenly found that, instead of helping to run the nation, it was their fate to spend night after night from about 10.30 p.m. until midnight, or later, listening to MPs filibustering on the opposition benches quite deliberately to keep Labour MPs there until a late hour. This was because as government members, and junior ones at that, they could be required to vote at any time to get government legislation through. The filibustering MPs knew this very well and could always divide the House if they so wished. This became one of the early reforms when standing orders were altered to allow discussion on orders to proceed as before, but the votes would be taken separately for the whole week, in writing and as early business the following Monday.

There have been many changes since which have moderated the hours of business. As a consequence of the earlier finishes some of the social aspects of Commons life have diminished, but a certain 'club' atmosphere still exists. Doubtless there is much modernisation and change to come both generally and with the more federal style of parliament towards which we are heading. Accepting the need for change and all the faults of the old system, it had its charm and the lifestyle could be very agreeable. I remember it with affection.

Three
THE BAR

Anyone who has been to an English public school will always feel comparatively at home in prison. It is the people brought up in the gay intimacy of the slums, Paul learned, who find prison so soul-destroying.
Evelyn Waugh, *Decline and Fall*, Part 3, Chapter 4, 1928

A political career in many cases means loss of income, financial insecurity or both. It was as true for Winston Churchill in his day, as it has been more recently for the rest of us and in spite of the increase in salary and allowances over the years. If one wants the right sort of people in the Commons then they must be properly remunerated, against a background where many of them could and will lose their seats. Should they be dependent on politics for their livelihood, then they will exist financially upon the changing whims of the electorate. There has to be a compromise between an appropriate salary and allowances and the freedom, if so wished, to have some sort of outside employment or occupation as a means of retaining a standard of living. Ignoring this will not provide the public with those best qualified by way of achievement and experience to represent them. The press do not help and do nothing but carp about and criticise any increase whatsoever in remuneration, which the public are encouraged to weigh against the fairly low levels of pay in the public sector. At the same time, those comparative few who can still earn money outside the House have to solemnly record how many hours a week they spend doing it. Who will bother with all this in the longer term? It is small wonder that we already get such vehement criticism of the standards of British politics. It is sad, and it is set to get worse, as many with talent decide there are more worthwhile things they can do with their lives than spend their time being financially deprived, shouted at and constantly criticised in the tribal and febrile atmosphere of British politics today.

The most important thing is to have some independence, or at least the freedom to act independently, when you choose to do so. If you are financially dependent on the system, it is very difficult indeed to maintain the necessary balance between your own views and those you are expected to have in order to preserve the unity of your party. In my case I was a reasonably free spirit, and this was only possible because I always had, in addition to an understanding constituency, the law and various advisory jobs either under way or to fall back on. To be something else as well as an MP gives you the confidence to be your own man when it is necessary to be so. Compared to the past, this advantage is not so evident today.

It was lunchtime on Friday. Payday for hundreds of construction workers, and the money would arrive in cash from the finance department of one of our largest construction companies, situated just outside Kingston upon Thames, near the bypass. Three men, walking side by side, in a manner resembling Burt Lancaster's Wyatt Earp approaching the OK Corral, headed towards the car-park and the main entrance. To the police eye, and even that of an amateur, it was obvious that the men were armed. In fact between them they had, all fully loaded, two pump-action shot-guns, two automatic pistols and one much-prized Smith and Wesson .44 Magnum revolver, hailed by Clint Eastwood's 'Dirty' Harry Callahan, in the film just out at the time, as 'the most powerful handgun in the world'. Later at the trial this monster of a weapon lay on the exhibit table at the Old Bailey, causing much interest amongst us *Dirty Harry* fans.

Behind the three was a back-up team and behind them two get-away cars, driven by the best the criminal world could offer. One of the arrests made over this very serious potential armed robbery was of a man called, I think, Jefferies, who was later given the annual and private title of the

Flying Squad's 'arrest of the year' 1972–3. There had been a tip-off and little did our trio, or the gang, know that a whole phalanx of Flying Squad officers were waiting for them on the first floor of the building, and the car-park and surroundings were heavily staked-out. The Flying Squad in a group were a formidable sight quite alien to the calm life of the average wages clerk.

The word went out that the robbery was on and then everything happened all at once. A number of wages clerks were returning from their lunch break across the car-park, and reaching the entrance came face to face with the Flying Squad rushing down the stairs to block the advancing robbers. Wages clerks tend to be of the gentler variety of human being and when they saw the Flying Squad coming straight at them they assumed a robbery was in process and the Flying Squad were the robbers. So they fled back across the car-park towards the real crooks, who rapidly realised that their caper had been blown. They drew weapons but on seeing the Flying Squad turned and ran back towards their get-away cars. All hell had broken loose and people were running everywhere. For the officers staking out the car-park it was difficult to tell who was who. One of my witnesses, a detective inspector, was sitting in a strategically placed car when a terrified wages clerk came sprinting towards him. I asked him what happened and I shall never forget the reply. Straight out of the mouth of Philip Glenister in that excellent BBC series, *Life on Mars*, set in the same period, it came: 'No problem, Sir. When he got level I opened the car door right into him. Down he went. One jab with my stick in his balls and he was as right as rain!' The outcome for this unfortunate wages clerk, streaming with blood, was to be bundled into a waiting police van with other 'suspects', in goodness knows what condition, to be taken off to the local 'nick', possibly with real criminals amongst them, for identification.

As for the leading three criminals they were caught between armed police behind them and the same in front of them. Very quickly their bravado collapsed and they realised that they were close to being shot. Throwing down their weapons, they put their hands in the air, literally screaming: 'Don't shoot, don't shoot.' They were arrested. The back-up squad made it to the get-away cars and, chased by the Flying Squad drivers, the best in the business on the police side, a car chase at over 100 mph ensued on the Kingston bypass. They were eventually cornered and forcibly halted, which was when the famous Jefferies arrest of the year was made. All were duly sentenced for conspiracy to rob.

This was a good example of the prosecution work I did with the Flying Squad between 1970 and 1976. They were terrific to work with and had an *esprit de corps* all of their own. One day I would be conducting a case for them at the Old Bailey and most of them would be there. When waiting they often played poker on any available surface, which seemed entirely in keeping. The next day they were gone and a comparatively junior officer would be left to instruct me. That day it is no exaggeration to say that when I sat comfortably watching the evening news there would be a report of some armed robbery – little shooting, hopefully – where an ambush led to the arrest of various villains. The next day back to court would come my squad, all smiling, and when I asked where they had been they politely apologised for not being present but they had been 'out on an operation'. They were great people and was I glad to have them around.

The fifteen years I had at the common law and criminal Bar were about the best introduction one could get anywhere to the vicissitudes of life. Much of it had the charm of youth, and we worked hard and played hard too. The drill was to check in with the clerk at around 5 p.m. and find out if there was work for you the next day. A brief might be given to you for anywhere in London or indeed the south-eastern circuit for the next day. Rapid assimilation of facts was necessary. This practice became extremely useful for me in politics and was accompanied with the associated skill of thinking on one's feet. Later on in my legal career, as the cases got heavier, preparation became more time-consuming but we were not deprived of the charm of our lives in the Temple.

A major figure in any barrister's life is their clerk. They called me 'Sir' in the manner of a sergeant-major but like their military equivalents they were in charge! I had two memorable senior clerks in my life, both of whom should be named. I did three enjoyable years at the Cardiff Bar, which gave me a wide variety of experience, better than I could have got in London at that stage. My clerk was Ken Gorman and I will never forget him. He knew exactly which cases to give me without overstraining my limited experience. He protected his barristers where necessary. One very distinguished member of chambers was Philip Wien QC, later a High Court judge, who had an enormous murder brief and asked for me, a pupil in chambers at the time, to 'devil' it for him; that is to read it up and point out the essentials, which would take me many hours but save him the same and more. No, said Gorman. He was not having his young pupils used like this when they could and should be getting wider experience in the courts. That was the end of it. Later when Wien became Mr Justice Wien, and incidentally a very good High Court judge, he was abrupt with a young member of chambers who needed encouragement. Ken Gorman went to see him privately in his judge's room and berated him, saying he could remember Mr Justice Wien in the same position as this young barrister. Wien said afterwards that he was deeply grateful and sent for the young man to give him encouragement.

My first London clerk at 5 King's Bench Walk was Stanley Hopkins, by then rather old, but who in his younger days had been junior clerk to the great Sir Edward Marshall-Hall KC. He was always kind, but tough too. I only had to stand up to him once when I was attracting work out in East Anglia, which I liked, but I had not left a promising practice on the Welsh circuit in order to get London to work near the House of Commons, and then find myself out on circuit all over again. It was a stand-off, but I survived and from then on was largely kept in London. Ironically, it was not such good quality work but a necessary sacrifice for the joys of a parliamentary career. One great moment came when he gave me a junior brief in a murder at the Old Bailey. His views on capital punishment were traditional, as one might expect. His great regret when it came to legal practice was expressed to me as a caution not to expect too much. 'If you takes away the rope, Sir, you takes away the glamour!'

The life of a young barrister in the 1960s and 1970s was very civilised. The company was agreeable and we had a great time together in chambers and out on circuit, where evenings could be somewhat indulgent. Our chambers was fairly typical, having when I joined in 1966 about twenty-two members, all of them male, including several QCs. These same chambers are now some ninety-strong, with about as many women as men. It has grown so big it has outgrown the Temple, being now in nearby offices and run by an administrator and his staff.

As we got more senior, the work got a lot tougher. Handling big cases could be very pressurised work. Some barristers could not cope. One sad case arose in our chambers, where a particularly gifted colleague, with first-class honours and legal prizes in addition, left his wife and, without her support, had a breakdown. Wasting himself on drink and casual relationships, he literally drank himself out and died. We all tried to help but it was to no avail. Sadly some enter a way of life they cannot sustain as the pressures mount. I suspect such pressures have not changed over time and will not do so.

The Bar, with its necessary introduction to the excesses of others, was a great education. As a young man I was introduced to all sorts of horrors of human behaviour. From murder to all kinds of violence, to bestiality and the rest. Standard pornography work was fairly normal and there was some light-hearted competition amongst young barristers to get the Scotland Yard briefs to prosecute such cases, not least because they involved a visit to the Yard and a private film show of the evidence. The great day arrived for one of my more eager colleagues. Down to Scotland Yard he went, having informed us all of his good fortune, and he was presented with a whole table full of films involving every sort of sexual excess. Having described them, the officer switched on the projector. Our hero settled back in his chair. On an enormous bed there reclined a waiting and expectant male to be joined by two young ladies. Dramatic action followed and just when it was getting to a breathless climax the projector broke down. A bored Vice Squad officer announced: 'You've seen enough haven't you, Sir. We've all got work to do', and that was the end of the show. Back to chambers he came.

One interesting part of my criminal work was prosecuting for the Customs and Excise. It mainly involved drugs and provided an education into their considerable variety. One routine case at the then Middlesex Crown Court in Parliament Square involved large-scale cannabis smuggling via Africa. As I pursued my duty to convict the villains responsible my two instructing customs officers were constantly leaving court and coming back to inform the others of a number. They seemed curiously gripped by the words five, then six, seven and so on. I eventually had to ask what on earth was going on. 'Well, Sir, last week we arrested a man at Heathrow who had swallowed some fourteen contraceptives full of liquid cannabis (or some such drug). We have him near the lavatory in the Station and we are counting them as they come out.' Well, well. The serious side of it was that if just one of them had burst inside him he would be dead. Apparently many of these 'mules' are followed and observed on the plane. Officers can always tell because they refuse all food and drink, which could have the effect of causing their bowels to open and out would come the treasure. Officers then tip off Heathrow customs, who prepare a friendly welcome. When the mule walks through he is intercepted and invited by the officer to drink a nice hot cup of tea. Motions occur and the count-down I witnessed begins. Before the end of my case we had reached, thank goodness, fourteen and all was well, subject to a stretch of time for the young mule.

The main feature of trials, and indeed many civil cases, is the constant exhibition of the human capacity to lie. My legal experiences were a very good preparation for politics and all the spin and slant that goes with it. Juries are a main target of all this, and many specious defences are aimed at them. Certainly in some complex, mainly financial, cases, a judge and assessors, conducting a more inquisitorial type of trial, would deal with such matters more effectively in my experience. Related to this is the key general problem of getting enough duly qualified people to serve on juries. In spite of the efforts of successive governments it is still very much a problem today. Now at least efforts are made to engage the professional and middle classes, with some success, but what chance for someone of position or with their own business if confronted by the prospect of, say, two months in court. Prior to 1988 the right of challenge made the problem infinitely worse. The defence had, when I started, seven challenges per defendant. In a case with multiple defendants, the number of total challenges available to the defendants could be sufficient to reduce the jury to the least capable it was possible to find from the pool available. It later got reduced to three challenges per defendant, which made only a nominal difference. A great event occurred at the Old Bailey when I was engaged there which was the talk of the Bar mess. A professional man had volunteered for jury service only to be challenged off again and again when called into court. He got the message and applied the antidote. The next day he appeared unshaven, in jeans and soiled shirt, with the *Daily Mirror* tucked under his arm and looking unwilling. In a flash he was accepted onto a jury. The trial was due to begin the next day and he duly appeared but this time he looked immaculate in a suit and tie with the *Daily Telegraph* firmly under his arm. He took his place in the jury box. The defence were mortified but it was too late. Since 1988 the right of peremptory challenge, that is without cause, by the defence has been abolished although the problem of getting a balanced jury of reasonable experience for the task ahead very much remains.

It is wrong to think that the system doesn't work. It can and does, but failures should not be assumed to be the fault of the jury. A jury needs a decisive foreman and depending on the presence of such a person, the role of prosecution counsel and the judge are vital to keep them from seduction by an able defending counsel. Those who have served on a jury will know what I mean when I say that being closeted in the same place with the same people, hour after hour, day after day, can create an unusual and even surreal atmosphere. An ideal climate for the defence to make the ridiculous sound just possible is formed and the voyage begins towards the creation of 'a reasonable doubt' and the final assault, asking how you, 'members of the jury, can possibly feel sure'. It is necessary for prosecution counsel to be alert at all times to prevent the defence crossing the line and for the judge to prepare a proper summing up as the case proceeds. In my experience some judges will not do that, and their summing up deteriorates into a massive read-out of the evidence. I can remember one judge reading out evidence for some three days. At the end, the jury, not to mention the rest of us, were so stupefied with boredom that an acquittal duly followed.

Many juries do try hard. The worst example I encountered of a failure of justice was no fault of the jury. It was a dramatic three-month Old Bailey trial of a known criminal gang for a succession of armed robberies. There were some ten defendants, all represented by Queen's Counsel. The prosecutor was the late John Leonard QC, later a High Court judge, and I was his junior counsel. All the gang had serious criminal records and the leader had already done ten years for the same offence of armed robbery. It was a colourful trial, featuring guns galore; armed robberies; female accomplices; and weekends passed in extravagant spending at casino hotels. The jury survived a three-month trial and a not very illuminating summing-up by a judge who assumed their guilt was so obvious that he did not really have to try. Out the jury went at the beginning of the day to consider their verdict and at 7 p.m. were still deliberating on the twenty-plus counts they had to consider. They came back with a few quite reasonable questions and had the majority direction from the judge that he would accept a verdict of ten of them if they were in difficulty. At about 7.30 p.m. when they were not far off being packed off to a hotel for the night they knocked on the door to speak to the usher who had been sitting outside the jury room all day. She was an extremely officious retired police officer who was by this time in a very bad temper. The jury said they were making good progress and could finish that evening but could they please have some coffee and sandwiches to keep them going. The stupid usher told them to get on with it and intimated that they were wasting everyone's time, implying that the accused were obviously guilty. She closed the door on them. All this was heard by the other usher, also a retired police officer, who was horrified but afterwards never let it go further than prosecuting counsel, who were to be quite shattered by a verdict they could not understand. Back to the verdict and ten minutes after the jury's request was refused they knocked on the door and announced that they were ready with their verdicts.

Into court they came. None of us had any idea of what had gone on 'backstage'. Everyone expected convictions on most of the counts. Silence reigned as the clerk of the court put the counts, one by one. 'Guilty or not guilty?' 'Not guilty, my Lord', came the reply to count after count. Three months of trial, two years of police investigation and goodness knows how much public money, all thrown away. A total 'not guilty' verdict, and as much to the surprise of the accused as everyone else. Out of the dock they walked. The male usher who told us later what had happened was standing by the jury foreman when he read out the verdicts as marked on the indictment, count for count. He saw that a large number of counts had 'guilty' marked next to them, only for this to be crossed out, and 'not guilty' substituted. Clearly the jury would not stand for the way they were treated by the usher after all those months, and therefore to hell with the whole thing. If they were not respected, then not guilty it was going to be. Never has a gang been so lucky in the game of chance.

The sequel to all this rubbed in this theme. I was left, as junior counsel, to tidy up the matter with a succession of some three subsidiary trials of the rest of the gang, who counted themselves lucky to be left off the main indictment. They were joined by some of the original defendants also charged on these additional indictments. These trials were smaller affairs, each a week or so long, with sentencing kept to the end of all trials as they were so inter-connected. They were all convicted to a man. When the jury went out in the last trial, all defendants were assembled downstairs in the cells for sentence. During these many months we all felt we had got to know each other and we, on our side, had tried to conduct a firm but fair prosecution and indeed quite a lot of humour crept in owing to the colourful nature of the evidence and the East London characters of the defendants.

When the jury in the last trial went out, my clerk had the brilliant idea of giving me a defence brief in the same court, thus gainfully employing me while we awaited the last verdict. It was necessary for me to go down to the cells to interview my client, and when I got down there who did I find but many of the gang I had been doing my best to convict for months on end. There they all were looking at me through the bars of their cells. There was a pause, and then lo and behold a sort of ironic cheer went up, followed by some jokes about the prosecution, and then friendly banter and questions about the completed trials. There was no animosity at all. This was reserved for the police and particularly the Flying Squad. I was seen as a player on the stage who could as easily have been representing them as being briefed to prosecute them.

Part II
A POLITICAL LIFE

Part II

A POLITICAL LIFE

Four

MRS THATCHER

You see things and you say, 'Why?' But I dream things that never were; and I say 'Why not?'

> George Bernard Shaw, the Serpent to Eve, in *Back to Methuselah*, Act 1, 1921

Part 1: Personal experiences

Mrs Thatcher was remarkable by any standards. That said, I record at the outset that I could never get on with her personally and never pretended to do so. She was not my type nor did she share my politics. At meetings she could be difficult and over-assertive, leader of a party which, at least at the outset, did not resemble her. She had a quick and able mind, with a tendency to take her basic opinion on anything and resolutely hang on to it. She would interrupt and contradict in such a way that you had to force your way through it all to get a point over to her. However, underneath all this there was a woman as human and sensitive anyone else. She certainly suffered from nerves before big speeches. To hear her in full flow it is difficult to believe this, but nervous she certainly was. On the occasion of one of her early major efforts in the Commons as leader of the opposition I had dinner with her afterwards in the Members' Dining Room. She had made a point of coming into the Chamber nearly an hour before she was due and just sitting there.

'Why?', I asked her. She frankly replied that to have nerves outside the Chamber was far worse than going into the atmosphere you had to face and preparing to get on with it. When her moment came, up she got and, with no nerves on view, she gave her opponents both barrels and more. As ever, it was splendid to behold.

She constantly needed reassurance, and Ian Gow MP, her first Parliamentary Private Secretary as prime minister, gave her this. When she needed support he made sure she had it. On one occasion in the early 1980s I was at an official dinner at Number 10 and came out with some compliment to Gow about how she had handled some difficult issue of the moment. To my surprise, Gow immediately gripped my arm and said that I should repeat what I had just said to the Prime Minister. Sweeping aside those she was talking to Gow said to me: 'Now repeat what you just said to me!' So repeat it I did, and of course she loved it. It was not my style to flatter, but Gow knew exactly what he was doing. When he left Number 10 after the 1983 election to become a Minister of State he was badly missed. He soon resigned his office over Northern Ireland and became a formidable but slightly eccentric figure on the backbenches. For her part she steadily got more and more difficult to deal with as the years of power went by. I believe Gow would have limited this trend but he was not there. He was murdered by the IRA in August 1990.

What follows are examples of what she was like in private meetings. Engaging with her was always a testing experience: little small talk and generally straight to the point and down to business.

In 1976 the Labour Party Conference undertook to abolish the House of Lords and, in reply, Mrs Thatcher, as leader of the opposition, asked Lord Home, former prime minister and doyen of the party, to produce a report on the subject. This he did in early 1978, only to have it placed in a lofty pigeon hole, never to be seen again. At the same time the Bow Group Home Affairs Committee, of which I was chairman, produced a fairly radical report on the same subject, launching it in time for the 1977 Party Conference in Blackpool. As I was standing alone in the large entrance hall of the Winter Gardens at a bookstand, the sound of marching feet attracted my attention and heralded the approach of the mighty. Up came

Mrs Thatcher plus entourage. She saw me, stopped, wheeled around and said: 'Peter, I have read your pamphlet on the House of Lords', wheeled back around and marched off in her own inimitable walking style, handbag in hand, without saying another word. Under her leadership Lords reform got nowhere.

Mrs Thatcher's technique in private meetings with her backbenchers was interesting. It perfectly marries up with how she was reported as behaving in Cabinet, and involved strongly asserting herself from the outset and being a party to any argument rather than an arbiter of it. This is well dealt with in Giles Radice's *Odd Couples: The Great Political Pairings of Modern Britain* (I.B.Tauris, 2015, at p. 189):

> In Cabinet, Whitelaw acted as de facto chairman. Thatcher almost always began meetings by the unusual practice of stating her conclusion first and challenging her colleagues to disagree with her. Some of them found her behavior intimidating, even intolerable.

He then quotes David Howell, her first Energy Secretary, as reported in Peter Hennessy's book on postwar prime ministers:

> Of course there is a deterring effect if one knows that one is not going into a discussion where various points of view will be weighed and gradually a view will be achieved, but into a huge argument when tremendous battle lines will be drawn up and everyone who doesn't fall into line will be hit on the head. (Peter Hennessy, *The Prime Minister: The Office and its Holders since 1945*, Allen Lane, 2000, at p. 405.)

Our backbench meetings tended to begin with some sort of mini-interrogation. Early in her premiership in 1980 the officers of the Conservative Foreign Affairs Committee were called to see her in Number 10 with her Foreign Secretary, Lord Carrington, in attendance. She literally sailed into us about who she had or had not heard on the *Today* programme. Fortunately I passed muster, as I had been on it a lot following the 1979 Iranian Revolution. The others somewhat desperately managed to recall some broadcast they had made on foreign affairs, except for the unfortunate Bill Shelton, the MP for Streatham, who had once been her Parliamentary Private Secretary. Apparently she had not heard him on any programme, and 'Why was that?'. Bill effected a strategic retreat by stating that he had been on the media regularly, but dealing with his other subject of education. Fortunately for Bill that appeared to satisfy our leader, who had once been Secretary of State for Education and Science, and we proceeded to our business with a definite idea of who was in charge of the meeting. This of course was the point of it all. That said, in the early days Mrs Thatcher was more restrained than later on, and not least as she was sitting there with Lord Carrington, who had great experience in a field in which our new Prime Minister was having to experience a rather sharp learning curve. We went through the problems of the moment and then suddenly the eyes flashed and we got our first taste of future dramas still to come. There she was, up and away, tearing into the French President, Valéry Giscard d'Estaing, who, mercifully for his sake, was not present and who had patronised her the previous week, at her first EU summit meeting. She was new upon the European scene and the all-too-grand President of France chose to talk down to her about the way it was all done in this high assembly of leaders, which at that point included no other women. We had a brief foretaste of the future as the mighty Giscard was put to the Thatcherite sword for our benefit. The prospect of foreign affairs becoming more exciting was abundantly clear.

A few years later there was a similar meeting in her Commons room when we were joined by her Foreign Secretary, Geoffrey Howe, plus all her Foreign Office ministers. This provided for an amusing example of the same technique, which is to assert oneself and assume a position of command, before the substantive meeting gets under way. Because of the ministerial presence we could be comparatively relaxed as she sailed into them, one by one, but discounting Geoffrey Howe with 'Oh, yes, Geoffrey, I know where you've been', as if she wished he had stayed there. She demanded to know where they had recently travelled to and why. She got to Malcolm Rifkin, who had mercifully been somewhere acceptable to her, and that left the remaining Minister of State, Baroness Young.

As Mrs Thatcher rounded on her, some recently half-read brief came to mind. She warmly congratulated Lady Young on the great job she had done in Uruguay. This produced complete consternation upon the visage of the noble Baroness as she stammered out the fact that 'I haven't been to Uruguay yet, Prime Minister, I am due to go next week.' We held our sides with restrained mirth as Mrs Thatcher ploughed on, totally unable to see the funny side.

Among the greatest difficulties in any discussion with Mrs Thatcher were her preconceived ideas, which she resolutely stuck to, and which made it very hard to have any sort of discussion. Some more courageous ministers found that she had to be stood up to so that they could get a contrary word, or any word, into the discussion. The good news was that if you got your point of view over in spite of a tight defence, she did give credit for it. One of the saddest aspects of the Thatcher period was that not enough of her ministers were willing and able to stand up to her.

As an example of her ways, a handful of us went to see her in 1981 over a visit we had made to the West Bank and Beirut during which we had met a crosssection of the Palestinian leadership from Yasser Arafat down. Try as we might to present an even and informative report, speaking as fast as we could to avoid constantly threatened interruption, we still had to face, after each point made, the rejoinder that the Palestinians were 'terrorists'. The meeting was a complete waste of time.

The 'one of us' attitude was always there. In early 1986 I was having a peaceful snack in the Strangers' Cafeteria, awaiting the ten o'clock vote, when in came no less a personage than the Prime Minister, with her Parliamentary Private Secretary in attendance, and both joined me and another Conservative MP at our table. The conversation rapidly got round to the AGM of the National Farmers' Union, whose dinner she was due to address the following evening. The new President of the NFU, Simon Gourlay, had just taken over, and before she could get going on the subject her PPS cautioned her that Simon, later Sir Simon, came from my constituency. I confirmed this and then off she went. A flow of criticism followed which included the fatal statement that he was not 'one of us'. She added that his wife, Caroline, was some sort of strange individual who 'voted Green' and added that Simon did not vote for us. This sort of divisive view was difficult to sustain but I held on to my anger, and just said gently and politely to the Prime Minister that I could not say whether Simon voted for us or not, but I was fairly sure he had voted for me. That ended the conversation.

This was not an untypical example of her thinking, which though endemic, was too often encouraged by those around her. It was not only partisan, but unnecessarily so.

The constant struggles during the 1980s to protect the BBC World Service in general, and its finances in particular, from the anti-BBC views of Mrs Thatcher and her allies, such as Norman Tebbit, provided a continuous cause for the left and right in the party to disagree on. In the same basket was the cause of the British Council. The winter of 1981–2 saw the first manifestation on the floor of the Commons of a very energetic campaign by the then Director-General of the British Council, Sir John Burgh. He created a body called the Friends of the British Council, with a parliamentary wing supported by a number of Conservative MPs, which led to us abstaining on an important relevant vote in 1983. At the time I little suspected that such a vote would have any lasting effect on the Prime Minister. How mistaken I was. A while afterwards in we went for one of our foreign affairs meetings with Mrs Thatcher, with the long-suffering Foreign Secretary, Geoffrey Howe, in attendance. Up came the subject of the British Council and Mrs Thatcher sprang into immediate action. 'Who was that man', she proclaimed, 'who caused my backbenchers to rise up against me? What was his name, Geoffrey, his name?' 'Burgh', came the reply, 'Burgh, Prime Minister.' This had to be repeated every time Burgh's name became relevant and which she affected to forget. Geoffrey Howe's replies, and he spoke in a low tone at the best of times, became lower and lower in repetition. But it was great theatre to watch!

Worse on this subject area came in 1985. The budgets of the World Service and the British Council were under threat. In we trooped with Geoffrey Howe in attendance. I had told him a few days earlier that I was going to raise both the World Service and the British Council with her. These are not the 'flavour of the month', he warned, and then helped me as to the best way to raise the issues to avoid sustaining serious political injury.

I decided to make my main pitch on the World Service and to put everything I'd got into creating the right impression. I had to use the minute-plus I had before interruption to engage her sympathy. I therefore played my strongest card, by stressing how much my wife's family had lost through the Iranian Revolution, a personal aspect she knew about. I continued that whilst I appreciated she held the World Service responsible, to an extent, for that revolution, we nevertheless respected its continuing role in the world. For a brief moment I thought I had got through. Not a bit of it!

In an example of the sometimes fickle, and unforeseeable, reaction of some leaders, the warning light came into her eye, as she launched her attack on the unfortunate World Service. It emerged that the Soviet Ambassador, Mr Zamyatin, whom I knew well, had come to see her the day before on the specific instructions of the Kremlin. This was to complain over references being made on the BBC World Service to Mrs Raisa Gorbachev's love of the good things in life, and not least expensive fur coats. This caught me completely unawares and it transpired to be a mere reference on the World Service programme *What the Papers Say* about something reported in the *Observer* about Mrs Gorbachev's sartorial preferences.

All of us who had anything to do with the Gorbachevs' visit to London in December 1984 knew this only too well. Indeed we had to organise shopping expeditions for Mrs Gorbachev during which vast amounts of cash would be produced by the Soviet Embassy to pay for her various purchases. Mrs Thatcher appeared to have no idea of all this and launched into another attack on the World Service, who had embarrassed her friend Mr Gorbachev.

All was not lost and I recovered just a little at the end of the meeting, when I risked double jeopardy by raising the British Council. This time the fates decreed in my favour. It so happened that, unlike Sir John Burgh, the new Director of the British Council, Dick Francis, ironically an ex-World Service man, had recently called to see her and his charm had obviously worked. For once the British Council could do no wrong.

As we tumbled out of her room this caused much amusement, and I remember Peter Bottomley, then Conservative MP for Eltham, congratulating me for only having one dagger sticking out of my back when I so easily could have collected two!

All these are but small examples of how Mrs Thatcher behaved in private meetings with her own MPs and ministers. As her eleven years of power wore on, her manner of doing things, always assertive, became more imperious in nature. I remember one of the new 1987 intake who was quite put out after an introductory meeting with her which he attended with some of his colleagues. They entered her room behind the Speaker's chair in a state of awe, and came out even more so, having been lectured from start to finish, without warmth, humour or the chance to participate. An amusing example at the other end of the spectrum was, as has been said, her tendency in Cabinet to enter into the fray of discussion with such partisan relish that it was difficult for her to then fulfil her role as PM and chairman, by summing up the arguments.

When all this is put together, with difficult political issues such as the poll tax and growing fears of the many MPs in marginal seats who had come into the House in her wake that they might lose their seats, then we have the perfect recipe for a crisis. In the period 1989–90 it all came to a head, and crisis there was indeed.

Part 2: The fall of the Iron Lady

> I returned, and saw under the sun, that the race is not to the swift, nor the battle to the strong, neither yet bread to the wise, nor yet riches to men of understanding, nor yet favour to men of skill; but time and chance happeneth to them all.
>
> Ecclesiastes 9:11

It was Tuesday, 30 October 1990. 'No, No, No', she cried, hammering the unfortunate dispatch box for emphasis at the same time. She was already magnificent in defiance of the forces of Europe, engaged as they were in pushing her towards Economic and Monetary Union and the single currency. She was making her statement concerning the EU Rome summit of the previous weekend where she had been out-manoeuvred by Italy's adroit, if not byzantine, Prime Minister Giulio Andreotti, who was in the chair. Her press conference from Rome on Sunday at the summit's conclusion was a Thatcherite classic, as with eyes flashing in anger and defiance, she fought back. She was accompanied by her Foreign Secretary, Douglas Hurd, whose body language, turn of the shoulders and pained look as he sat beside her clearly indicated, for all to see, his wish to be somewhere else at the time!

In the chamber her defiance continued, but, though she was unaware of it, she had a lot she would need to be defiant about. Feeling against her had been steadily mounting, the catalyst being the poll tax. Now we had continued clashes and tantrums over Europe. The process leading to her removal and resignation had begun. It is amazing to think that this whole process, from the end of the Rome summit to her resignation took a grand total of twenty-five days. When I told some experienced American political friends this fact they were almost speechless. 'Good God, Peter, it takes us four years to get rid of a President!'

My first thoughts that change could be on the cards belong, of all places, to the Savoy Hotel. In the spring of 1989 we were all summoned to a grand celebration lunch. It was to be in honour of our leader's ten years at Number 10. To get there in time it was necessary for our chairman, David Howell MP (the Rt. Hon. Lord Howell of Guildford), to adjourn the Commons Foreign Affairs Committee early, which he did, so that we could get to the lunch. He was not going to it. I had always viewed David Howell as a sensible weather vane indicating where the Conservative Party stood at any particular time. He was not content. All was not well.

The lunch added to my apprehension. During President Reagan's re-election campaign of 1984, the standard chant of supporters was: 'Four more years, four more years.' At the lunch the chant went up from the ranks of the devoted, 'Ten more years, ten more years'. It somehow summed up the division amongst us. Some wanted more and more of the same. The rest of us would have appreciated some gesture of humility and at least keeping open the possibility that sometime in the future there might be a change. After lunch I strolled back along the Embankment with others, feeling profoundly depressed. I was not alone.

This simmering discontent surfaced later that year, in October/ November 1989, when Mrs Thatcher was obliged to stand for the normal ritual of her re-election as leader of the Parliamentary Party. She suddenly found herself opposed by a prominent pro-European and senior MP, Sir Anthony Meyer Bt., which was a very brave thing to do in the face of the entire Conservative establishment. In those days you needed only two signatures, of a proposer and seconder, to stand. Who they were remains an interesting question to this day. I had my considered suspicions, but with no real evidence to support them they have to remain unspoken.

At that time the Lollards, an organisation of Conservative MPs on the centre-left of the Party, of which I was chairman, always gave an opening of session party at Lollards' Tower, Lambeth Palace, in the flat of Sir William Van Straubenzee MP, one of our founders. Sir Anthony was expected as usual. I got there early as co-host, to find Lollards' Tower, and come to that much of Lambeth Palace, bathed in the bright lights of the media, with eager camera crews awaiting the arrival of the challenger. This was the last thing we all wanted; the warning went out and Sir Anthony and others eventually arrived via circuitous routes from within, and through, the palace. The joke of the evening was that Sir Anthony must have passed through the archbishop's bedroom and hopefully picked up a needed blessing along the way. Perhaps he did, because in the election two weeks later he picked up sixty votes, either directly or by way of abstention. This was a clear warning to the leader, and by all inside accounts, her campaign adviser, the much-liked George Younger MP (the Rt. Hon. Lord Younger of Leckie), tried to warn her of the significance of all this. She took not a blind bit of notice.

A year later the same leadership election came around and there was enormous media and general pressure on Michael Heseltine to stand. One particularly graphic piece of journalism came from a leading commentator, who told of entering the Commons through the St Stephen's entrance with his young son. They duly walked past the statue of Charles James Fox on the right. 'What was that man for, Daddy?' asked the boy. The clear inference was then imaginatively created that Heseltine had no other purpose in life but to seize this, his great chance. On the other hand, whilst Heseltine necessarily made all contingency arrangements to stand, he had no great wish to do so. It was highly likely that Mrs Thatcher would lose the next election and he would be the leading candidate for the succession without any question of splitting the party. However, events, always the most difficult thing to deal with, developed a momentum of their own. On the morning of Thursday, 1 November the Cabinet met as usual and Mrs Thatcher chose to quite gratuitously bully Geoffrey Howe, her Leader of the House, when his turn came to deal with parliamentary business. This turned out to be just once too often and the resentment caused by years of loyal service, rewarded by a lack of gratitude bordering on contempt, boiled over. At about 6.30 that evening his resignation was announced. All hell then broke loose.

I wanted change. I had never been 'one of us' and had never felt part of Mrs Thatcher's Conservative Party. The issue of Europe, and her attitude to it, was around with a vengeance, and causing increasing disharmony for us all. What was more, without a new leader we were likely to lose the approaching General Election. Mrs Thatcher was even seen by many as a liability. Now we were propelled into a campaign to end her leadership. There was little time to think whether this was the best time or way of doing things. It was 'Events, dear boy, events!' and we were in it almost before we knew it was happening. As for the Heseltine campaign, he was by far the best option for progressive Conservatism and for pro-European change. For my part I was automatically drawn into it by my views and connections as chairman of the Lollards. At the centre of the campaign were Michael Mates, as director and main 'name cruncher', and Dr Keith Hampson, Heseltine's former PPS and a valued adviser on the various issues that arose.

On the evening of Geoffrey Howe's resignation I found myself on the 'Green' opposite Parliament doing a succession of interviews, one after the other. The lesson here is that the more interviews you do in succession on the same subject the more you have to watch what you say. You get a bit too relaxed with the repetition. My basic line was that the party had to unite and that it should be led in such a way as to make that possible. Risky, but just all right if I stopped at that. In my last interview with *Newsnight*, conducted by James Cox, I went a bit too far and appeared to suggest the Prime Minister would have to change her ways to achieve that unity. Quick as a flash James pounced on my words and asked 'But will she change, Mr Temple-Morris?' Equally quickly I replied 'No, she won't!'

I knew I had over-stepped the mark but mercifully got away with it on that evening's programmes. The following morning I went into the BBC news studio, to appear straight after the main 8 a.m. news on *Breakfast Time*. The golden rule here is to always get into the studio and listen to the news if you are about to pontificate concerning it. To my horror there I was with my comment of the evening before leading the news, and indeed the whole tenor of the programme was whether Mrs Thatcher would change. Needless to say, I did not have an easy time.

A good example of the importance of this rule came shortly after all these events when the new chairman of the party, Jeremy Hanley MP, arrived too late to see the relevant news programme. He was due to speak about violent crime and the news had featured a load of louts literally breaking up the site of a boxing match. When immediately asked about this he described the behaviour he had not seen as 'somewhat exuberant'. He never lived it down!

For the campaign I did my bit by canvassing my share of the somewhat personal electorate of Conservative MPs. A number held doubts about Heseltine, who was regarded by some as aloof, cold and impetuous. In personal terms I exploited weakness which usually amounted to reluctance to disturb the status quo. I used strength in my targets to emphasise the need for change and their opportunity to do something about it at last, and so on it went. Basically here were all the essentials of a political campaign amongst a small, but very personal and connected electorate. One thing I never did was to offer any hint of possible preferment. I always felt that those voting with that in mind could work out their own chances without my help. We had visits to Heseltine's Victoria Street office, from where progress was monitored, and virtually daily meetings down in Room J, in the basement below the Members' Lobby, a room with an almost matchless history of being at the centre of dramatic events because of its handiness for the Chamber. However, my main role was with the media and there ensued an exhausting period doing some six to ten broadcasts a day, including the regulars and after that anywhere from Ireland to New Zealand. At weekends in particular, various journalist friends would call and it was vital to talk and set the tone for the week ahead. Before and during the courses of Sunday lunch, one could emerge having contributed to anything from straight coverage to the line to be taken in a leading article. It was necessary, but very bad for the digestion.

Some facts about such campaigns emerged. Those who wrote major pieces or books about the campaign afterwards tended automatically to go straight to the doings of the mighty. They would start with the famous meeting Mrs Thatcher had with her Cabinet, going in to see her one by one. This was of course vital, but that point was only reached because we foot soldiers had been constantly fanning the flames, and adding to the crisis, so that this was able to happen. It was only because of a well-organised campaign within the Commons that the situation was there to exploit.

Another interesting aspect, particularly involving an effort to depose an established leader, is the ability of the press to assist a candidate and, if necessary, to fight dirty on his or her behalf. An example of this occurred during the challenge of Sir Anthony Meyer in 1989. Sir Anthony was a wealthy man and our right-wing press uncovered some earlier sexual exploits of his in Paris. I was told about this at the time but it never came out as it was judged to be overkill. However, once Mrs Thatcher was duly re-elected, a tabloid used the material, as it was obviously a good juicy story, and helped the process of speeding up Sir Anthony's deselection by his constituency. The following year, when the Heseltine challenge to Mrs Thatcher was warming up and I was spending a lot of time in the media, a good journalist friend came to see me. He was the late Anthony Bevins, a respected figure who at various times wrote for the *Guardian*, the *Observer* and the *Independent*. To my innocent surprise, he warned me to destroy anything I might have in my possession that might indicate anything but a completely regular personal and private life. I found this a quite chilling aspect of our democracy and I have never forgotten his words: 'These people fight dirty and you have to be ready for it.'

Sure enough the first ballot drew near and stories started to appear referring to the allegedly wayward lifestyles of the Heseltine family, with particular reference to his daughters. Fortunately for everyone this all ended with Mrs Thatcher's withdrawal from the contest. The remaining campaign between Heseltine, Hurd and Major for the second ballot was as friendly and above-board as you could get. An amusing side is that there are always a few who try to get around the system and have it all ways. They try to give the impression when approached that they are in favour of whatever candidate may be approaching them. This may be for reasons of personal advantage, or because they have insufficient confidence to face up to it and say 'No'. Little do they realise that they have become marked men, and as the election gets close each team has the same problem. In such a closed election, we all have friends in the opposing teams, and towards the end of the process we get together to check out those we believe to be cheating. It is a rewarding part of the process as the double-dealers are all too easily found out. They deserve their fate, which can be serious: from resignation from government to little chance of promotion within it.

Going back to the day of Geoffrey Howe's resignation I was still in Ireland that morning on the business of the British–Irish Inter-Parliamentary Body, of which I was British chairman. I was phoned at my hotel by Michael Mates, telling me that all was in place with the organisation and we were ready to go. All that remained was Geoffrey Howe's speech that afternoon. We didn't know what it would be like, but we needed a boost from it. Had Howe appealed for calm and a united front for the General Election it would have been very difficult for us to proceed. I have no inside information but I have always suspected that Geoffrey Howe, old hand that he was, knew perfectly well what his resignation would do. Collusion was unnecessary. He had had enough of her and his speech proved that. The effect of it was electrifying and, as far as we were concerned, the starting gun had been fired and away we went with no delay at all.

Michael Heseltine was a marvellous campaigner. Having been obliged for so long to say that there were no circumstances that he could foresee that would cause him to stand against his Prime Minister, he was now liberated. Evasion and silence was now the fate of others. Geoffrey Howe contrived to lose his voice. John Major, well appreciating that he could be a candidate in a second ballot, suddenly developed a raging toothache and was confined incommunicado in hospital. Poor Douglas Hurd needed all his diplomatic skills to fend off the press, and so it went on. A number of members and junior ministers were already positioning themselves for a second ballot. In the main this meant voting for Heseltine as the best way of defeating Thatcher and then the way was clear to go for John Major on the second ballot. We knew what was going on, but we needed votes and could not be choosy about personal motivation.

The chosen day for the ballot came around. The date was hers to choose, and Mrs Thatcher was badly advised by those close to her. It was considered best for her to appear above it all as a world statesman, and therefore the date chosen was that of the G7 summit in Paris, where she would be clearly seen with other world leaders. This was the fatal error of a leader who had been too long in post. Had she mixed in and campaigned for the votes of the doubters, she would have won. As it was, the way was left completely clear for us to operate on the ground. Democracy belongs with the relevant electorate and not in the grandeur of a Paris summit. Her decision was excusable, as those in her entourage by that time of her period in office were in too many cases mediocre, and certainly detached from the realities of the situation. Her Parliamentary Private Secretary, Peter Morrison, was, of all people, the one responsible for overseeing her campaign and telling her how it was going. None of us knew how he was getting any real figures for her, but some would emerge according to his inspiration of the moment. When the truth was announced, with the leadership being at the Paris Embassy that fateful evening, it must have been a quite dreadful experience for him, let alone Mrs Thatcher.

Her reaction provided one of the most splendid items of news coverage I have ever seen. Down the stairs and out into the Embassy forecourt she strode, with minions scrambling to keep up with her. There before her were the pack of the press with microphones trembling in anticipation. 'This microphone, Prime Minister, this microphone', called out the BBC's John Sergeant, and she duly obliged. Out came a message of defiance of the result, and totally without any sign or show of humility. Back in London, the effect amongst media and politicians broadcasting amidst the frenzy taking place on the Green, adjacent to Millbank, was electric. I was very much there, going from broadcast to broadcast, as were others, and the looks of regret, and in some cases anger, when she was seen on the monitors, and endlessly repeated thereafter, was ominously clear. Even as we spoke, the Whips went into conclave and rapidly fanned out around the palace and to their telephones, sounding out opinion. By the end of the evening their findings were not at all good and such was the mood when Mrs Thatcher returned the next day. The stage was set for the Cabinet to deliver the message, one by one, and at about 10 a.m. the following morning her resignation was announced.

That was effectively the end of the Heseltine campaign for the leadership of the party. We all knew, even if we did not say it, that with Thatcher still in the ring we could win. Without her a completely different scenario was about to play out. Michael Heseltine had wielded the knife, and against the same opponent this would have been a badge of courage. With the victim of the knifing departed it was a different story. The whole Conservative world reached for safety and did its best to deny what it had done. Members had been brave but their constituency officers saw a rat when they looked at the results. Perhaps their member had voted for Heseltine without telling them. If he had he should not do so again. Most of these rank and file, so vital for the vote, were no longer in the fight. They, and their constituencies, wanted a safe pair of hands, blessed by Mrs Thatcher into the bargain. They had this safe package in the form of John Major, who was about to emerge, in these extraordinary circumstances, as the leader and the Prime Minister. Surprising, but his chance came and he took it.

In the Heseltine camp all this had been foreseen and winning was a somewhat hopeless concept, but we had the people to put up a good fight. We suddenly had a new and rejuvenated team. Gone, in a sense, were our cosy meetings amongst political friends. In came a number of the Thatcherite right who saw Michael as a leader qualified to succeed Thatcher. They had doubtless been wooed by Heseltine over his years going around the constituency 'rubber chicken circuit'. They represented the more cavalier elements of the right, sadly not enough to cater for the more mundane electorate in our midst. It was beyond that element to wield the dagger twice and, having put themselves right in their constituencies, they voted for Major. Democratic politics therefore got us a prime minister who really could have been an excellent chief-of-staff, and a number two, Heseltine, who could have been an excellent leader.

With the second ballot over and the result finalised we then came into the deselection stage. Heseltine had made a heroic exit at our last meeting in Room J after the result. Quoting from some epic classical source he told us that the good fight, which he said we had won, was worth it, and so it was. We stood and applauded him with genuine warmth before he went off to return to government as Environment Secretary. Whilst his ministers in the department were rearranged, with one resignation in anticipation of his wrath, he took not one of his supporters with him into government. For me that had not been the point, but for others, such as Michael Mates, it was deeply resented. It also said something about Heseltine, who sadly inspired support but seldom affection. His warmth towards his fellow man was limited. Following complaints this situation was rectified after the 1992 election, with Mates going to Northern Ireland as Minister of State. For better or worse he did not survive very long, and the loyalty to the fraudulent Conservative donor, Asil Nadir, ended his brief period of office.

After the second ballot, we were all taken up by constituency moves to secure our deselection for the part we had played in removing the much-revered leader. Under the standard Conservative Association rules, it took the votes of fifty members to have a Special General Meeting. My media prominence guaranteed my fate, and even before the second ballot result, signatures were being gathered against me. It only took one member of the association, a former PR man who wanted to cut a dash in the public eye, to do the trick. He was aided and abetted by, of all people, the younger brother of Norman Tebbit, who was the superintendant of a care home on the Worcestershire side of my constituency. The press went wild, thinking that Norman Tebbit and I were having some sort of personal fight. We had done so and could have done so again, but in this instance, as could be the way in the Tebbit family, there was no love lost between the two brothers. So, for once, Norman Tebbit was of help to me in denying any involvement, and his brother was seen as the maverick he was.

These deselection battles went on into the New Year. Before Christmas one after the other we came to judgement before our associations. Julian Critchley came first, followed the evening after by Michael Mates. A typical scene ensued, as the gruff Colonel Mates marched into his meeting, scattering all before him, including a large group of assembled media. One brave cameraman from the BBC back-peddled in front of the advancing Mates and held his ground in spite of the order to 'Get out of my way!' Unfortunately for the cameraman, he could not see behind him, as he back-peddled, a formidable step that lay in his path, which he quite spectacularly fell backwards over, plus camera and equipment. The BBC news duly recorded a film of the advancing Mates, which suddenly ended with the camera somehow pointing to the sky. It was not until the later ITN news that it was reported, with relish on the part of ITV, how the BBC cameraman had met his fate, fortunately without injury. Colonel Mates marched on undaunted to a difficult meeting from which he successfully emerged.

The next night it was my turn. I had taken the threat very seriously, not least thanks to the advice of concerned Labour friends in the Commons. Most of them had just passed through their damaging deselection period, when they had to beat off the challenge of the extreme left in their constituencies. They were connoisseurs of constituency troubles in a way that, at the time, was completely alien to Tory MPs, and particularly those of us with traditional county seats. I had lots of sympathy from Labour and I particularly remember two bits of advice. I followed both to the letter and it paid off. First Stuart Bell came into my room and gave me a pep talk. It ended with him saying there was only one thing that mattered, which was to make sure you had 'bottoms on seats'. In other words, make sure you get your people there. 'Organisation, organisation' was the order of the day. I walked over to the Commons from the Norman Shaw Building on the Embankment with my old friend Giles Radice of the Labour Party, who had been through it all and recounted to me the realities of a divided constituency party which I, as a mere Tory, had little if any appreciation of. 'Get ready to prepare a counter-cheer', he sagely advised. I did not know what he was talking about, but it steadily dawned that I had entered that strange realm of internal conflict. He then explained to me that on entry, or at the start of the meeting, I would be cheered. There was then likely to be a jeer from opponents. This was the point when the counter-cheer came in. All this was unthinkable for a county Tory like me, but I took it all in, knowing that this strange world was about to apply to me. I was told it was important for me to have some of my people at the flanks of the meeting, a controlling position, to lead the 'counter-cheer' after the jeer. I followed this to the letter, and to my amazement, the experience Labour predicted was exactly what happened.

My preparation for all this was thorough. We had had a constituency executive meeting with ninety people present which I had come through by a majority of seven to one, so I started well. I had on my side my entire constituency establishment, and we organised, with the help of my agent, Don Preece, to get our people there. Sunday after Sunday during the period before, my then Chairman, Henry Moore, and President, Philip Verdin, plus a chosen team met at my home, and we made a good job of it. When the meeting came around we met at the Leominster Sports Centre and a total of 616 members were in attendance under the able chairmanship, thank goodness, of Henry Moore. When I arrived I found that the usual crowd of media were gathered at the doors, no doubt hoping for some dramatic defeat of my position, which would be news. In I went, not in the manner of Colonel Mates, but smiling away and giving interviews, which is more my style. What I did not see was that one of the press had even climbed onto the roof at some risk to reach a distant skylight, sufficient to provide inadequate pictures whilst the meeting was a progress.

I had a coffee on arrival and then the time came for my entrance as the gladiator of the moment. As I went in to face the assembled masses, sure enough a great cheer went up, to be followed by a lesser jeer as forecast by the streetwise Radice. Immediately my plants on the sidelines put up a lusty offering and I appeared victorious from the outset. The meeting then got under way and it was the nearest thing to a trial that a Member can experience at constituency level. My accuser spoke first and then me, followed by the floor. A hand-microphone was passed around and I sat there hoping for the best. It transpired that seven speakers went against me and sixteen spoke in favour. We then proceeded to the vote. The result was 159 in favour of the motion, which meant against me, and 457 against the motion and in my favour. It was one of the most substantial victories achieved by any of the Heseltine brigade and I was proud of it. During all my years in the constituency my association never failed to back me up through my various adventures. When I left them for New Labour I did so with the full knowledge of my main players, to whom to this day I remain close. To officially cut myself off from them was the one thing that most upset me during the whole saga. However, friendship remains.

As for the rest of our small group who had been brave leaders in the Heseltine cause, we all survived. The last was Patrick Cormack, after Christmas, and then it was all over.

A finale

The progress of the demise of Mrs Thatcher and its aftermath has been much written about. However, as a finale three great occasions and speeches in the Chamber must be mentioned. The first, already referred to, was Mrs Thatcher's defiant 'No, No, No' after the Rome summit. The second was Geoffrey Howe's resignation statement, which was a classic by any standards. One resident wit coined the, no doubt apocryphal, story that the speech had taken his wife, Elspeth, long angry at the way Mrs Thatcher had treated her husband, ten minutes to write and Geoffrey ten years to make!

The last great speech was Mrs Thatcher's reply to the opposition's motion of No Confidence, made days after she resigned, but still in power, pending the election of her successor. For the whole House, friend and foe alike, wherever they sat, it was a dazzling performance, bold, defiant and incisive. Whatever you might think of her, this was a speech from a person who was capable of leadership. When she ended there was a brief moment of comparative silence before cheers rang out. During that brief interim came an agonised cry from a very Thatcherite backbencher, Michael Carttiss, 'What have we done, what have we done?' Yes, indeed. What had happened over those last twenty-five days was quite remarkable by any standard.

Five

LABOUR CONNECTIONS, SOUTH WALES AND BEYOND

Author as new MP in Chamber: '… and over there is the enemy?'

Sir Derek Walker-Smith: 'No, Peter, over there is the Opposition. Your enemy is behind you!'

What is an old former Tory like me doing in the Labour Party? The answer belongs with the fates, but an important part of my background is that I come from South Wales and from Cardiff. My family has been for generations professional, Anglican and politically Conservative. That said, Wales is not a Tory heartland and I grew up in a comparatively non-partisan political atmosphere where Conservatives coexisted in a largely Labour-dominated area. My father, Owen, was Conservative MP for the then constituency of Cardiff East from 1931 to 1942, when, in bad health at the time, he accepted an early County Court judgeship. He was never politically dogmatic and was primarily a lawyer, seeing both sides of any question. He always had many friends in both the Labour and Conservative parties, and I grew up in a very apolitical atmosphere.

My first contact with Labour began at the age of eight at the highest level. In the spring of 1946 I was taken by my father to view the World War II Victory Parade from a stand outside the splendid City Hall in Cathays Park, Cardiff. I had earlier celebrated my birthday, and had been given my first wrist-watch, which I was proudly wearing and relentlessly timing everything going on. Just before the parade began my father introduced me to the Prime Minister, Clement Attlee, who was in the capital city of Wales for the great occasion. I can remember the meeting but I was reminded afterwards that as soon as I met the Prime Minister I tapped my precious watch and complained that the parade was three minutes late! Mr Attlee retorted that something would have to be done about it, whereupon the music suddenly started and round the corner came the marching men. I went home much impressed with prime ministerial powers.

My father's friendships in South Wales were extensive and very much included members of the Labour Party. During long evenings in the Commons, he frequently had legal work to do as a practising King's Counsel and would have poached eggs on toast at the then Annie's Bar, sometimes with Sir Stafford Cripps, also a practising King's Counsel, before they went back to work in the library. When going into places like Monmouth to address Conservative meetings my father ended up more than once having tea with Labour MP Arthur Jenkins, father of Roy and later Parliamentary Private Secretary to Prime Minister Attlee. Later, as a judge, my father was for many years chairman of Monmouthshire Quarter Sessions and one of his leading magistrates, who he said was a very formidable lady, was Roy Jenkins's mother, Hattie. When I joined the Labour Party, I had a very warm letter from Roy Jenkins on account of those early family contacts.

During my father's years as MP in Cardiff, a local teaching union representative was a young man from Tonypandy, namely George Thomas. They got on well together, both before and after George became MP for Cardiff West in 1945. George had known me from a very young age and never failed to ask after me, and later on, when I entered the Commons, to help and advise me from his then position as the Deputy Speaker of the Commons. Apart from his warmth and ready Welsh wit, he was well known for his ability to disarm his political opponents. This talent served him well during his distinguished tenure as Speaker of the Commons which ended with his elevation as Viscount Tonypandy. For the first half of the 1959 General Election campaign, before I had to return to Cambridge for the Michaelmas term, I was rash enough to volunteer to help the Conservative cause in George Thomas's constituency of Cardiff West. One evening I was dispatched with a friend from Conservative HQ to cover George's meetings and to give him a 'hard time'. We were late for the first meeting, having been to the wrong venue. Arriving at the correct school somewhat ruffled we found George's meeting over and walked straight into him and his entourage as they hurried out to get to the next meeting. There I was, covered with blue rosettes and badges, to be greeted: 'Hello, Peter, how are you and how is your Dad? Come for the meeting have you? You're too late for this one but you can certainly come to the next one.' In the circumstances I was quite put out by the warmth of the greeting, but the knockout was still to come: 'You don't know how to get there? Well, join up with our cars and we will guide you to the meeting.' The public were then treated to the somewhat bizarre sight of a Conservative car, swathed in blue, in the middle of a motor cavalcade abundantly decorated in Labour colours, sweeping out of Cathays, Cardiff and on to the next meeting in Grangetown.

That was not the end of it. We arrived just after George, who called me over and said, 'Peter, I've got to get in there quickly. Would you be kind enough to take Mam in?' Mam was the elderly mother of George Thomas, who did everything with her son, who always referred to her as Mam. She had become, within and beyond the Welsh Labour Party, something of an institution. Years later her funeral was one of the best-attended Labour events South Wales had seen for many years. So there I was, still with my blue rosette, solemnly holding the arm of Mam and progressing to the front row. The amusing thing was that nobody seemed in the least put out, and the fact that this nice young Tory was helping Mam added to the general warmth of the occasion. As for me, I was completely disarmed and there was no way I could even attempt to ask awkward questions. At the conclusion we saw George off with cheery goodnights and happily went our separate ways. Game, set and match to George Thomas! I often think it could only happen in Cardiff or perhaps Wales generally.

I cannot mention George Thomas without mentioning the other great figure representing Cardiff from 1945, namely James Callaghan. He was elected for my father's former seat of Cardiff East in 1945, although when my father left to become a judge in 1942 the seat was given to James Grigg, under the terms of the wartime coalition. Churchill wanted Grigg in the Commons to become Secretary of State for War, having been Permanent Under-Secretary before. My father and Callaghan always got on well over the years, which helped me when I got to the Commons and found myself with a personal line of contact to a Labour Prime Minister who could not have been nicer to me whenever we met. My father exchanged letters with him each Christmas and it was amusing for me to see the references Jim Callaghan made to my humble interventions at Prime Minister's Question Time and to my efforts on the media. It obviously gave my father great pleasure and it amuses me to think of how better placed I would have been if I had been Labour from the start! The last thing Jim Callaghan said to me about my father was at a Speaker's dinner in the 1980s when he made a point of saying that he would drop in and see him as soon as he could. Sadly, my father went into his final illness soon after, before he died at the age of eighty-nine.

As earlier recounted, in January 1962, at the age of twenty-three, I was selected as Conservative candidate for Newport, Monmouthshire. I found myself opposing Sir Frank Soskice QC, the sitting Labour MP, a man of charm and considerable distinction. He had been Solicitor and then Attorney General in the Attlee government and was heading for great things, should Labour win the approaching 1964 General Election. Legal connections came into the picture immediately. I had met Sir Frank some years before when my father took me to a Magistrates' Association meeting, over which he was presiding, and Frank Soskice was a speaker. When I was selected as his opponent he wrote to congratulate me and invited me out to lunch at the Tredegar Arms Hotel, just opposite Newport station, where he always stayed and referred to as his 'Club'. Whilst Sir Frank obviously wanted to size up his young opponent, he had no electoral problems and the episode signifies a more civilised and bipartisan approach to party politics which I think we could do with more of today.

The veteran and the young challenger maintained the most cordial of relationships up to and including the October 1964 General Election campaign. Neither attacked the other and where necessary we spoke privately during the campaign. At the beginning of it he phoned me to say that he would prefer not to debate publicly with me and would I agree to this as a favour to him. This call was unknown to all but my agent, Joe Morris, and the reason for it was clear, in that Sir Frank was ageing and very arthritic, to the extent of being permanently stooped. He had no wish to be physically compared to a then vibrant twenty-six-year-old, even if he had won any debate, which he certainly would have. I readily agreed, and we both refused every occasion to debate in some bleak church hall or other with our supporters making up most of the audience. In future elections how I wished I had similar arrangements as I spent precious Sunday evenings in some desultory debate that few noticed.

The election ended with the usual count and I quickly learnt that local and national considerations are two very different things. Locally Sir Frank did not have to worry but nationally he had everything to worry about. Because of his age and health this was his last chance of holding a high Office of State. As the count progressed the probability of a Labour government became clearer and once more, as he relaxed on that front, local considerations came to the fore. He confided in me during the count that his increasing fear and dread was that his supporters would insist on picking him up and carrying him shoulder-high to the nearby Labour Club. For someone with bad arthritis this could be a very painful operation and as the result was declared in front of the Town Hall, and the applause rang out, I held my breath for him. There was a pause and I thought for a moment that he might have got away with it. No such luck! From the midst of the assembled multitude a lusty shout went up: 'Good old Frankie. He's our man' and with that a group of stalwarts surged forward, picked up a wincing Sir Frank, like a sack of potatoes, and bore him painfully away to the Labour Club.

Sir Frank survived the experience and the next day was appointed Home Secretary in the first Wilson government. I continued to see him regularly for the rest of his life, which was always a pleasure. Once he came out of government in 1966, he went to the House of Lords and also became treasurer of my Inn, the Inner Temple. Such were the fates that we went to live in Redington Road, Hampstead and lo and behold around the corner in Church Row lived Sir Frank. During our talks strolling around the streets of Hampstead and at the odd local function he was always kind enough to tell me that I would achieve the status of Queen's Counsel and Member of Parliament and even attain high political office. I may not have fulfilled all his ambitions for me, but he would certainly have been surprised to learn that he was speaking to a future Labour member of the House of Lords.

One of the most accomplished of South Wales figures was undoubtedly Leo Abse, a very successful solicitor, who became MP for Pontypool in 1959. Like a number in those days he had no great ambition for office, was financially independent and, even if his abilities were more than sufficient for ministerial office, far preferred the freedom of the backbenches, which enabled him to take up the causes he wanted to promote. This led to him proposing substantial Private Member's legislation in the fields of matrimonial causes and homosexual rights and to his permanent memorial in their realisation. At a personal level he could be described as exotic, first making his name in the Commons by dressing up in various specially tailored Regency costumes, including stovepipe top hats, for Budget Day. This may have infuriated his then leader, Hugh Gaitskell, but it gave Leo great pleasure as awards flooded in from various organisations of tailors and cloth manufacturers. At the personal and family level we spent time together with Leo, Marjorie his wife and my parents. He gave me my first brief at the Bar, in front of my father, the County Court judge, in 1963. He left the House in 1987 and continued to write various psycho-analytical books that more than kept him in the public eye. I was in personal contact with him until he died and a more practical man you could not wish to meet. Marjorie sadly died in 1996 and he missed her dreadfully. Some years later he was working on his front garden at his fine house beside the Thames, at Strand on the Green, when along the towpath came a young Polish woman, Ania, and they talked. This led to a second marriage of great contentment in which Ania cared for him and helped him lead the wider social life he loved.

One Conservative in South Wales politics with whom I was always agreeably connected was Michael Roberts, MP for Cardiff North, and later Cardiff North West, 1970–82. When I entered the Commons in February 1974 he was Welsh Whip, and without too many Welsh MPs to look after he was given the Borders in addition, which included me at Leominster. During my early days I decided to go in and listen to a Welsh debate and in my innocence I got a shock when someone asked me what on earth I was doing there? I responded by asking the same question of him, to be told that he was trying to make a speech and saw no other reason for him, let alone an English MP, to be in the Chamber. The fact that I had a prominent Welsh background did not matter. I was an English MP! That was that and it was not for me to spoil the rather inward-looking fun of a Welsh debate. Michael explained the realities very tactfully to me and that was the end of my early experience of Welsh affairs at Westminster. Some years later in 1982 I was at a Speaker's Dinner when an emergency message came through that we might have a doctor present and would he immediately go down to the Chamber. It was the St David's Day Annual Debate and Dr Maurice Miller MP was immediately dispatched. It turned out that Michael Roberts, then a Welsh Office Junior Minister, was speaking in the Chamber when he had a heart attack. I found Michael flat on the floor of the Member's Cloakroom, with Maurice Miller frantically trying to revive him with heart massage. These were the days before defibrillators. Very sadly he died, and ex-Prime Minister Jim Callaghan, who was also present at the dinner, went straight away to see Michael's wife at their Dolphin Square flat to break the news to her. Jim Callaghan was the de facto 'Father' of the Welsh MPs, and this was another good example of the bipartisan nature of Welsh politics.

I always maintained friendships across the floor of the House and particularly those relating to my foreign affairs interests. I first went to the Soviet Union with the Cambridge Afro-Asian Expedition 1961, which gave me a lasting interest in Russia. I returned many times, and became chairman of the All-Party Group for the Soviet Union at Westminster and joint vice-chairman of the then GB–USSR Association with the late John Smith MP, later leader of the Labour Party. The Soviet invasion of Afghanistan in 1979 limited political contact for a period, but in the autumn of 1981 a delegation was formed under the association's banner. The purpose was to put a toe in the water without any commitment, which is perfect territory for a quasi-parliamentary exchange. governments cannot do this, we can. At the end of the day, how we are received will be noted by our Ambassador, and if it goes well then relations can be improved by our government without embarrassment. If it goes badly, then nothing is lost. The association was ideal for this purpose, as it was created on the orders of Harold Macmillan after his successful visit to Moscow in 1958 and received Foreign Office support and funding. Four of us were chosen to go, namely John Osborn, MP for Sheffield Hallam and then chairman of the Soviet Group; Arthur Bottomley MP, former Labour Colonial/Commonwealth Secretary; John Smith MP, then Shadow Trade Secretary; and myself. John and I were both barristers and of almost exactly the same age and we hit it off immediately. We had many a good laugh around all the formal meetings and it was a real pleasure to be with him. His premature death was a blow for me and for many others. What a contribution he could have made.

As for the visit itself, it went well. We got the full treatment, which meant lunches, dinners, food and vodka in abundance. We were treated at senior Supreme Soviet level, with meetings at the Foreign Ministry with ministers and officials and at the associated policy institutes, which were very important. It was clear that the Soviets were ready to improve relations, if we had recovered sufficiently from Afghanistan. Soon after this relations were normalised. In charge of us day by day was a diplomat who had served in London and knew John Smith and was clearly marking John for the future. He was also a senior KGB operative, which we knew only too well and therefore could relax in his company. He had high tastes generally: well-cut suits, designer ties and all the rest of the adornment of the privileged in the Soviet Union. A very engaging figure who was interesting, but also amusing in his overt dislike of the provinces. To venture out of Moscow and visit Belorussia was an ordeal for him. He forgot his coat, as he was not an outdoor type, and I can see him now shivering in his fancy suit in Minsk, as he waited for the cars to arrive. When we visited rural areas I got my first experience of the egalitarian ways of the dominion of the workers. As our convoy approached, traffic coming the other way would head for the hedges on either side of the road, so that we could have the whole thing to ourselves.

Our KGB friend took John and me to his home on the way to the airport, to meet his family and no doubt for us to see the style in which he lived. It was fully up to the Western standards of the prosperous USA middle class. The latest equipment everywhere for television, recording equipment and so on. We also visited the senior party shop so we could see he had access to everything we ourselves could want on the consumer side of things.

John had been the youngest Cabinet minister in the Callaghan government. He made his name in the Commons as Minister of State, under the Leader of the House, Michael Foot, in handling that government's ill-fated devolution bills. Interestingly the equivalent Shadow role on the opposition side was played by Leon Brittan MP, who similarly made his name. Having two up-and-coming lawyers opposite each other doubtless spurred them both on to even better performances. They did indeed have an appropriate respect for each other. John had a wife and family to support in Edinburgh, and as with so many of us, being an MP involved loss of income at a rather expensive time of life. On top of everything else, he struggled to keep up what practice he could at the Scottish Bar, which became quite impossible when he became Shadow Chancellor. This was yet another pressure he had to contend with as, all things considered, he drove himself far too hard. Over these years he did not spare himself in political life, let alone the pleasures of social and family life. His national responsibilities were conducted all over the UK, and then were accompanied by a rush back to Edinburgh to spend all possible time with his family. Whether he overdid it or not, he was great company. We even shared a first-class Russian sleeper, being always in those days for two people, between Moscow and Minsk. We both had a good sleep. More than a decade later I made another such journey, this time between Moscow and Kiev, with none other than Geoffrey Howe, and I wish that one had passed as quietly. I got to bed late as it was my birthday, and found Geoffrey already in the full melodious flow of luxurious snoring. Fortunately the festivities had blunted my sensitivities, but I thought at the time that it was my wife's revenge for all of the same that I have inflicted on her over the years. That said I would not recommend her to trade me in for a Geoffrey Howe.

After we returned from the Soviet Union, John and I used to have the odd drink together in the House, as he steadily rose within the ranks of the Labour Party. The last one was on the Terrace in the summer of 1991 when he was still Shadow Chancellor before the 1992 General Election, after which he became leader. Much has been written about John and alcohol. Having spent time with him at home and abroad, there is no question that the man was anything other than a normal *bon viveur*, whose body could not take the strains that his hard-working lifestyle placed upon it. He, like me, enjoyed his drink, and on occasion relaxed with a whisky or two in a very normal way. All went well after the first heart attack in 1989, but from 1992 that demanding job of leader of the opposition, involving all the strain of office and little of the necessary support, took its tragic toll.

Out on the Terrace, on a lovely summer evening in 1991, we talked about this. At that time he was mercifully over his heart attack, was taking a lot of exercise and limiting his alcohol intake. Of all things he was drinking spritzers, and managed his diet on a straightforward calorie count, rather than the fancy diets people like me would get into at that time. The key to it was that he could manage the job of Shadow Chancellor with a controlled lifestyle and was doing well. Becoming leader of the opposition after the 1992 General Election was something else, and gave him one of the most demanding and stressful jobs in British politics. Unsurprisingly, he began to feel the strain, and a few drinks were always there to help with the tension.

Another sad and unavoidable factor was that his wife, Elizabeth, three daughters and family life were away in Edinburgh. All of us who have experienced this artificial separation from our families don't like going home to empty flats. In John's case, the temptation to wind down with the odd Scottish journalist in the leader of the opposition's room was an all-too-enjoyable option. Norman Lamont, as Chancellor, well appreciated John's talents, and went up, at his invitation, to do a debate with him at Glasgow University, where one of John's daughters was president of the society in question. After the debate there was the usual mix with undergraduates, and it was noticeable how much wine was consumed by John. A need for relaxation no doubt, but it was too much.

In my experience, it was only like this when he was under strain, most particularly as leader of the opposition. Well before this, with him having to lead off an opposition debate that afternoon as Shadow Trade Minister, we were at an annual luncheon of the GB–USSR Association, as joint vice-chairmen, with our wives, adjacent to the president, Harold Wilson. Geoffrey Howe as Foreign Secretary was with him at the top table. Harold Wilson brought us upstanding for the Loyal Toast and all seemed well. Ten minutes later he brought us up again for another such toast and we wondered what on earth was going on. Afterwards Geoffrey Howe told us that Harold Wilson spent lunch telling the same stories over again. His dementia was taking hold. It was sad that one of the finest minds in the country had to deteriorate so publicly. Better perhaps to call it a day, but always difficult. As for John, quite relaxed, he went straight back to the House to lead off the debate.

The loss to British politics was as sad as it was considerable. As leader of the opposition, John Smith rose to being easily the best performer in the House of Commons. The last time he responded to the Queen's Speech in 1994, he landed all the right political blows while keeping us all laughing, and on occasion convulsed, at the same time. It is classic in the Commons to observe the other side of the House wanting to laugh when it feels it should not. This circumstance is not good for the health of members, and on this occasion the dam finally broke, to the relief of us all. What did it was when he said, 'Who would want to live in a country where the Grand National doesn't start and hotels slide into the sea.' He did not get more than half-way through before the laughter started and one could hardly hear the end. The day after, I went up to the Committee Floor in the lift with him and congratulated him. With typical modesty he replied, 'Well, if all else fails, at least I can become a busker.'

In 1996, I was asked to preside over the John Smith *Observer* Mace Debating Competition, when it was held in Trinity College, Dublin. Elizabeth Smith and one of her daughters were there as guests of honour and I was able to pay a public tribute to John for the first time. I included some of the experiences mentioned here, and made clear the considerable affection I felt for him. Elizabeth responded with grace and the Irish hosts much appreciated having them there. Respect across the floor, not to say friendship, is always there in the Commons, something I don't think the public always realises. They imagine that all the shenanigans we put on, at Prime Minister's Question Time for example, are serious rather than the play of democracy, accepting the necessary clash of strong views.

Had John Smith survived he would have undoubtedly won the 1997 General Election, if not by the enormous majority achieved by Tony Blair. Matters would have taken a normal course, with reform of the Labour Party proceeding under a more traditionally minded Labour prime minister than his young and dynamic successor. We might also have seen a beginning to the reform of the House of Commons. The Blair–Brown saga would have been played out before the succession, when I am quite certain Tony Blair would have achieved his deserts and proceeded with the job of modernising the Labour Party and constitutional reform, without the impediment of war in Iraq, which I am sure John Smith would have had nothing to do with. But an '*if*' doesn't grow, as a wise Persian proverb tells us.

Six
PARTY COMPARISONS

All conservatism is based on the idea that if you leave things alone you leave them as they are. But you do not. If you leave a thing alone you leave it to a torrent of change.

G. K. Chesterton, Orthodoxy, 1908

The most conservative man in the world is the British Trades Unionist, when you want to change him.

Ernest Bevin, speech to the TUC, 1927

Having seen both our major parties in operation I am in a good position to compare them. The most important point is their similarity, rather than their difference. This is what most struck me and was not what I expected beforehand. But then they have exactly the same problems to deal with, the same ministries to run and the same democratic elections to contest. They also have the same problems of running major parties in the close-knit circumstances of Westminster politics. How they set about it is different, but nothing like as different as is generally assumed.

The differing styles are mainly due to the traditional class system. This is steadily getting less as the backgrounds of many Conservative and Labour members become more similar. After Labour's troubles of the 1970s and 1980s, and particularly under Tony Blair, Labour has steadily become more middle class. The Conservatives accomplished a similar thing but from the opposite direction. Throughout the 1980s and onwards until about 2001 the 'Gentlemen' steadily retired. In their place increasingly came Thatcher's image, being aggressively middle class, self-made and in general more right wing and nationalistic.

More about differences of style later, but some history may help here. It may also help illustrate the similarities of opposites. The Conservative Party had a long tradition of 'Gentlemen and Players'. The so-called 'Knights of the Shires' were influential because they didn't want anything. They entered Parliament almost 'as of right' but with their lives mainly outside Parliament, be it county, City, inherited interests or a combination of all three. They regarded the Commons as a civilised way to do something useful. They would no more dream of taking on the Under-Secretaryship of Social Security, or whatever, than they would be prepared to give up their leisure pursuits. Jack Weatherill, when deputy chief whip, well before becoming Speaker, told a not untypical story. He wanted to get a particular county Member, and champion of the hunting field, into the Whips' Office to help deal with rural issues. He approached the gentleman concerned to be told in no uncertain manner that he could not possibly accept, much as he would like to help, as the job would interfere with his hunting. This type of county member has all but disappeared, and we now have a comparatively young crowd of 'career politicians', most of whom can't wait to be an under-secretary.

On the Labour side the concept of the 'Knights of the Shires' seems out of place, but consider for a moment. In the 1970s, just opposite the Smoking Room, there lurked a room of separate privilege, known as the Trades Union Room. There sat once-powerful figures who had, for whatever reason, missed out on the general-secretaryship of their union and as compensation had been agreeably provided with a union seat in the Commons. Did any of them want to be Under-Secretary for Social Security? No, not a bit of it. But the Labour whips had a very useful resource in gauging the mood of the unions and the working-class elements of the party and how far they could go without trouble. All this has now disappeared, and the room, a sad relic of working-class camaraderie, became a ladies' sitting-room until it was absorbed by the Commons establishment.

Although my theme here is underlying similarity, one could assume that these social differences meant that we did not get on with each other. Not a bit of it! We all had a common bond, which was having had to survive elections and the ways of the electorate. I have often seen politicians grouped together in receptions or similar, socialising across party lines and often amongst themselves. One can carry the point a bit further, in that the working-class elements of the Labour Party got on surprisingly well with the upper-class Tories. Each had no middle-class pretensions to get over. A classic historical example of this would be the relationship of Harold Macmillan and his socially grand Conservative friends had, as backbenchers in the 1930s, with Jimmy Maxton and his Clydesiders. Warmth, plenty of teasing and more than a little understanding.

In my own case, I formed friendships with many Labour MPs, and not least trade unionists, whom I always found straightforward and unpretentious. As a very new member I went off to lunch at an embassy with various Conservative and Labour MPs. I did not know what to expect, and to my agreeable surprise we all got on like a house on fire. On return I walked up to the Members' Lobby with a northern trade unionist, older and more senior than me. As we were about to enter the Chamber a glint came into his eye. He rubbed his hands together and said 'Nice lunch, Peter, now let 'ostilities commence.'

In 1965 Edward Heath was the chosen natural leader for the steady modernisation of the Conservative Party. A grammar school boy of high achievement and with a good war record, he was indeed to gradually change the image of the party, but very sadly the whole game plan went wrong. The one thing this very able and moderate man lacked was any sort of glamour or promotional ability in an increasingly television-conscious age. One story that appeared in the press during the 1970 General Election, which took place during a very hot June, was of Heath's plane arriving at Cardiff airport, and while he was walking across the tarmac to the terminal, a supporter jumped the barrier with a nice cold pint of beer for his leader. On seeing what might have been a welcome sight, and certainly a marvellous photo opportunity, Heath said, 'No, thank you very much' and marched on! This may have been invented, or otherwise apocryphal, but says it all, nevertheless. To everyone's great surprise he won that election, but thereafter he was a sad electoral failure, falling easy prey to the eventual Thatcher challenge, so ably managed by Airey Neave.

With the arrival of Thatcher, the two basic elements of the then Conservative Party became more clearly visible as the so-called secret weapon of loyalty was gradually lost in the face of increasing division. Those two elements were the traditional Tories, basically moderate, gentle and loyal by instinct, on the one hand, and the new, aggressive, middle-class Thatcherite Conservatives on the other. Over the years of Thatcher and beyond, the latter steadily took over. From this change came a narrow, right-wing, nationalistic, anti-European outlook which always lurked within the party, and which the leadership of old always took upon itself to contain, rather than to encourage. Under Thatcher, the party in the country leapt at the opportunity to connect with its conservative instincts and the stage was set for a right-wing journey.

The old traditional Tory had his views, but these tended to be limited and policy could safely be left to the ambitions of the more intellectually gifted. After all, 'views' were potentially dangerous things, and somewhat disturbing to the rhythms of high Tory life. For them it all came down to 'pragmatism'. Along came Thatcher, and suddenly they were all expected to be 'conviction politicians'. This gave a terrible shock to many traditional Tories as they sat at peace in the Smoking Room. The new wave was unkindly described by the late Julian Critchley as the advent of the 'Garageistes', which, although a disagreeable comment, hit home. They had views in abundance, and worse, were intent on getting their own way, and worse again, on inflicting their views on others. The associations in the country followed suit. In the county seats many gentlemen of the shires found the new party disagreeable and quietly backed out of active service. The difference was that their replacements sought recognition, whereas those they replaced did not need it. So the colonels and the grandees were replaced by the socially ambitious. The divisions at the centre were thus replicated outside, in the body of the organisation, with the result that they got deeper and potentially more factional.

The weakness of the Labour Party in the 1970s and 1980s greatly helped the Conservatives to get away with all this, and become more rather than less popular for much of the period it was going on. Many don't see Labour as a progressive party of the centre-left, indeed had the Social Democrats got off the ground in the 1980s they might well have been the second major party. As it is Labour still has a chance to find a social democratic formula, which could well deliver greater electoral success.

Labour grew up as a movement, but have had difficulty developing into a truly national party. They are dependent on the unions for finance and are stuck to the public sector, and in English terms to the industrial north, which in turn has often made them unattractive to the aspirant south. This is at the heart of the argument of Lord Radice, who as an MP wrote *Southern Discomfort* (Fabian Society, 1992), which put the case so well regarding the importance of gaining southern voters if Labour is to truly succeed.

Devolution has introduced new problems for Labour in its Celtic heartlands. For many years they have collected automatic votes from Scotland and Wales, where the Conservative Party is seen as the 'English' party. England is to be beaten on the rugby field at all costs, and never to be voted for politically. Devolution has changed much and comes along with the fact that an automatic Labour vote does not necessarily deliver a government at Westminster. For many the alternative is to vote for the available nationalist party rather than Labour, and after the Scottish Referendum and the 2015 General Election Labour is seriously losing out in Scotland, and is not so dominant in Wales either. This has led to a serious decline in overall electability and needs to be addressed urgently and on an United Kingdom basis. In party terms this has to start with the Southern Discomfort question which must deliver a party that can win in England and establish itself as a truly United Kingdom party.

Historically the Labour Party has only succeeded in getting into government when the Conservatives have been visibly flagging, and the Labour Party has possessed what was recognised at the time as the best leadership in the eyes of the electorate. This combination gets them over the problems of the north–south divide and enables them to win in England. Harold Wilson accomplished this in 1964/66 and Tony Blair from 1997. Such times and leadership are not always available, and we get into the depressing area of government by default, as in the 1974–9 period.

Back to the Commons, where, whatever may be the diversity of friendships, behavioural patterns still have their differences. The Labour Party sanctum still tends to be the first two sections of the Tea Room, which is the territory for snacks and a high tea. Conservatives have as their equivalent the Smoking Room, which was popular for drinks before dinner in the Members' Dining Room next door, and for further refreshment afterwards, if the hours make that appropriate. However, it was not by any means a total Tory preserve. Throughout my time the more classless members of the Labour left, such as Michael Foot, Ian Mikardo and their friends, were often there. Later on, the new wave of Blairite 'professionals' blended in so well that you could not tell the parties apart.

Downstairs is the Strangers' Bar, with access on to the Terrace, and the place for a good pint of beer, the favourite being 'Fed', a brew from the northern working-men's clubs. This tends to be a Labour preserve, although some Tories who prefer the atmosphere to that of the club-like Smoking Room used it on a regular basis. In the old days it was down the corridor from its present site and was always referred to as the Kremlin Bar. This was because during the celebrated visit of Bulgannin and Khrushchev in 1956 they were taken down there by their Labour hosts of the moment. One amusing by-product of this bar was that the Conservatives always deputed one of their more beer-loving Whips to go down there for long periods to gain information, which tended to flow freely the later it got.

The 1970s and 1980s represented a quite dire period for Labour, which included the attempted takeover by the Social Democratic Party on the one hand, and the ultra-lefties and Trotskyists on the other. The combined threats were beaten off by many devoted representatives of the Labour Party. However, had just a few more Labour figures of influence decided that the Labour interest lay with the Social Democratic Party then the outcome could have been very different. As it was the 1987 election was a watershed and Labour had survived.

They had now to begin the deeper process which the SDP had attempted to short-cut. They have still not got there. In 1987 the first Queen's Speech of the new Parliament was remarkable. The Conservatives had an overwhelming majority but looking over at Labour you would have thought they had won. It did not take a genius to work it out. Quite simply they were still HM opposition and that, essentially, was what counted. They had survived, and with an overwhelming majority in Scotland as a bonus. Ironically this woke Scotland up to the brutal fact that their overwhelming vote did not deliver them a government at Westminster.

From 1987 Neil Kinnock consolidated his leadership and gradually shepherded the party in the direction of government. The fact that ultimately the British people did not want him at the head of that government is another question. A manifestation of what was happening overall was seen in the increasingly middle-class appearance of the Labour members. Both sides were converging on the middle ground, and somehow their appearance went the same way.

As has been said, the operation of the two main parties was surprisingly similar but different in style. The respective Whips' Offices are a case in point. The Conservatives were initially gentle but hard if necessary and appropriate, and the effects on a career were the same. Labour was much more upfront, accompanied by colourful language and a pro forma asking for the reason why a vote was missed. By contrast, the first time I innocently missed a three-line Conservative whip I received a note inviting me to see Humphrey Atkins, the chief whip in the 1974–9 period, and on arrival was promptly offered a large gin and tonic. All civilised, but not always so in later years. Tension and unpleasantness can go both ways. When Emma Nicholson defected from the Conservatives to the Liberal Democrats in 1996, she had a dreadful time which included one heavily built Conservative moving deliberately to the side as he passed her from the other direction in a crowded corridor, thus administering a painful barge to her chest and shoulder. As for Labour, they managed to put the fear of God into their post-1997 defector to the Liberal Democrats, Paul Marsden, MP for Shrewsbury, late one evening in the Strangers' Bar.

Contrasts between the present day and days of old show differences of style, but the name of the game is to keep the party's MPs on side and as contented as possible. The quality of the chief whip of whatever party is crucial, as is that of his or her whips. Backbench committees also play a vital role as the sounding-boards of backbench opinion and the place for private reservations to be put in order to see whether colleagues are prepared to voice their opinions on the record and in the presence of Whips. This role is similar in both major parties and the chairmanship of these committees is important and influential. Access to the media is part of the role which makes these positions sought-after, particularly at times when the party concerned may be going through a difficult period involving division. In the old days they were often in the hands of grandees on the Conservative side, and their equivalent with Labour. The old knights of the shires viewed it as their task and responsibility to ensure that their troops were content and fundamentally loyal to the cause. Methods varied. Before 1964 it was the custom of a distinguished chairman of the 1922 Committee, John Morrison, MP for Salisbury and later 1st Baron Margadale, to sit for some minutes in the Aye Lobby immediately after Prime Minister's Questions twice a week, to be available to any Member who might wish to see him. In Conservative terms the chairman of the '22 is a key personage, with regular access to the leader and/or Prime Minister. On the Labour side the same applies. In the 1970s, Cledwyn Hughes, Labour grandee and later a peer, as chairman of the Parliamentary Labour Party (PLP), was relaxed and approachable at all times, as was Jack Dormand, later a peer, in the 1980s. In recent years the task is the same even if it is less grand, and not quite so party-neutral as it used to be.

Outside the House the chairman of the Conservative Party is of considerable importance and performs the same role for the party at large. Access to the rank and file and the ability to speak on a wide brief gives the incumbent a considerable advantage over most Cabinet ministers in any potential leadership contest. For obvious reasons leaders are therefore very careful as to who they place in this role, which can provide a vehicle for a rival as well as a friend. The Labour Party, with its history as a movement, has an elected chairman of the National Executive Committee responsible for the movement as a whole during a short term of office, and with little concentration of power as back-up. Under him the general secretary is potentially a powerful figure, as Morgan Phillips was in the 1950s. At the urging of some, including myself, Tony Blair did appoint a chairman as head of organisation (Charles Clarke MP), but it did not last and never overcame the relative power of the established role of the general secretary in what was still the 'Labour movement'.

What said a lot about the old Tory Party was the way party committees reported dissatisfaction. A whip is normally present at all party committee meetings but where necessary the secretaries or even the chairman would call in to see the chief whip should there be a particular problem. At one meeting in the 1960s a particular committee was upset and the chairman, at the end of discussion, magisterially pronounced: 'Send for the Chief Whip', whereupon secretarial minions were duly dispatched and the chief whip was found and brought forth. He listened to the problem, reacted and went on his way. A balance of equals was present, which the current system, based on more professional politicians, has no call for. In my time from 1974 I never saw this happen as part of the system. Whips and chief whips attended committees as required by situation or problem but never by command.

The Labour Party was more democratically structured, and certainly not content with the old ways of proceeding according to accepted lines of unwritten authority. They needed to be democratically elected in all things, which could be a complete pain for the executive, which had to live with the process. Elected committees for everything, including regular access to the Prime Minister for the Parliamentary Labour Party. The Conservatives believed in the culture of the 'Old Boy' network, which was endemic to Tories and lay at the heart of the government of this country until recently. Labour is not like that. For example, the meetings of the Parliamentary Labour Party are open to all members, ministers and backbenchers, and I think all the better for it. In the party of the people, nobody seems to care too much about rank and station and people fire off regardless. Splendid to watch for an ex-Tory.

On the Tory side the niceties of the separation of powers were observed. The 1922 was attended by backbenchers and whips only. Invited ministers, including the Prime Minister, waited outside and were called in when they were reached on the agenda. It is announced on the whip that they 'will attend', and attend they most certainly do. These little habits are the remains of a very different system.

The pairing system is a parliamentary classic. Over the twentieth century demands on members had steadily got greater. Until 1945 they were virtually unpaid, whereas ministers were in days of old comparatively well paid by the standards of today. Members were expected to earn their living, and with the increasing difficulty of the hours of sitting, this could not be managed without pairing between members of the two major parties. Many were wealthy men and others had the means to earn their living, but that took time. So the pairing system was very necessary and helped us both financially and socially. It involved a close bond of trust between two members of opposing major parties who paired with each other for votes when they agreed for one or both of them to be away from the House. Each vote was registered with the Whips' Offices, who were well aware of the individual pairing arrangements and had to consent in each case. Until about 1983 barristers were excused committee work as they were liable to be in court in the mornings and frequently paired with each other. Sir Hartley Shawcross QC, formerly Attorney-General and Cabinet minister, then Lord Shawcross, told me as a young MP and barrister not to worry about the difficulty of sustaining my practice at the Bar. For his part he 'never went near the House' unless necessary, and always paired with Gerald Howard QC, later Mr Justice Howard. In my time I always had a pair, but we did not abuse the process, which was in any event under pressure, as the whips increasingly frowned on the practice as the House got so much more professional. Indeed the large majorities of Tony Blair gave the whips on both sides an excuse to close down formal pairing, even if it still exists unofficially. With Mrs Thatcher's big majorities of 1983/88, the Tory whips were confounded about what to do, but not for long. They devised a system called the 'bisque system' which gave a night off every ten days or so to government members. The big joke was that nobody knew what a bisque was and most of us stopped at lobster soup. It turned out to be an extra turn at croquet and was so devised by the Tory whips that any prowling tabloid journalist would not have any idea what was happening. Having said all that, there was something noble about the pairing system. It was a bond that was not to be broken. Many have remarked that it is the nearest thing to matrimony. My own pair was the late John McWilliam, MP for Blyth, and we became the closest of friends, as did others in the same relationship. The irony for him was that I came over and joined the Labour Party, thus depriving him of his pair, however delighted he was to welcome me into the fold. In his memory I will state that he took the trouble to phone me from Italy, while on honeymoon, to congratulate me on my much publicised defection. Thereafter he never lost an opportunity to declaim that he had performed the ultimate sacrifice for the Labour Party in losing his pair.

Outside the House it was again a question of style rather than substance. Meetings were a case in point. On the Conservative side these could include vigorous political discussion at quarterly Executives and AGMs, but all were expected to observe the Conservatives' secret weapon of loyalty, and most did. The rest of the time politics were not allowed to overburden the system. There were numerous constituency association functions and many could be enjoyable. The main purpose of the occasion would be social, and through that to raise money for the association. It was also a valuable opportunity for the Member to socialise, and the last thing most would want from him would be some serious oration. Things would often run a bit late and the chairman for the occasion would be a bit hassled by the need to promote and announce his all-important raffle. In possible conflict with this was the fact that this was the traditional moment for the Member's speech. I would be warmly if briefly introduced with the words: 'Here is the moment we have been waiting for ... our raffle. Before that we will have a speech from the Member – not too long this time, Peter. Here he is ...'

In contrast the atmosphere at a Labour meeting was very different. Monthly management and other formal meetings were treated very seriously, with parliamentary, local government and other reports accompanied by copious minute-taking. With Conservative meetings short minutes were treated as an art form which covered differences, and gave the troops less to argue about in the future. The local Labour Party meetings were different. They tended to have some agenda and people definitely expected me to speak. Whilst there generally was wine, and the dreaded raffle, at the end, people came with something specific on their mind and every intention of saying it. This did not worry me, but nevertheless as a former Conservative of many years' standing there was something terrifying to be directly confronted, in your own backyard, by an irate staff nurse or angry schoolteacher with strong views and seeking serious change. That was after all why they were members and were there. They wanted change and to make things, as they saw it, better. Conservatives, on the other hand, were in general content with their lot. That was after all why they were Conservatives. To my mind each party's ways were completely understandable. One party was there to change things and the other to ensure that change came at a reasonable pace and in the right direction.

Party conferences, of whatever party, were always a considerable travail to me. A few moments of enjoyment in the midst of interminable events, too much bad food taken during functions as 'in-flight refuelling' and accompanied by often bad and mixed drink of all kinds. The added problem was the sheer expense of it all, which, to do it properly, necessitated staying at hotels or guest houses for three or four nights plus various meals there or in restaurants. It had its charms. On one occasion at a boarding-house in Blackpool I emerged reluctantly from my habitat for breakfast, to be greeted by a flow of Hawaiian music and a middle-aged landlady stripped down to regulation Hawaii clothing, with a little dance to match. With rain and red brick outside and a day in conference ahead of me, I took time to recover.

Like so much else the conferences of the major parties have become more similar, whereas in the not-too-distant past they were very different. Conservative conferences, which I regularly attended from 1962 to

1995, began for me as deceptively old-fashioned affairs, in that under the surface little was more professionally controlled. They were run by formidable dowagers and established men with impressive war records. The main bars were full of these often large men ordering equally large gin and tonics, sometimes with the hope of some honours recognition for their services, often deserved, and without the envious press clamour of today. By convention the leader and/or the prime minister did not attend until the occasion of a special rally on the last day, and after the conference had formally closed. This merciful release for him was ended from 1965 by Edward Heath, and conferences became an exhausting treadmill for the leader. The handling of a carefully arranged agenda was at a level of 'state of the art' that I have never seen bettered, and still chuckle about today. A classic example would be allowing the conference to be carried gently down the road of objection when, at the vital point of balance, a known objector would appear as a speaker, and to everyone's profound shock would have miraculously changed his mind and seen the light. He would then deliver a resounding speech confessing the error of his ways and would be followed by some popular figures in support. The platform would conduct a mopping-up operation and the day was won.

From 1979 the old skills remained to be used as necessary, but a heavier emphasis was placed on the increasing number of fringe meetings. Within both major parties these were frequently used to float controversial views or to air policy differences. It could get bitter. Great figures out of favour for the moment would appear for large meetings and be cheered to the echo by their partisan supporters. Things got so bad over the European disputes within the Conservative Party in the pre-1997 period that bread was thrown over a partition separating two rival events in the same large ballroom. At one conference around 1993, Norman Tebbit made an anti-European and anti-platform speech involving a long approach to the dais under a balcony packed with Euro-sceptic Young Conservatives cheering him all along the way. As I emerged afterwards I was recognised in the street as a pro-European by a group of banner-waving sceptics and jeered. This was not the Conservative Party I had joined.

A couple of conference examples give an illustration of the change in the Conservative Party. Back in the late 1960s it was still seen as the duty of the leadership to rescue the party from its own excesses. Brilliant speeches came forth from the likes of Macleod and Hailsham which by oratorical power controlled the omnipresent excesses of the rank and file, and produced an acceptable conclusion for the great British public. I never forget Lord Hailsham avoiding a vote on capital punishment by sheer flat-out oratory. In comparison, in the early 1990s and the Major government, one was treated to the most miserable display where ministers, one after another, played to the lowest common denominator, thus encouraging the very tendencies that their predecessors had used their considerable talents to control. The farce of 'Back to Basics' was a lamentable case in point. This involved an admirable plan for John Major to guide us towards the traditional ways of honour, tradition and the family. It became hopeless as the tabloid press saw it as an opportunity to discuss the extra-marital affairs of Conservative ministers and MPs, which were much more numerous and colourful than we all imagined. The press had a field day and the policy became a laughing stock.

The Labour conferences over the same period provide an interesting contrast. Eventually under Tony Blair, they changed quite remarkably into responsible affairs for the promotion of the Labour Party in government. Before that it is not an exaggeration to say that Labour conferences with their various motions, the agony of 'Composites' and the unlimited use of the opportunity to vent views and differences presented an absolute nightmare for the leadership, not least when in government. The party structure was such that the conference was under the control of the National Executive, and it was their members who had the floor for longer periods. Mere government ministers, who were not members of the Executive, had only the five minutes' of a floor speaker. This was quite extraordinary for a party in government and indicated that the Labour Party was more concerned with itself than the country whose votes it needed. The most famous example of this was Denis Healey as Chancellor, en route to Washington for the annual IMF conference, having borrowed from the IMF and with important work to do to secure their backing. That was not appreciated by his party and he understandably overshot his floor time, which was all he had, and ended up with his microphone cut off. It was a classic display of the differences between the two parties, with one wanting to always remain in power and the other feeling, if anything, uncomfortable with government, which was far less interesting than being a party of protest.

By the time I arrived on the Labour scene, it was clear to me, attending a full Blackpool conference in 1998, that the monster had been tamed. Indeed it was a model conference, with none of the unhappiness I had left behind in the Tory Party. Being a recent arrival on the Labour scene, and having spoken at several fringe meetings and to the conference itself, I was a known figure. I spoke to all manner of delegates, from trade unionists to professionals, and enjoyed myself. On a number of occasions I was told by old veterans that I had arrived too late. 'Peter, you have missed all the fun. We used to come to conference and have a wonderful time, eventually leaving with blood all over the floor. Those were the days.' Well meant and amusing to hear in retrospect, but quite awful to have to go through if you wanted Labour in government.

To sum up, I have enjoyed being in both the Conservative and the Labour Party and appreciated their differences. Obviously I was brought up in the Tory Party, and felt socially at ease within it. At constituency level a county seat was hard work but had very agreeable rewards. The people were naturally easy and a social life came with the job: functions, dinner parties, shooting parties and so on, as well as the more conventional constituency functions. The knights of the shire had plenty of opportunity to act as such, and being 'the Member' gave them that extra bit of status in their chosen habitats. At Westminster, life for them could be equally agreeable in the club, with continuous entertainment provided. Good company and pleasant dining clubs were everywhere, and when I started in 1974 one could just about pursue another career as well, but only just.

All this steadily changed as conviction politics took over at Westminster. During the period 1974–2001 the social change in the party was considerable. We became less grand, more meritocratic, more middle class and more right wing as a consequence. As my differences with the Conservatives had been aired all too publicly, the Labour Party was in a sense expecting me. During my first week, I went to a reception at Number 10 and the powers that be were worried about my welcome, as the party was for lifelong supporters from the West Midlands. As I entered the main reception room one old salt came up to me and said: 'Peter, what took you so long!' Relief poured off my allotted minder, who then dropped away and all went well. I also had a lot of friends in the Labour Party through years of work in foreign affairs and on various bipartisan committees. For my part I worked at being one of them, and for their part they welcomed me in. At parliamentary functions, I always appreciated that there would be some Labour people somehow on hand to see I was not alone or in any way isolated. During one discussion someone said in answer to me: 'But, Peter, you are a toff, after all!' I immediately replied: 'And why can't a toff be a member of the Labour Party?' That was accepted, and I think the essence in life generally is to be yourself. I found little hypocrisy in Labour members and they did not expect any from me.

To speak generally of Labour members as I found them, and I was a Labour backbencher for three years, I would say that they have a certain warmth and sympathy that you don't necessarily find in the same measure on the Conservative side. They are also direct and straight and will generally say it upfront. I like that. Whatever their views, I would stand on the barricades with most of them.

Part III
AN INTERNATIONAL LIFE

Seven
REVOLUTION IN IRAN

Louis XVI: 'Is this a revolt?'

Duc de La Rochefoucauld-Liancourt: 'No sir, it's a revolution.'
> Exchange after the fall of the Bastille, in F. Dreyfus,
> *Un philanthrope d'autrefois: La Rochefoucauld-Liancourt,*
> *1747–1827,* 1903

Take care to get what you like or you will be forced to like what you get.
> George Bernard Shaw, 'Maxims for revolutionists',
> *Man and Superman,* 1903

Introduction

During 1978–9 Iran was consumed by a mounting crisis that developed into a full-scale revolution. Too much had been expected from Iran, and far quicker than could be accomplished. Iran's turbulent history was compounded by occupation during the World War II, the Cold War that followed and constant political difficulties. Rapidly growing oil wealth added to an all-too-complex scene. Politically the Shah and his country were encouraged by the American-led West to think of itself as the protector of Western interests in the whole region. Massive defence contracts ensued and oil wealth enabled development at a pace which led to severe economic indigestion. Every hotel became packed with businessmen, and wheels, deals and opportunities for corruption were everywhere. Last but not least development towards democracy was far too limited to satisfy a population whose expectations were rising, with many having been educated abroad at the expense of the Shah's government.

Traditional Islam, with many reactionary Shia mullahs, was waiting in the wings. Their chance came and in an unholy alliance with liberal elements and the discontented, the Shah and his government were overthrown in February 1979. The final stage of the revolution involved a virtual civil war as the Islamic interest brutally overcame the more secular elements that had supported them in the revolution, and by 1983 they had assumed full power and authority.

The last act began in January 1979 when an Air France chartered plane delivered Ayatollah Khomeini from Paris to Tehran, an act echoing the closed train that carried Lenin across Europe after World War I to take command of the Bolshevik Revolution. As Churchill put it at the time, a poisoned and toxic substance was being permitted to travel across Europe. How often history repeats itself to the detriment of people and countries who have to put up with the inadequacies of their leadership. A serious revolution got under way. Arrests, execution and persecution followed their familiar revolutionary course. Setting the trend for the somewhat bizarre nature of this revolution, the early executions took place on a school rooftop adjacent to Ayatollah Khomeini's initial headquarters. A little later on, the habit was formed of hanging people from mobile cranes in public. Many died and many others managed to escape, often dramatically. Some elected to stay, such as Amir Abbas Hoveyda, the Shah's Prime Minister for many years, who suddenly found his prison cell opened up in the initial chaos of revolution, as had happened at the Bastille some 190 years before. He elected to stay and was executed later for his pains. Anyone of prominence in the Shah's regime was in severe and often mortal danger. In a revolution the fact that one may not have done anything wrong is as nothing compared to who you might be in your connections with the previous government and system. Not only the elite were affected, but also the emerging professional and upper middle classes, so nurtured by the Shah. They fled virtually en masse to set up large expatriate communities, not least in both California and Canada. For them it was to preserve their standards and to live in freedom. For the old ruling class and the *prominenti* it was a matter of life and death.

The family

My wife, Taheré, is of the Khozeimeh family, being the eldest child of HE Amir Hussein Khozeimeh Alam. Her mother, Mme Fatemeh, was of the Alam side of the same family, as was her distinguished brother, HE Amir Asadollah Alam. Until the early twentieth century the family had ruled substantial parts of Khorasan, Sistan and Baluchistan. Their ancestors had come to the region from Mesopotamia, as part of the ruling Caliphate, some 1,300 years before. At its height in the eighteenth century the Khozeimeh amirdom included most of the east of Iran, starting from above Mashhad in the north and stretching down almost to Chah Bahar on the Gulf coast. It included great tracts of what is now Afghanistan and Pakistan.

In the early part of the twentieth century the family still ruled substantial areas. Amongst the family, the senior figures, and cousins, at this time were Mme Fatemeh's father, the Shokat al- Mulk II, and Amir Hussein's father, the Hesam al-Doleh III. When Reza Shah abolished the old Qajar dynasty titles they became HE Amir Ebrahim Khan Alam and HE Amir Masum Khan Khozeimch respectively.

Amir Ebrahim, during Reza Shah's centralisation of power throughout Iran in the late 1920s and into the 1930s, kept himself close to the new Shah and served as one of his Ministers. If not as rulers, the family's position and influence in its region was preserved. Amir Ebrahim's son and Taheré's uncle, HE Amir Asadollah Alam, became a governor, minister, prime minister and latterly a powerful Minister of the Shah's Court. In 1963 as prime minister he forcibly put down the first Khomeini-inspired uprising, which climaxed in a march on Tehran from the holy city of Qom. It never reached Tehran and Khomeini ended up escaping execution and being sent into exile to the holy city of Najaf in Iraq. He remained there until 1978, when he was ordered out of Iraq by Saddam Hussein, at the behest of the Shah, ironically ending up in Paris, which gave him a far better base from which to ferment revolution, sitting under his tree in the suburbs of that city.

Taheré's father, Amir Hussein, became a governor, minister, Member of Parliament, senator and a chamberlain to the Shah. He had ended his education at the Royal Agricultural College, Cirencester, attached to the University of Bristol, and put his knowledge to good use as a modern and effective landowner. Amir Asadollah sadly died in 1977, just before the revolution. This was particularly unfortunate as he was perhaps the one person who could have best advised the Shah during the vital years running up to the revolution. As for Amir Hussein, he suffered the full drama of revolution, months in hiding and a daring escape in October 1979 into Turkey.

Part 1: How are the mighty fallen

Istanbul, October 1979

It was an overcast day at Istanbul local airport. We waited anxiously for the internal flight from Van in the east. It arrived and two men in their sixties, still with a certain manner of authority about them, walked towards us across the tarmac. Dressed in dark raincoats, and with only the clothes they stood up in, plus one small travelling bag each, two of the more important men of the Shah's Iran had arrived as illegal refugees. My brother-in-law Darioush and I were there to meet my father-in-law, HE Amir Hussein Khozeime-Alam. His companion had been, until February, Governor of Isfahan and its province, one of the most beautiful cities of the world, let alone of Iran.

Greetings were warm and just a little emotional. Once these were over, we relaxed and the governor turned and asked me directly, 'And how is Mrs Thatcher?' I was surprised by the direct question and replied, saying I had just come directly from the Conservative Party conference in Blackpool where she was celebrating her great election victory of the previous May. 'If you get the chance please remember me to her. I was her host when she visited Isfahan last year.' It was at that moment that the reality of the situation was brought home to me. How indeed are the mighty fallen!

A year ago these two men could have been in the glittering gold-inlaid uniforms of the government and court. Now raincoats and the little bags. Inside his, Amir Hussein had one spare of each essential item of personal clothing, plus toiletry items and essential medication. Within the straps of his bag, the seams of his raincoat and his belt were sown lines of gold sovereigns and gold pahlavis. These were for eventualities and for smoothing out the obvious difficulties that could and did arise in such a difficult and dangerous journey. They had crossed the mountains above Lake Van, taking it in turns to ride the one available mule and conducted by drug- and people-smugglers who carried their very illegal cargo in addition to their two distinguished passengers. Some three weeks later this particular gang were caught on the Iranian side and promptly executed.

That evening, sitting out on the comfortable terrace of our rooms at the Inter-Continental Hotel, overlooking the beautiful sight of the Bosphorus and Istanbul by night, we heard some of the detail of what had transpired during and after the revolution. The revolution finally occurred over the weekend of 11–12 February 1979 and within two days the Revolutionary Guards turned up at the family home at 16 Avenue Alam, Dezashib to arrest my mother-in-law: they were starting with those who had royal connections. These were followed by the court, government, parliament and so on down the line. Her great crime was that she had been honorary chairman of Queen Farah's charities. Fortunately she had left for London on the same day as the Shah left in January, together with her youngest daughter, Ziba, and two little grandchildren. Amir Hussein promptly made himself scarce, and by the time they came to arrest him the following day he was in hiding. He had made a potentially fatal mistake in the face of revolution by assuming that because he had done nothing wrong, he could take his chances and try to safeguard the family property. He was even chairman of the Senate's Ombudsman Committee dealing with complaints against government, a task he took seriously.

Immediately after the attempt to arrest his wife he went into hiding, ending up in a flat he borrowed from Belgian friends who had returned to Brussels. He remained there, with one family servant who looked after him, for some eight months without ever going out. The sum of his exercise was going up and down the staircase a set number of times per day. Whilst he was there his eldest son, Parviz, who had also stayed behind, was eventually able to arrange his escape. Parviz himself was later to literally crash out of the country in a Range Rover across the Pakistani border.

The message came through to London in September that Amir Hussein's escape was imminent. We all went on stand-by, although I was at the party conference in Blackpool when we heard that it was in progress. I left immediately, met Darioush in Geneva and off to Istanbul we went. There we waited in the comfort of the Istanbul Hilton for some ten days, in a somewhat tense state, as word of his arrival had to come through via London from Tehran. My role was to help Amir Hussein out of Turkey and into the UK on a passport that was all too obviously a fake!

Getting out of Turkey was easy. The Turks knew that a lot of Iranians were coming through, and as long as they were in transit they turned a blind eye. An overweight official looked at the passport in a somewhat bored way and promptly stamped it. At that moment I was frantically thinking of the best response to the challenge that never came. We were on our way, but the UK could be more difficult.

At Heathrow I decided that a direct approach would be best. I got through my shorter queue of UK/EU passengers as early as I could and quickly doubled around to introduce myself to the somewhat surprised immigration officer handling Amir Hussein's queue of foreign nationals. I outlined the situation, told him who Amir Hussein was, that he owned a flat in Cheyne Walk, Chelsea and was only wanting a three-month standard tourist visa. I would handle matters thereafter. It worked. When Amir Hussein's turn came he was waved through without demur. This was just as well, as with all the tension of recent events and months I don't think Amir Hussein was in any condition to suffer questioning.

The lift doors opened with an old-fashioned clang at Carlyle Mansions, Cheyne Walk and Amir Hussein was greeted on the landing by his waiting family. It was a very emotional moment, but he had arrived unharmed at what was to be his home in exile for the rest of his life. He was very lucky. Many of his rank ended up in prison and/or lost their lives.

As a postscript, my parents-in-law continued to live in Carlyle Mansions until old age took them peacefully away in the early years of the new millennium. Their servants, loyal as ever to this day, managed to occupy their Tehran compound for several years after 1979 on the grounds of homelessness but eventually had to give in and move out. The main house was bulldozed and the gardens were ploughed up and turned into two blocks of flats. Their lands were all confiscated and the lovely Old Persian main houses outside Birjand were looted. Almost immediately several antique shops sprang up in the town. Fortunately, because the family were popular and charitable landlords, ways were found by the local leadership to save the houses, one becoming a museum, one municipal offices and another the basis of a new university. It is some consolation to the family, who have lost so much, that their main houses remain in reasonable condition. Similarly a family cemetery was unmolested, whereas those of many landowners were ploughed over and disappeared without visible trace. When I led the first official Westminster delegation since the revolution in 1999 my Iranian counterpart told me he had enquired about the family from the Revolutionary Guards in Birjand out of curiosity and was told 'Please don't let them come here. They are still very popular.' Even in great loss there can be some satisfaction.

It is a tribute that I never heard my parents-in-law complain about their lot. They accepted it and got on with their lives.

Part 2: Revolution is awful

This was a revolution in every sense of the word. As distinct from coups d'état, the major revolutions of the twentieth century can be limited to those in Russia, China and Iran. To understand better what happened we can take a brief look at recent Iranian history and most particularly the rivalry between the British Empire and Imperial Russia. Iran became a victim of the 'Great Game', with Britain protecting the 'Jewel of the Empire', India, from any threat from Russia, and Imperial Russia set on expansion and always with an eye out for a warm-water port. Iran was effectively divided into two zones of influence between the two Powers, was exploited, deliberately kept weak and effectively denied any much-needed progress towards gaining a more effective and centralised government. Arguably Iran suffered the disadvantages of de facto colonisation without the benefits of being left with a centralised administration and a more modern military tradition.

By the early twentieth century the British effectively ran the financial administration and the all-important emerging oil industry. A badly declining Qajar dynasty was replaced in 1921 by a *coup d' état* headed by Reza Khan, commander of the Persian Cossacks, and with the support of the British. He was a strong leader, with little formal education, who rapidly created a dictatorship, emerging as Reza Shah Pahlavi, the first of the two Shahs of the Pahlavi dynasty.

From this point everything happens far too quickly for stability to prevail. What should have evolved gradually occurred at an increasingly fast gallop. The administration of the country had to be centralised, which took time and struggle, and parallel with that it was more and more necessary to develop a modern infrastructure. The 1930s saw the rise to power of Nazi Germany. The Germans arrived in some force at this geopolitically well-situated country, to trade, build railways and give military advice. Reza Shah was partial to their authoritarian ways and the stage was set, all too soon, for Iran to be caught once more between the interests of Great Powers.

The concern of the British was exacerbated by the outbreak of World War II. The geographical situation of neutral Iran was pivotal, and had the German armies broken through at Stalingrad and headed south through the Caucasus, the oilfields of Iran and indeed the Gulf would have become an obvious target. In addition Iran's geographical position made it a vital supply route for Allied assistance to the Soviet Union, to check the German advance and secure victory on that crucial front. Reza

Shah had declared Iran neutral, but his pro-German sympathies were well known. In August 1941, to secure Iran for the allies, British and Russian armies invaded Iran, occupied the country and sent Reza Shah into exile. His son, Mohammed Reza Shah, became Shah at the age of twenty-one and never saw his father again. He inherited an occupied country, and governed with limited authority in the midst of a World War. He was virtually ignored by the Great Powers during the Tehran Conference of 1943, and clearly felt humiliated in the eyes of his people. No reign could have had a more dreadful beginning.

The Shah, still very young at twenty-one, had his personal confidence shattered. He never really recovered, however mighty he may have seemed later on to Western observers. As time went on this weakness was fatal for a ruler who needed every talent and sophistication in the book to survive politically, and deliver his country at the same time. Events demanded qualities that were beyond him and for which he was never given time to prepare or train.

The end of the war in 1945 did not end foreign occupation, as the Soviet Union remained in Iranian Azerbaijan, plus Kurdistan, and would not budge. They eventually withdrew in May 1946, under formidable pressure from the Allies, and Iran was able to reoccupy its territories and defeat its rebels, who had been fostered by the Soviets. However, the country was in a state of turbulence and constant Cold War pressure from the Soviet Union, allied to Iran's domestic Tudeh (Communist) Party. In 1951 the Prime Minister, General Razmara, was assassinated while attending a funeral, with amongst others my wife's uncle, Asadollah, a Cabinet minister at the time, standing beside him when he was shot. The guilty party was a member of the extreme Islam Fedayeen, a party of the extreme Islamic right, which were active for years and killed a number of American servicemen in the run-up to 1979. From 1951 Iran increasingly came under the influence of the nationalists and the left, headed by Mohammed Mosaddeq, leader of the National Front and prime minister. Had his rule been consolidated it is a matter of conjecture how long he would have lasted before more extreme elements took over. The Anglo-Iranian Oil crisis continued and there followed the famous CIA/

MI6 coup of 1953. The Shah, who had left the country, was brought back and restored by the West. That began the final chapter, leaving twenty-six years, before 1979 arrived, to modernise a country and install a stable system of government. This was difficult enough but it was destined to occur in the midst of an oil and gas boom in the economy. This caused a pace of progress that Iran was ill-equipped to handle and the West did everything to increase, rather than having the foresight to moderate. Change came so fast that the people could not keep up with it. The traditional ways of much of Iran and the considerable power of the clergy were forgotten in the rush to Westernise. It was a recipe for disaster.

In considering what transpired, the personality of the Shah becomes very important. Contrary to popular belief he was not the dictator his father had been or even a particularly strong leader. Ironically, much of his father's formidable strength of character was invested in his twin sister, Princess Ashraf. He so surrounded himself with the trappings of power, and his ego was so much flattered domestically and internationally, that he was assumed to possess a strength that he did not have. The biggest example of this was the Nixon–Kissinger doctrine that placed Iran, under his leadership, as the Guardian of the Gulf and indeed the whole region, on behalf of the West. His rather gruff manner on British television was not, as people thought, arrogance, but rather shyness and deep suspicion of the British, who had conquered his country, exiled his father and placed him prematurely on the throne at the age of twenty-one. The redoubtable Miss Palmer Smith, English teacher to the Shah and the other royal children, once perceptively remarked when he was a boy that he could do well, but only if he had the strength to withstand the flattering ways of the Persian court. Sadly he did not survive this test, although one can have some sympathy for a man who had everybody, at home and abroad, constantly telling him how marvellous he was. governments of Iran increasingly did virtually everything overtly in his name: 'His Majesty has ordered so many houses to be built ...'; 'His Majesty has done this, commanded that ...', and so on. Fine when things go well, but if they don't, who picks up the blame? As for the court, he permitted other power centres to develop around other royals and tolerated corruption which then became more endemic in the system than it might have been. When the revolution came this was an important factor used to justify it.

In 1963 he was establishing himself on the throne when the first uprising inspired and led by Ayatollah Khomeini took place. It centred on the holy city of Qom and culminated in a dramatic march aimed at Tehran. The Prime Minister was Asadollah Alam, my wife's uncle, who put down this revolt, which was intended to develop into something bigger and more dangerous to the regime. Whilst always respectful, Asadollah was one of the few to whom the Shah would listen and would treat as a relative equal. When the crisis arrived, he advised the Shah to go to his palace, do nothing and keep out of it. He, Alam, would deal with it and if all went well the Shah could claim the credit, and if it didn't he, Alam, would take the blame. The Shah agreed and left Alam to it. Alam deployed the Army and forcibly put down the revolt, stopping the march well before it was any threat to Tehran.

Khomeini was arrested and was in some danger of execution. A serious plea to the Shah on his behalf was led by Grand Ayatollah Shariat Maderi, which ended with him being spared. He was sent into exile in the holy city of Najaf, Iraq, from where he continued to do whatever mischief he could to the Shah and his government. This was a mistake compounded later by the Shah getting Saddam Hussein to remove Khomeini from Najaf as the revolution was building up in 1978, and from where he went to Paris with free access to the world's media.

The humane side of the Shah's character came out at the time of the revolution. It is fair to say that during the horrendous period of 1978–February 1979, being the run-up to the revolution, at no time did he formally let loose the full power of the military on the people. The revolution was allowed to gather momentum and whilst undue force was employed in the later stages, it was never full force, and in any event was too late. The military commander of Tehran was four-star General Gholam Ali Oveissi, later exiled in France and assassinated by the Khomeini regime in the mid-eighties. On several occasions early on, he 'literally begged' (as he told me in his own words in conversation around 1984) to be given a free hand to use sufficient force to restore order on the streets while there was still time to do so. The Shah refused and said he would not be responsible for killing his own people. He later said that his refusing to do this was the best legacy he could leave to his son and heir, Crown Prince Reza.

As has been remarked in a historical context, the main factor in the approach to the revolution, and particularly during the 1970s, was the sheer speed of events and change in a country insufficiently developed to absorb so much so quickly. There was not a hotel in Tehran that was not flooded out with Western businessmen; there was not an Iranian bank that was not expanding into Western capitals; a massive amount of military equipment flowed into the country to support the Nixon–Kissinger plan, including the latest US jets and from the UK specially designed Chobham armour and the tanks to go with it; ambassadors rushed to promote their country's commercial interests; renovated former US Navy ships helped to create a modern navy; and not a word of warning came that such a pace could not be sustained. As an aside the Iranian Navy personnel spent a year in the USA training and learning how to handle the ships. To show them that they had a long way to go, when they had nearly completed their training the accompanying US ships electronically blotted out the entire communication and computer systems on the newly acquired Iranian assets and then played some tune like 'Singing in the Rain' to emphasise the point. The Iranians took it well, treating it as both a joke and a lesson, which it was. (This account was related to me by Naval Lieutenant Kayhan Khosravani.)

In the autumn of 1973 came the Arab–Israeli War and the resulting hike in the price of oil. Virtually overnight the Iranian budget almost doubled and matters got rapidly worse. Great queues of ships waited to unload at inadequate Gulf ports. Greed and corruption got worse, fortunes were made and all in an economy lacking the capacity to absorb so much of everything so quickly.

On top of all this came social and cultural excesses which served to alienate the people from those who ruled them and to awaken increasing anti-Western feeling in a traditionally Islamic nation. In 1972 the *folies de grandeur* of the court reached their height with the celebrations of 2,500 years of Iranian monarchy centred on Shiraz and Persepolis. It became one of the world's most extravagant parties and, even if it was fantastic to watch, it was politically unwise, to say the least, in a country where so many were poor. Some wise heads at court and in government were very uneasy about it, but the Shah became absolutely set on it and there was no changing his mind.

One of the principal guests from the UK was Lord Shawcross, then President of the Iran Society in London. The annual dinner at the Savoy followed soon after this great event and the president was so struck by the celebrations that he spent the first ten minutes of his speech regaling us with the joys of Chateau Lafite 1945, caviar and all the rest of the delicacies consumed at the main banquet. Bearing in mind that we had just consumed a typical, and not very spectacular, offering from the Savoy banqueting department, many of us found his enthusiasm somewhat galling.

On the cultural side of things it was decided that Iran had to have its own major festival. This became the Shiraz Festival and featured the latest from East and West. However, to conservative Islamic eyes it appeared decadent and gave the clerics even more ammunition for their Friday sermons. An extreme example of unnecessary excess was a live theatre group from Poland, who roamed around the streets of Shiraz doing 'Live Theatre' which included simulated sexual intercourse. The effect on the locals that witnessed it was horrendous.

Sadly the Shah went wrong on the all-important political side. As education improved and with many from the emerging middle classes being sent abroad on scholarships to study, there arose an increasing desire for more democracy. As a cover for this, under constant urging from the Americans over the years, the Shah had created a governing party, Iran Novin or New Iran, and a token opposition party, the Mardom or People's Party. One of its members once showed me the committee room in the Majlis (Parliament) where they met and remarked: 'This is where we decide what to say and, more important, what we can't say!' Because Iran Novin was favoured it grew powerful, and the Shah had to decide in 1974 whether to limit Iran Novin by democratic means, and bring on Mardom to challenge it, or start again in some way. Sadly he decided on the latter course by abolishing both parties and establishing a single new party called the Rastakhiz (Resurgence) Party and the word was given that everyone was expected to join it. The result was that Iran became a one-party state. I remember my senator father-in-law complaining that he had never been a party member in his life but always an independent. However, he was obliged to join up. This decision of the Shah was very unfortunate and denied democracy to a talented and vibrant people who were ready and waiting for at least some progress in that direction. Ironically this was because of the improvements in education and living conditions introduced by the very same Shah.

From 1976 on it all began to go overtly wrong. Expectations were too high and the capacity of the infrastructure too limited. No firm sense of direction was established in a highly talented but very technocratic government, full of ministers with US PhDs, but at the end of the day far too deferential to the Shah. The writing was on the wall, even if the world at large was blissfully ignorant of the seriousness of what was unfolding in Iran. The great exception in 1977 was the London *Financial Times*, which ran a supplement on Iran within which a talented journalist called Robert Graham got it right, way ahead of governments and their Foreign Ministries and Security Services. It was obviously noted, but very few, Iranian or foreign, could quite see that this was not just another difficulty, which, as so often in the past, Iran would eventually get over. Iran and its Shah had reached such an eminence that it must all work out in the end.

In July 1978 the British Ambassador in Tehran, Sir Anthony Parsons, came home on leave with the object of decorating a house he had bought in Dulwich. The British Group of the Inter-Parliamentary Union, of which I was then an Executive Committee member, entertained him informally to lunch in the House of Commons. As I knew him well, I was placed next to him. The object of the lunch was to hear about Iran, but much to my surprise, rather than telling me the situation, he somewhat anxiously asked me what I thought was happening in Iran. He obviously wanted to know what my wife's family thought about the situation, which would represent the inside track. However, it gave me a shock as it did indicate how starved of information, if not confused, the highest levels of government were. We now know that the same went for the Americans and others. At the time I had little to tell him, as I had been far more consumed with my own very busy domestic political life.

We went out to Tehran in August 1978 for what was to be our last holiday there. The atmosphere was very uneasy. Downtown Tehran around the Bazaar was heavily patrolled by armed police and eerily silent. It was in effect the lull before the storm and years later I was reminded of it when on a visit to India. Our plane landed at Mumbai the day after the Ayodhya Mosque had been stormed by Hindu extremists in December 1992. The run-down Islamic areas on the way in from the airport were heavily patrolled by armed police and soldiers. All was quiet in the same eerie way. That night mosques and temples were burnt down and several hundreds lost their lives. Back in Tehran demonstrations were beginning and then came the Abadan cinema fire, when an entire audience, unable to get out of the building, was incinerated alive. The government, through Savak, the Shah's intelligence service, was blamed by the rebel elements and they in turn were blamed by the government. However, I suspect that the rebels had much more to gain than the government did by stirring up the situation, which this fire surely did. The revolution gathered momentum towards its bloody conclusion six months later.

Even then, most refused to accept the seriousness of what was happening. One of my favourite stories is of a Friday lunch party, in well-to-do north Tehran, with the guests enjoying pre-lunch drinks by the swimming pool. Revolutions were far away as upper-class Tehran life pursued its normal course. Suddenly one of the sons of the house appeared, filthy and covered in dust. The guests looked at him disapprovingly and asked him where on earth he had been to get into that state. 'Marching', he said. He had joined a demonstration at Tadjreish Square, north Tehran, and had marched all the way downtown with the demonstrators. The assembled company, still clutching their drinks, looked suitably pained that he had joined a demonstration. He turned to them and said: 'You don't seem to know it, but there's a real revolution going on down there.'

The same atmosphere prevailed in most such houses, including our own. At least part of the reason was the fact that over the years Iranians had endured so many crises in their history, most recently from World War II and then to Mossadeq and beyond, that they were in a sense inured to it all. They had seen so much that it could not get worse. For example, my wife's family, for a period under Mossadeq, were confined to their country seat at Birjand, and some were not allowed near Tehran. When we were engaged my wife staggered me when I took her to a funfair and we patronised a shooting gallery where I expected to show off as a former member of my school shooting eight. She went first and shot down everything in sight, collecting all sorts of prizes in the process. I was outclassed. It turned out that during the period of exile, at the age of thirteen or fourteen, she had thoroughly learnt how to shoot both rifle and pistol. With that sort of background, the family in 1978 were obviously concerned but not too alarmed, and discussed the future, including the approaching senate elections, quite normally.

During our stay the cycle of demonstrations got into its stride. After a death, Shi'a Muslims have set mourning periods, first after seven days and then forty days, followed by one year. The clergy craftily adapted this practice to cause the deaths of the Abadan fire, and later events, to be remembered by demonstrations after these set periods. These became increasingly massive. It seemed as if everyone was joining in. My sister-in-law went to her local hairdresser as usual to find a notice on the door: 'Gone to demonstrations. Back at 6 p.m.'

People often wonder about the sheer size of these demonstrations. They understood the participation of the engaged political elements, but why were they so enormous? The Shah, whatever may have been his faults, had after all done much to improve living standards, the same with women's rights and education, and had started the process of developing a middle class. All this was secular and anathema to the clerics, yet out onto the streets they all went, one out, all out, be they clerical or secular, identifying the Shah with everything which in their eyes might be wrong with life. As to the size, with millions on the streets, I can only invoke the completely unrelated comparison of the death of Princess Diana in 1997.

An enormous shared communal grief descended on the United Kingdom and fed on itself. Its intensity was quite unexpected by most people, from the Royal Family down. It took hold and multiplied, as did events in Iran. People forgot the realities and joined in. It became unstoppable, and Iranians woke up to discover, when they suddenly thought about what they had accomplished, that they had a full-blown revolution on their hands. It was too late to go back.

Going back to our family holiday in August 1978, the penny finally dropped for my wife and me when a very old friend of the family, Professor Mohammad Hassan Ganji, who was from Birjand, came calling and asked to see us in particular. We had a private talk with him at the bottom of the garden and he explained the level of anti-regime feeling amongst the clergy. A year before, in 1977, my wife's uncle, Amir Asadollah Alam, the former prime minister and more recently Minister of Court, had died. As one of the most powerful men in Iran, and his native Khorasan, he was duly laid to rest in the family vault at the holy shrine of Meshed. In 1977 there was still no problem with this, and he was given a state funeral and remains in that vault today, at rest with his ancestors. However, there is an ante-chamber above the vault, with memorial plaques to those interred there, and all the names and inscriptions have been erased. Professor Ganji explained that difficulties emerged after the state funeral in dealing with the clergy over the formal memorial service at their home and seat in Birjand. The mullahs, led by one awkward individual, were reluctant to officiate, whereas a few years before they would have been honoured to do so. This was not a good omen. We returned to London with some foreboding.

It was at this point that the revolution really took hold. Demonstration followed demonstration, government followed government, with the Shah in retreat and always giving too little, too late. His increasing isolation was compounded by the vacillation of the West. The Americans divided into two schools of thought: the hawks under National Security Chief Brzezinski and the doves under Secretary of State Vance, with President Carter somewhat ineffectually in the middle. The Shah did not know where he was in terms of US support when he really needed it. It is an interesting thought that had it all occurred but a few years later, Reagan would have been in charge, supported by Thatcher in the UK. Things might well have been different, but as it was the Shah felt he had been abandoned by the West and left the country in January 1979. No doubt he wanted, as has been written, to talk to the Americans and always had the idea that he might be recalled, through Western power, to resume his rule, as had happened before in 1953. In the circumstances this was as naive as it was mistaken.

Back in the UK, I found myself in demand to talk about Iran. In February 1979 I went to speak to the Conservative students at both Durham and Newcastle universities about the unfolding revolution and saw how fashionable it had become for middle-class Iranian students, no doubt on scholarships from the Shah's government, to oppose the Shah and all he stood for. Both were open meetings because of the interest in the subject. Durham went well and I was then driven to Newcastle. The chairman of the meeting was waiting for me in a state of some agitation. She explained that they had expected an open meeting of their own students, but some forty to fifty Iranian students from all over the UK were waiting for me in the hall. Apparently they were not in a charitable frame of mind and she was uncertain about how the situation might develop. My family relationship to the Iranian establishment was of course known and this was the very weekend of 9–12 February when the revolution finally came to a head.

Up and into the hall we went. Sure enough it was full of Iranians, with Newcastle student Conservatives very much in the minority and somewhat overcome at that. I knew I had the natural politeness of Iranians on my side but the whole thing could easily have gone sour. Sadly, but necessarily, I came to the conclusion that the best thing I could do was to hit them below the belt at the first available opportunity. All Iranian students were well monitored by the Iranian Security Service, Savak, and their informants were in every university. So at an early stage in my speech I exploited this by deploring it, and said how wrong it was that they were put in a situation where they did not know whom they could trust. They started to look worried, and when I finally added that by the law of averages Savak would be present at our meeting and 'could even be sitting next to you', they absolutely froze. From there onwards it was fine and we had an excellent meeting in which they asked very good questions. We parted good friends, and I went off to do a party meeting before catching the sleeper to Euston. When I boarded, lo and behold the carriage was full of the same Iranian students, who gave me a genuinely warm welcome and said how much they had enjoyed the meeting. As I went to sleep, I had to spare a thought for the Shah, who had sent them to the UK, and their parents, who were no doubt paying for their first-class rail fares, while they denounced their government. Little did they know it, but within a matter of months they would be thinking again about what they had managed to achieve and within a year or so would be desperately leaving Iran or seeking to remain in the UK. I myself had to help several political leaders on the left to get political exile status. The revolution was turning out to be so awful that they had to be protected, as did the more establishment figures of Iran.

Over that weekend the dam broke in Tehran. A group of cadets fired on the Shah's Guards Regiment, which had been sent to oppose them. The Guards by this time were low in both spirit and morale. The Shah had left the country weeks before, and though they were his personal 'Imperial Guard', they were without their leader and their officers were disillusioned. The Guards did not return any effective fire or take further action. They went back to barracks and that was the end. Revolution now took over. Arrests and executions followed as the Khomeini regime moved to establish its power. From the beginning, the clergy moved to dominate their secular allies in the revolution, which they duly did. They had a national network through the mosques and it was their organisation that had promoted the revolution. The secular side was as ever divided and their ideological aspirations were no match for the 'hard-right' approach of the ayatollahs. The liberal government of Bazargan was immediately dispensed with and, as with other revolutions, the liberal elements had only provided an interim stage before the less well-meaning took over.

The more secular Mujahedin led by Massoud Rajavi had been an actual part of the revolution and were the leading left-wing element involved.

I had several meetings with Massoud Rajavi when he was exiled in Paris from 1983, and what he told me rapidly dissipated any glamour of revolution as far as the left were concerned. He said he only had about four nights in his own bed before having to live like a fugitive, sleeping at a different address each night. Iran descended into a virtual civil war, with the Mujahedin going underground. There was a lot of bombing and their big hit was to blow up both Khomeini's Prime Minister and the leading political cleric, Ayatollah Beheshti. This virtual civil war situation lasted until 1983, when the clerics finally won, and Rajavi, the secular President Bani Sadr and the Mujahedin leadership either got away or stayed and faced execution if caught. Many were killed.

The Mujahedin became the National Council of Resistance and still exist today under the leadership of Rajavi's wife, Maryam. Massoud made the great mistake of going off to Iraq in the late 1980s under the pay and patronage of Saddam Hussein, a Sunni Muslim, and founding Camp Ashraf. During the Iran–Iraq War he made the further mistake of fighting for his patron, Saddam, against his own country. Onto the world's newsreels they came with smart women in military fatigues directing lorries and tanks, their uniforms unstained by any trace of combat. It had a lasting effect on Iranians, within and outside Iran, whatever they thought about the revolution. Their country was at war and there were these compatriots, claiming to be liberating them, fighting, or pretending to, with the enemy. It had fatal consequences for them within Iran from which they have never really recovered. When the Iraq situation changed as a result of the 2003 Anglo-American invasion, Camp Ashraf was isolated and increasingly under heavy and often very unpleasant pressure to disband from the Shia-dominated government of Iraq. The problem is that they have nowhere to go and nobody wants them.

From 1983 onwards, having won the internal battle, the Iranian regime began to open up and I had many meetings with them over the years, first as chairman of the British Group of the Inter-Parliamentary Union and later under a variety of hats. I led the first official parliamentary delegation to Iran post-revolution, in 1999, which went extremely well. Whoever might rule Iran you can always expect warmth both of welcome and hospitality. We stayed with our Ambassador, Sir Nicholas Browne, in what is one of our nicest embassy residences, in this case built by Indian Army engineers in the mid-nineteenth century and decorated with lovely Persian plaster work within. It was the fine setting for part of the celebrated Tehran Conference of 1943 between Churchill, Stalin and Roosevelt. Sadly this embassy residence was ransacked and violated in 2011, as an act of spite against Britain which was clearly permitted and encouraged by the Iranian government. It has now been renovated and is being brought back into use. We saw plenty of the Iranian government but also the people, who were for me unchanged through all they had endured. I had a surprising example of an amity that I had little right to expect when, in a brief interlude in my schedule, I escaped to see those of my wife's family who remained in Tehran. I had been with the Ambassador before and he let me continue in his official car. What was forgotten was that Her Majesty's official coat of arms was still fluttering away on the car, with only me in it. Perhaps with my white hair I looked like an ambassador but suddenly there appeared on our flank a motorcycle with two young men astride it. I had images of the classical modern assassination, often carried out from fast-moving motorcycles, and had a few moments deliberating the possibilities of eternity. The two men came right alongside the official car and smilingly conveyed to me by signs and shouts that they thought that the UK was very good. It was a charming interlude in retrospect, after a tense beginning.

I again went out to represent the government at the 2002 Oil and Gas Show, when relationships were so bad that we had no Ambassador *in situ* and could not send a minister. Throughout this time I had meetings and contact with Iranian ministers, clerics, businessmen and ordinary people. I always found them willing and able to try to improve our relations. That said, the regime they had to live in was not so helpful.

Sadly from 1983 onwards it could have been different had the Americans chosen to engage. But the USA finds rejection very difficult to come to terms with. They have established their promised land, and find it difficult to understand why people do not want the same things. Iran, Cuba and even Vietnam are good examples of this thinking. The larger problem is Israel and its interests as championed by the very powerful Jewish American lobby. From the time of the revolution, Iran has been seen as the 'bad guy', with cause, but the Americans have never consistently tried to get in there and get on with the Iranians. Had they done so, and the earlier the better, things could have been very different today. It also suits Israel to have a 'bad guy' about, to distract from the Palestine situation and their actions in connection with it. Such are the realities of international politics, and problems that could have been solved remain, sometimes with tragic results. The worst recent example of serious American error was President George W. Bush's statement that Iran was part of an axis of evil. This did untold, lasting damage. President Obama is trying to rectify some of this and we must hope that current developments in this difficult situation are successful.

The Iranian regime continues and the outcome is far from clear. The irony is that the bulk of ordinary educated Iranians want to be connected to the West and are not anti-American in the least. Their country has been borrowed by an inappropriate regime and the middle classes that remain at least have their illegal satellite dishes from which they watch the BBC World Service and various Iranian exile productions. In 2013 near two million of them voted by telephone for an Iranian version of the *X Factor* broadcast from the UK. A post-revolutionary middle class in Iran has to speak to us like this, after the failure of their more militant attempt at change, forcibly put down in 2009. They live in hope, and sanctions have finally bitten, with the regime beginning to realise that it must accommodate change to stay in power. They have few places in which to hide. There are grounds for some optimism.

Eight

RUSSIA AND THE SOVIET UNION

Part 1: Mikhail Sergeyevitch Gorbachev

A state without the means of some change is without the means of its conservation.

Edmund Burke, *Reflections on the Revolution in France*, 1790

In 1961, whilst still at university, I became a member of the Cambridge Afro-Asian Expedition 1961 and off we went on an odyssey to the USSR, the Balkans and the Middle East. Innocently pursuing pretty Russian students around Moscow State University, camping and generally mixing teaches more about a country than many meetings and first-class hotels later on. Over some five weeks I formed a great affection for Russia which has remained to this day. In the early 1980s I became joint vice-president of the GB–USSR Association, sharing the honours with the late John Smith, later leader of the Labour Party.

My particular interest continued with my election as chairman of the British Group of the Inter-Parliamentary Union (IPU) in 1982. This was one of the few executive jobs available on the backbenches and presented many opportunities. We were responsible not only for Inter-Parliamentary Conferences but also for Westminster's relations with world parliaments and delegations to and from them, apart from the Commonwealth, which has its own Commonwealth Parliamentary Association (CPA). We could take our own initiatives independently of government and were less restricted than government in our discussions, which was useful in itself.

After the 1983 General Election Geoffrey Howe became Foreign Secretary. The government decided that the UK would undertake a major effort to improve relations with the Soviet bloc in general and the Soviet Union in particular. Quite independently of this, we, at the comparatively humble parliamentary end of things, decided to do the same thing. Our efforts became complementary to each other over Mikhail Gorbachev.

Gorbachev in 1983 was a member of the most powerful ruling authority of the Soviet Union, namely the Politburo of the Communist Party. He had risen to particular prominence under the patronage of General Secretary Andropov, and had become recognised as the heir apparent to the ailing current General Secretary, Chernenko. Up to then Gorbachev had only once travelled officially outside the Soviet Union, which was to Canada in furtherance of his then responsibilities for Soviet agriculture. To get him to the UK as an individual guest was not as simple as it might sound. We, and other Western governments, did not recognise the Soviet Communist Party as having any constitutional significance. The fact that it ruled the USSR was quite immaterial! Official relations were conducted with the Soviet State via its president and officers of government, who were in reality executive servants of the Politburo. The Foreign and Commonwealth Office (FCO) under the able Minister of State responsible, Malcolm Rifkind, aided and abetted by our then Ambassador in Moscow, Sir Iain Sutherland, discovered that one of Mr Gorbachev's more honorary titles was Chairman of the Foreign Affairs Committee of the Supreme Soviet (Parliament). It was therefore decided that Mr Gorbachev could be invited to the UK in that capacity, which made the whole thing a parliamentary visit. As the IPU was responsible for parliamentary delegations, acting in the name of the Speaker, that put us, and for that matter me, at least nominally in charge. Malcolm Rifkind, who had been told of the IPU's interest in the Soviet Union, invited me in and explained the plan. I was delighted, and immediately agreed for the IPU to play its full part, and for the FCO to pull out all the stops to get Gorbachev to the UK, and to help us with the extra resources necessary to organise such

1. Cambridge Mafia. Leon Brittan's Union Presidency, 1960. Colin Renfrew (sitting second from left), the author and Norman Fowler (standing right).

2. Prime Minister Harold Macmillan at Cambridge, 1960. L-R: the author, John Selwyn Gummer, Peter Viggers, Norman Fowler and Macmillan's Parliamentary Private Secretary, Knox Cunningham, QC, MP.

3. Cambridge Mafia and Bow Group. Dinner party at Michael Howard's house on occasion of Leon Brittan's departure for Brussels, 1989. The author forgot his dinner jacket!

4. The young candidate for Newport, Monmouthshire, at Llandudno Conference, 1962 with the Earl of Home, foreign secretary and later prime minister.

5. With wife Taheré after the count when first elected as MP for Leominster, February 1974.

6. The new Hereford-Worcester MPs take their seats, February 1974, with Peter Walker, MP for Worcester and outgoing Secretary of State. L-R: Esmond Bulmer, Michael Spicer, Peter Walker, the author, and Hal Miller.

7. Mrs Thatcher's visit to Leominster, 1980.

8. Mrs Thatcher at the Rankin Club, Leominster, 1980.

9. Parliamentary Regatta for St Margaret's, Westminster 1986. The Foreign Affairs Boat. L-R: Tom Clarke, (Lab.), Bowen Wells, (Con.), Tim Renton, (Con.), Andrew Faulds, (Lab.), Linda Chalker, (Con.), Robert Jackson, (Con.), Alan Beith, (Lib.), the author and George Robertson, (Lab.).

10. Record Early Day Motion for the BBC World Service, 1993. L-R: George Robertson (Lab.), George Foulkes (Lab.), David Steele (Lib.), Bob Phillis, M-D, BBC World Service, the author, Russell Johnston (Lib.), and Michael Marshall (Con.).

11. Geoffrey Howe with Leominster farmers, 1975.

12. Michael Heseltine at Leominster, 1989.

13. The old Iran at the court of the Shah. HE Amir Hussein, Senator and Chamberlain to the Shah with his cousin HE Amir Asadollah, Prime Minister of Iran. Both are in the appropriate court dress of their office.

14. HM the Shah at home. A good man but exceptional times.

15. Gorbachev's arrival at London Heathrow, December 1984. With the author, Chairman, Inter-Parliamentary Union, British Group, and Sir Anthony Kershaw, MP, Chairman, Commons Foreign Affairs Committee.

16. Gorbachev's arrival at the Palace of Westminster, December 1984. With the author, Sir Anthony Kershaw, Raisa Gorbacheva and officials.

17. The author with Ambassador Popov of the Soviet Union, 1985.

18. GB-USSR Society Parliamentary visit to the Soviet Union, 1981. Breaking the ice after the invasion of Afghanistan. L-R: John Smith, later leader of the Labour Party, John Osborne, Arthur Bottomley and the author.

19. IPU Parliamentary visit to the Soviet Union, 1986. Far left, Denis Healey, Willie Whitelaw speaking and the author second from right.

20. British–Irish Body visit to Edinburgh, 1993. Jim Tunney and the author, founding co-chairmen, with Ian Lang, Secretary of State.

21. British–Irish Body at Dublin Castle, 1995. Author with then co-chairman Paul Bradford and Austin Currie.

22. British–Irish Body. Peter Brooke and the author in Killarney, 1993.

23. British–Irish Body in Dublin. Press Officer Mike Burns and his wife with the author.

24. Foundation photograph in Westminster Hall of the Body, 1990. It was launched by the Deputy Prime Ministers Geoffrey Howe and Brian Lenihan, photographed with the author and Jim Tunney and senior representatives of all major parties of Britain and Ireland.

25. British–Irish Body, Dublin 1994, Albert Reynolds, Taoseach/Prime Minister, with the author and Dermot Ahern, then co-chairman and later Irish Foreign Minister.

26. In East Germany as IPU chairman with Horst Sinderman, former prime minister and then president of the Volkskammer (Parliament).

27. IPU/CPA South Africa election team, 1993–4.

To Peter Temple-Morris
With appreciation and best wishes.

Ronald Reagan

28. The author with Ronald Reagan at White House; representing the Conservative Party for Conference on Latin American Democracy.

To the Hon. Peter Temple-Morris
On a most pleasant occasion with best wishes

George Bush

29. The author with then Vice President George Bush at the Dallas Republican Convention in 1984.

30. The author with the Pope, as Leader British Delegation, IPU Conference, Rome 1982.

31. The author with Yasser Arafat in Beirut, 1981.

32. The author with then Foreign Secretary Francis Pym, 1982. Ioan Evans, MP, is in the background.

33. Prime Minister Tony Blair with Labour peers, 2006.

34. Entering No.10 for first time as a Labour MP. With Labour West Midlands Group officers L-R: Peter Snape and Dennis Turner.

35. The author speaks to Chelmsford Labour Party, 1999.

an important and grand visitation. For the best part of a year approaches were made at all possible levels, which included us raising it constantly with the Supreme Soviet, whom we met up with at IPU conferences.

Eventually it was on. On Saturday, 15 December 1984 at noon a Soviet government Ilyushin aircraft touched down at the VIP arrivals area at Heathrow and a visit that had historic implications for the end of the Cold War began. The welcoming party was headed by our Speaker, Jack Weatherill MP; myself as IPU chairman and host for the visit; and the chairman of the Commons Foreign Affairs Committee, Sir Anthony Kershaw MP; with other luminaries and a large press contingent that was present throughout the visit. The government was nowhere to be seen, to preserve the occasion as a parliamentary visit.

Out stepped Gorbachev, a new figure to the Western world, immediately striking me as possessing the confidence and personal assurance of leadership. At the time I felt I was part of something special. It does not happen very often, but here it was. The delegation, as is the way in more totalitarian societies, stayed some 20 metres behind him. They were distinguished in their own right, but knew they had to play their part as extras in a greater show. It was relaxed from the start, with constructive speeches for the benefit of the eagerly awaiting press. The security detail moved in and Mr Gorbachev swept off with the Ambassador to the Embassy in Kensington and the delegation followed, destined for the nearby Royal Garden Hotel, in a twelve-car convoy with police outriders securing our swift passage.

The reality of change was all too evident at the welcoming dinner we gave to Mr Gorbachev and the delegation at Claridge's that Saturday evening. Fortunately I had secured the presence of enough MPs, always difficult at the weekend, and altogether there were some fifty people present in a private room. I had been used to dealing with the Soviets over many years at social events, and under Soviet auspices it was usually a very alcoholic affair. When it came to the inevitable speeches they were delivered from a lengthy script, with the KGB minder checking it out. It was a dull process which quite spoilt the effect of the vodka previously consumed. Claridge's did not work out at all like that.

I speak from headings at such events, which include names I might forget. Apart from that I speak extempore. I got a few laughs and established the informal nature of it all. Up stood Gorbachev to reply without a single note. What a change! He made a light and witty speech which delighted us all. As he sat down to our applause it was by then perfectly obvious that we had something very different on our hands. We were off to a good start, and had played our part in setting the friendly scene before the all-important meeting with the Prime Minister the following day.

The Chequers meeting has been much referred to and is well documented, not least by Professor Archie Brown of St Anthony's, Oxford, who followed this visit and its aftermath in some detail. Suffice it to say here that Gorbachev came out well in convincing a difficult Prime Minister of his good intentions, although both she and her advisers had more than seen the possibilities of all this. Mrs Thatcher's statement summed it up: 'We can do business with him', she said. With that she went off to Hong Kong the next day to sign the Sino-British Agreement and after that to see President Reagan in Washington, to whom she reported on her meeting with Gorbachev. The end of the Cold War had begun.

For Mr Gorbachev the visit to the UK continued. It was a glittering affair involving Hampton Court Palace, the Royal Opera House, Lancaster House, various visits and trade talks plus political exchanges at the Palace of Westminster. Throughout Mr Gorbachev kept up the constructive tone and good humour in numerous speeches and remarks. His arrival at Westminster Hall, via the main door off New Palace Yard, provided an early example. An absolute mass of press photographers confronted us. I stood between the Gorbachevs, with Sir Anthony Kershaw alongside Raisa. On and on went the clicks and the flashes and the ending of it all was accomplished by Mr Gorbachev. He raised his hands and the press immediately calmed down. 'Gentlemen', he said, 'we must now stop this or your cameras will die of exhaustion.' Everyone laughed and the press went away content.

Later came the public session with the Commons Foreign Affairs Committee in the Grand Committee Room off Westminster Hall. Other meetings, for example with party leaders, were in private, but this one was not. We were concerned over the issue of human rights in the USSR, about which there had been press comment and some small demonstrations. It was a good and wide-ranging meeting, but sure enough up came human rights. Mr Gorbachev's reply was vigorous to say the least. He used the standard Soviet counter-attack on this subject by referring to the British treatment of the Irish historically, and of the Northern Irish Catholics in particular. A no-score draw was achieved, and a touch of steel shown which helped to explain how he had climbed so high within the Soviet Union. From the Soviet point of view human rights were seen as an irritant which got in the way of what they considered more serious matters. The nearest we got to temper from Mr Gorbachev was after a lunch the Labour Party gave for him. He was having a final conversation with Neil Kinnock, then leader of the Labour Party, who brought up human rights again in the form of a leading but diminutive Soviet Jewish dissident, Mr Sharanski. 'Why', asked Mr Gorbachev, 'does he keep asking me about this little fellow that we're packing off to Israel anyway?' The words were accompanied by a choice expletive or two, but the two interpreters present were well used to smartening up the words of their politicians and the reply given to Neil Kinnock was as immaculate as ever. The FCO interpreter could not resist telling me this later in the week.

During that afternoon Mr Gorbachev's twelve-car motorcade was proceeding along Whitehall when he suddenly indicated he wanted to stop. He had been told of the Downing Street Christmas tree and he wanted to see it, and Downing Street itself, which he had missed, as Mrs Thatcher had seen him at Chequers on Sunday and was by now visiting China and Hong Kong. All the cars came to a sudden stop, with police running around everywhere thinking there was some sort of emergency. Into Downing Street he went, with no gates in those days to obstruct him, and stood before the Christmas tree. The word got about within Number 10 and he was taken in to meet the staff. Everyone was delighted with this impromptu visit and his pleasant words, coming from a communist leader for whom the festival of Christmas was officially unrecognised.

Another example of his free thinking came the next day, when part of the morning had been allocated to the usual dull ritual for Communist delegations of a visit to the tomb of Karl Marx in Highgate Cemetery. Mr Gorbachev excused himself from the visit at the last minute and, leaving the wreath-laying to his delegation, disappeared off with Raisa on a rapidly arranged visit to St Paul's Cathedral and the Tower of London. This was a good example of his considerable confidence, as he was not yet General Secretary.

After London the visit was due to end in Scotland on the Friday and Saturday. Early on Friday morning the Ilyushin, which had been on stand-by all week, flew Mr Gorbachev and his delegation to Edinburgh. A tour of Holyrood Palace was to be followed by an informal lunch I was to give at the Caledonian Hotel. The grandest event, due to be hosted by the Secretary of State, George Younger MP, was to take place at Edinburgh Castle that evening. However, during the morning Mr Gorbachev was informed of the death of the Soviet Minister of Defence and Politburo member Marshall Ustinov, and decided he had to return immediately. No doubt this was for appearances but also to safeguard his position during the changes at the top that would follow such a demise. So my lunch became the official farewell event, with both government ministers, George Younger and Malcolm Rifkind, in attendance. After lunch Mr Gorbachev gave sincere and dignified thanks to us all, thoughtfully mentioning our secretary, Captain Peter Shaw RN, who had worked so hard to make the visit a success. Then out we went to get into the vast convoy of cars that awaited us and unfortunately the trip to Scotland somehow caused me to have no car. I was talking to the Gorbachevs at the hotel entrance whilst everyone hastened to their vehicles and suddenly realised I had nowhere to go. Instantly seeing the problem, Mr Gorbachev, still outside his leading vehicle, signalled for me to get into it. This I did, with Raisa between us on the back seat and just a plain-clothes protection officer beside the driver in the front. No interpreter. Mr Gorbachev spoke no English and Raisa just sufficient to get by. She assumed the role of interpreter and we talked through her all the way to the airport. 'Mikhail Sergeyovitch, he says ...', she would begin, and I seem to remember that it was not at all hard going and we managed quite a few laughs over the events of the previous week. I don't think all world leaders would have acted with the same generosity and warmth.

This was not to be the end of my contact with Mr Gorbachev. The next time I met him was during the return parliamentary visit that we made to the Soviet Union in 1986, by which time he was very much General Secretary with *glasnost* and *perestroika* getting under way. At the request of Mrs Thatcher this visit was boosted by the inclusion of senior government and opposition representatives. I remember that John Biffen, then Leader of the Commons, was hoping he might lead it but the Prime Minister requested that the delegation be of the same seniority as that led by Mr Gorbachev in 1984. So Viscount Whitelaw was nominated leader, as Lord President of the Council and Leader of the House of Lords, and the nearest thing she had to a deputy at the time. His Labour counterpart was ex-Chancellor Denis Healey MP, then Shadow Foreign Affairs spokesman. The relationship of the two of them, of which more later, was completely relaxed. The rest of us were all MPs and peers and as my term as IPU chairman had expired the year before, I was but a foot soldier on this particular delegation.

Willie Whitelaw proved a marvellous leader. A big man in every way and a gentleman of the old school, he exhibited during the trip a care and concern for us individuals that I put down to his warm personality. Each morning before we went out somewhere, he would individually ask as many as he could how we were, even if he himself was finding a full and even gruelling programme steadily more tiring. An impressive man, as indeed was Denis Healey. He and Willie Whitelaw seemed to get on very easily. They usually breakfasted together at our hotel of the moment and I occasionally joined them. There was an obvious camaraderie that transcended politics, which I put down to World War II. Whitelaw had fought through Europe as a young Scots Guards Officer. Denis Healey had been beachmaster at the famous Anzio landings in southern Italy and fought right on up Italy with the Eighth Army. They both emerged as majors.

In Moscow the two of them provided a very good example of unity across party lines when abroad. While Healey loved to put on an act as the old bruiser when it suited him in the Commons, he was in reality a highly intelligent and cultivated man of wide interests. Whitelaw had the laid-back approach of the upper-class grandee, but underneath was very wise indeed and absolutely invaluable to the Thatcher premiership. One of our more important meetings was with the Supreme Soviet, who fielded a team of some twenty very distinguished heads of institutes, professors and so on who were all desperate to discuss disarmament in general, and intermediate-range nuclear missiles pointed at the Soviet Union in particular. We had made no particular preparation for the meeting and Lord Whitelaw decided to open up on domestic issues such as our Health Service, and be as non-political as possible. Whatever his many attributes, the details of nuclear defence policy were not amongst them. The other side of the table started to fidget and clearly were dissatisfied with the choice of subject. Denis Healey sized up the situation, and when his turn to speak came next, saved the day. He began by saying that, as he was a former Defence Secretary, Lord Whitelaw had asked him to deal with this subject, and he spoke for the whole delegation. He then launched into an excellent and succinct statement of the defence policies of the Conservative government and then the Labour opposition, even numbering the points as he went along. It was a formidable performance and as good as any Conservative specialist could have managed. But the old Healey had to emerge somewhere, and when he got to the end of dealing with Conservative and Labour he turned towards Alan Beith MP, who was present representing the Liberals and proclaimed: 'Gentlemen, I have not troubled you with the position of the Liberal Party on these matters as they have no policies at all!' This of course brought the house down and even poor Alan Beith did not know whether to laugh or cry.

During the visit we had one long meeting with General Secretary Gorbachev at the Kremlin, in a palatial room decorated with, amongst the marble, pillars of solid malachite. Mr Gorbachev and his interpreter sat on one side of a large table and we on the other. Speeches were made and he took a number of questions, without any notice or preparation. He referred to me by name, which I appreciated because, although I was only a relatively junior member of this delegation, I was the one he knew best amongst its members. When the meeting was over we stood chatting on our side of the table and around came Mr Gorbachev and to my surprise and pleasure straight up to me. After a bit of small talk he said: 'My wife Raisa and I will never forget you. We have your photograph in our house.' This must be the famous one of his entrance to Westminster Hall, but what a nice and very human thing for the General Secretary of the Soviet Union to say to a backbench MP.

I met Mr Gorbachev several times subsequently at Downing Street functions and lastly at a reception we gave him at Westminster after he had lost power as General Secretary. He came into a crowded room, looked around amidst a very warm reception, and said: 'I have every respect for your democratic system but looking around me I am relieved that it has had so little effect on the presence here of so many of my friends.'

A remarkable man by any standards, to whom we all owe a lot. He has had little domestic thanks for this, but has, because of it all, enormous international status. I have no doubt that one day Russia will give him the full recognition and respect that he so richly deserves.

Part 2: The old and the new

Travel is fatal to prejudice.

Mark Twain, *The Innocents Abroad*, 1869

During my last year at Cambridge I was invited to go on the Cambridge Afro-Asian Expedition 1961. A well-illustrated book of our exploits, *The Kombi Trail. Across Three Continents in a VW Van*, was published in 2013 by I.B.Tauris with the support of Volkswagen Commercial Vehicles. To travel at that age is a solid basis for further travel later. This formidable trip gave me five weeks in the Soviet Union as a student, and before I had occasion to visit it many times in a political capacity. While 1961 may seem a long time ago, countries and peoples don't change that much. Certainly their politics, economics and, in the case of the Soviet Union, governance can change; but underneath people are the same. We ate with Russian students, drank with them, debated with them, played sport with them, took out Russian girls and generally lived a full life, which, in terms of visiting the Soviet Union, would have been impossible for us later on. Afterwards during official visits, I often longed to be back travelling and camping as in 1961, rather than receiving the best of party hospitality. But the events of youth can never be repeated, although our understanding of the present is immeasurably strengthened by them.

Our visit, comparatively rare in those days, had the concurrence and support of the Foreign Office and the Moscow Embassy, who arranged our programme. It was a strong Embassy under the redoubtable Sir Frank Roberts and whose young diplomats, including Sir Christopher Mallaby and Sir John Fretwell, went on to great things thereafter. We were well briefed.

In 1961 Nikita Khrushchev was in power as General Secretary and with him were historical figures such as Mikoyan and Gromyko. We were lucky enough to see them all close up at the opening night of the Royal Ballet performing at the Bolshoi in Moscow on 2 July, with Dame Margot Fonteyn and Michael Soames dancing the leading roles. The Soviet leadership led the applause, amounting to some thirty curtain-calls from a standing audience. A triumph for Britain in the land of the Bolshoi and also an early lesson that Russians could be generous and even emotional in their praise. In the face of such cultural contact the Cold War was not very evident that evening.

The Soviet Union in 1961 was a world power and knew it. There was international recognition of that power, with perhaps an element of fear attached. They had played the major role in the military defeat of Nazi Germany only sixteen years before; were a nuclear power with vast military resources; were ruled by an all-too-firm political machine; and, most important, were motivated by the task of promoting their system in the direction of world domination. They were practical enough to recognise the technical superiority of the West, and, with their comparatively drab existence, were fascinated by the glamour of its ways. They wanted and expected our respect as equals but knew that, for all their power, they had some catching up to do. That feeling still exists today and is not always respected and understood by those dealing with Russia at the highest level.

Russian pride, and accompanying Slav emotion, will never allow them to tolerate being perceived as anything other than a developed country. Today, given the background of former power and empire, it is understandable that they want to be respected within their traditional spheres of influence. They don't like being lectured, particularly by the well-meaning West, about democracy and human rights. To do so gets nowhere, and harms the wider and more important relationship. They have a defined policy towards their allies and particularly important to them is any question of NATO and EU expansion in Eastern Europe, as with Georgia a few years back and Ukraine more recently. This is Russia's backyard and former empire, and they remark that the United States might remember how it has felt, and does feel, about their own in Cuba and Central America. We need to be pragmatic, rather than evangelical about the virtues of Western-style democracy.

Back in 1961 the power of the Soviet state was absolute. But the aspirations of the people included a fascination with things Western, at all levels. One bizarre example was of a young man who was introduced to me because he looked like Marlon Brando, and could I help him get to Hollywood. Western clothes at that time fetched exorbitant prices and, in spite of serious penalties for those caught dealing in it, a considerable black market existed. We could have financed our entire stay with a suitcase of M&S Y-front underwear, had we wished to take the risk. More serious were the official efforts to contain those students who kept company with us, and insisted on doing so, in spite of threats from the KGB. Young Russians getting used to Western ways was not to be encouraged, and it is a tribute to our friends from the university that they continued to see us. Fortunately for them and us we were something fairly new, and the authorities did not want bad publicity. I only hope our friends did not suffer after we left.

For all the warmth, hospitality and even affection with which we were received, official Russia in 1961 was all too ready to bully its way out of any political argument. Our contacts with Komsomol, the young communist national movement (for those aged fourteen to twenty-eight), led to many discussions where there was an anti-capitalist argument for everything. Discussion of political subjects led to a wall of dogmatism descending, and, try as one did, it could not be broken down. They had fixed positions which were rigid, and would be repeated as necessary. However, it is important to note that after vigorous exchanges and some tough accusations, things would return quite easily thereafter to conviviality all round. Vodka would be drunk, everyone would laugh and smoke, and we would stroll on a lovely summer's evening in the university gardens in the Lenin Hills. Today it reminds me of repairing from the exchanges of the House of Commons to the Smoking Room.

As mentioned, the Russians do expect to be treated and understood as equals. There are repeated examples in recent years of neglect to do this. A classic is the imposition of a peace settlement on the Slavs of Kosovo in 1998–9. Russia expected to be involved over what she considered an affair involving her allied Slav brothers and was ignored. When the settlement came they mounted a mad dash southwards to be the first to occupy Pristina airport and, under the command of NATO, British airborne troops were ordered to get there first and got as far as waiting around for hours at their take-off point on a very hot day. The wisdom of their commander, General Sir Mike Jackson, was shown in going over the heads of NATO command and, via Prime Minister Blair, to President Clinton, to abort the order. This was accomplished, the Russians got there first, and then we arrived to join them and in effect take over, but with Russian honour intact and goodwill dominating rather than enmity. This was as good an example as one will get of the right leadership being in place at the right time.

It avoided a very nasty and unnecessary confrontation. Later in 1999, soon after this drama, I was asked by the government to be one of four MPs, of all parties, who were to go to Moscow and test the political atmosphere. Parliamentarians are well placed for this job and we did some good. It was an opportunity to see the emerging capitalist Russia, with many associated problems and a far from democratic mentality. Treatment of journalists and others was bad, as was the distribution of state assets, creating the oligarchs that we are familiar with today. Non-payment of taxes was all too general, as was corruption and even murder in connection with it. That said, their main concern remained as it ever was, namely the security of Russia and no intrusion by the West. They wanted their space, which in days gone-by we would have called a buffer zone, be it Ukraine or elsewhere. The USA, effectively in charge of Western policy, has other ideas which remain more related to the Cold War than to today's realities. Meanwhile the European Union struggles to make itself felt. Its main officers tend not to be from the major players and like to be appreciated more than they may be in the major countries of Western Europe. They journey to the East and there at last is recognition, together with gratitude for the largesse they bring and engagement with the question of the boundaries of the European Union, which they feel is their just preserve. As far as the Russians are concerned they have very different ideas for those same boundaries. However, our differences are not worth a major falling out and both sides need to display a level of sophistication for the common good.

At a personal level how did I find the Soviet Union and the Russians in 1961? The answer is that few places have so taken my mind, enthusiasm and imagination as the then Soviet Union. Of course it was a ruthless dictatorship, with the base of a somewhat dreary Communist system to support it. But the warmth of the Russian people came through. How they suffered under their leadership was clear to us but, sadly, such has been the lot of Russians throughout the ages. However, as a young man it did not appear all that dreary, far from it. The young people and students we spent a lot of time with were highly motivated and dedicated to the success of their country, and, right or wrong, its system. They enjoyed their food and drink in plentiful quantities; they danced and sang as if the problems of the world hardly existed; played sport; and enjoyed their many parks. A regular sight there, which to me signified the timelessness of a great people, was a reserved chess area where old men with flowing white hair and beards played chess with young schoolboys. All this was way beyond politics and systems of government.

That said, there was another side to the story. This can best be illustrated by the story of our friend the late Vladimir Afonichkin, a Russian from Kiev in Ukraine. He was a young engineering student, spoke fluent English and then as now was a committed Christian. We met him at the Moscow Film Festival of that summer, where the chief guests were Elizabeth Taylor and her then husband, Eddie Fisher. We got talking and spent some time with him. His fluent English, school- and self-taught, was valuable in explaining a lot to us and we met up with him again in Kiev. We were invited to his grandmother's house, a small but immaculate place which she had specially prepared, including getting out the family icon as 'English people like the God'. When we ended our stay and went on to Romania, Vladimir came with us to the last city bus stop and we said farewell. In our final conversation he at last expressed dissatisfaction with the leadership, a longing for freedom and for knowledge of the West. He almost apologised in saying 'Peter, I have no choice but to be a good Communist and hopefully by that means I shall eventually be free', which I took to mean that his only chance was for the system to change gradually. I gave him a book on the British constitution and political system and we said our farewells. I later sent him various books he wanted, which miraculously got through to him. We kept in contact for some years, followed by a gap, but we picked up again when he saw my picture with Gorbachev in the Soviet press during the 1984 visit already described on pp. 129–32. Later when the Cold War ended he was able to come to London as guest of one of the evangelical churches that operated in Ukraine and I was able to enter- tain him and talk freely about all that had happened over the last thirty years. A remarkable and very sad story came out which he had not been able to write about. It started when we dropped him at the last bus stop in Kiev on that day of our departure. As soon as our Volkswagen Kombi disappeared over the horizon, and he turned towards the bus stop, a KGB car screamed to a halt and he was bundled into it. He was taken in for interrogation, but managed to get to the lavatory to destroy and dispose of the book I had just given him. The interrogation about his association with us could have turned nasty, but he was saved by the fact that his father had fought through the 'Great Patriotic War' and became a colonel in the Red Army. So severe warnings were administered and that was it. Later on when his studies concluded, he applied for a job as an interpreter for which his English abundantly qualified him. He was again brought before the KGB, who asked whether, as an international interpreter, he would report to them and work with them. He asked them whether this meant he should report private conversations and the expected answer came back: 'Of course'. He said he would not feel able to do that and was immediately told that they would block him from the job and any other such job for the rest of his life.

He did not give in, got married and to increase his meagre earnings went to live and work in Sakhalin Island in the Russian Far East. He returned to Kiev in the mid-1980s, and being an engineer was sent into the nuclear site of Chernobyl to clear it up after the disastrous leakage and explosion. Those doing such work were given no proper protection from the radioactivity, with a small increase in their pension as their reward. Many of them have died prematurely, and Vladimir suffered bad health ever since, eventually losing a leg to diabetes a few years back. He became bedridden and, with no health service to look after him, sadly died in July 2014. That bright young student with all before him comes to mind, yet he never grumbled about his fate and the difficult life he had.

Nine

PARLIAMENTARY DIPLOMACY AND THE FOREIGN OFFICE

Forever poised between a cliché and an indiscretion.
Harold Macmillan on the role of a Foreign Secretary, 1956

Introduction

Often the press exploit some story about parliamentarians abroad. This coverage conceals the usefulness of parliamentary visits, in all their different forms. In the 1980s the term parliamentary diplomacy came in, within the wider description of cultural diplomacy, now referred to under the unattractive expression 'soft power'.

International parliamentary contact is growing. In the diplomatic sense, as part of conduct of our international relations, it breaks down into two areas: the select committees of both Houses on the one hand, and the independent organisations within parliament of the Inter-Parliamentary Union and the Commonwealth Parliamentary Association on the other. These also operate a multiplicity of bilateral groups with various countries.

The role of the select committees is different, in that their job is not so much diplomacy, but the monitoring of the work of the FCO and the preparation of reports on matters of concern. Diplomacy comes into it but fostering good relations is not the main purpose of these committees. The IPU and the CPA decide their own agendas, and have considerable flexibility. This can include a number of very useful activities.

Their conferences are formidable gatherings, with many opportunities to do political business in the margins, as I will refer to later. Bilateral delegations can discuss frankly any issue without prejudice to government, so that feelers can be put out and difficulties assessed. Gibraltar and the Falklands would be two examples of recent years. Election-monitoring missions are undertaken and tutorials can be offered to emerging democracies. Heavy politics can be involved such as the Irish peace process and Mr Gorbachev's visit, to give two examples from my own career. All this is parliamentary, but very useful to the government of the day, who can get many useful indicators from comparatively unscripted international parliamentary exchanges. Some examples are instructive.

Southern Africa and the winds of change

In early 1980 I went to Southern Rhodesia, as it still was, to observe the elections taking place prior to independence. The visit included South Africa and Namibia. I was particularly interested in Namibia, about which I had been involved in an investigation back in 1977 for the Inter-Parliamentary Union. Suddenly over the intercom in the departures hall at Heathrow came the sound of my name, calling me to the phone. For a moment I felt rather important, until for all to hear came the dreaded accompaniment that it was the government whips on the line. They did the expected and tried to get me to call off my trip with the first No Confidence vote of the new Parliament coming up the following week. I told them I was definitely going but I would arrange a pair, as the Labour Foreign Affairs spokesman, Peter Shore, was on the same flight to observe the same thing. Peter Shore readily agreed on the plane and all seemed well.

We arrived in Salisbury and found a surprisingly normal and attractive country with no visible effect of any sanctions. There was an interim administration under a governor, Christopher Soames, and everything running smoothly for the elections. Had I then known what a mess was due to be made of that country by its inheritors I would have been both surprised and appalled. Suffice it to say that the British Rhodesians made a good job of it and, with the help of South Africa, made a complete nonsense of the sanctions Britain placed upon them. Their economy was thriving while they fought a guerrilla war at the same time. We stayed in a fine hotel called the Monipapata and discovered that the basement bar was the unofficial headquarters of the by then stood-down Rhodesian Special Forces, the Selous and the Gray Scouts by name. They were the SAS equivalent, and wreaked absolute havoc with Mugabe's guerrillas out in the bush. It was sad to see them with nothing to do but drink too much in their bar and act to excess. While we were there one of them was shot and killed playing Russian roulette for real, which gives an example of the acute frustration involved. Once independence was certain most of them went down to South Africa, where, for better or worse, their skills were a valuable help to the South African Special Forces.

Official observers, to whom we were attached, abounded. We travelled widely: functions, good food and wine and even a cathedral service on Sunday, all seemed to fit the old ways. One official trip we made was down to Bulawayo to see how the elections were going on in primarily Matabele territory. After lunch I had the unexpected honour of travelling up in the hotel lift with an amiable and very talkative black clergyman who turned out to be Dr Canaan Banana, the future Matabele first black President of independent Zimbabwe for a period before he was duly dumped by Robert Mugabe as being of the wrong tribe. As we flew there and back to Salisbury the management of the whole thing was immaculate and clear for all to see. Various British administrators walked around in tropical kit and short trousers with clip-boards, and it was plain who was running the show. I asked who the leading man was and was told that he was the clerk or chief executive of a Midland county council, seconded for the duration, and conducting himself and the operation as if the Empire, of which he would have had no personal experience, had never departed. To the manner born, effortless, and amusing to behold.

We were also taken to a rally for the official candidate, Bishop Muzarewa, which seemed superficial and contrived. It did not take an electoral genius to see he was going nowhere. By contrast we were privately shown that evening, an American NBC film of Mugabe's guerrillas coming in from the bush, armed to the teeth, to settle into a prepared encampment. They were nominally guarded by a couple of battalions of Coldstream Guards, who I was told afterwards were somewhat nervous as they were heavily outnumbered and outgunned should there be an emergency. However, it was meant to be low-key and it worked.

Our briefing from Rhodesian intelligence was professional and to the point. Looking back, they were correct on everything. Our own people knew it well, but what was more important to them was an orderly retreat out of the country. The basic message was that it was all going Mugabe's way and we should take note that he was ruthless, malign and would cause nothing but trouble for the future Zimbabwe. How right they were. On a large tribal majority, he easily won the election and it did not take long for him to put down the minority Matabele under Joshua Nkomo. However, before he took power and divided and ruined the country, the atmosphere was remarkably good. The late Michael Onslow (Earl of Onslow) and I made a point of getting a taxi and making a private visit to the then Harare, which was the name given to the African township adjacent to the city of Salisbury. We could not have stood out more, not least as Michael Onslow, ever the eccentric aristocrat, was walking with the full glory of a silver-topped cane. The taxi driver took us to his family house and the whole family came on parade in the garden, not to mention the whole street. Within the past year the Smith government had been hanging rebels, termed terrorists by the government, but that seemed to make no difference. They were all Mugabe voters, gave us a terrific welcome and lined up to wave us goodbye. The absence of any sort of enmity towards us was very impressive.

Then to South Africa we went, for me to get another call from the government whips demanding that I return for the vote. My protestations that I was paired with Peter Shore cut no ice as they had 'reserved him for a minister', so, courtesy of South African Airways, I returned to London, voted and returned to South Africa in time for a peaceful Sunday. The next day we were off to Namibia, which was a part of the trip I was especially looking forward to, as I had done a lot of work on the problems there for the Inter-Parliamentary Union, as referred to later. It was the period of South African military occupation supporting a mixed-race government under white leadership in the form of the agreeable Dirk Mudge. After meeting the powers that be in Windhoek, the most interesting part of the visit took place when we were taken up to the war zone in Ovamboland, where the South African Army was confronting and containing SWAPO, the Namibian freedom fighters, based in Angola and raiding across the border. We were to stay at a forward military base and command centre in the middle of the most beautiful savannah vegetation.

To get there we flew in a World War II Dakota which had to travel at a couple of hundred feet to avoid any SAM 7 missiles that might show an interest. Apparently they could not explode that quickly to cater for low altitude, which was reassuring to know. That said, one of our group, Bill Cash, later an MP of Euro-sceptic fame, announced that he would not go on such a trip as he was not insured. Such a thought had not occurred to the rest of us, but he stuck to his guns and stayed in Windhoek. A fascinating flight ensued as the Dakota, the great transporter of World War II and afterwards, roared across the most beautiful savannah. Its young British-South African pilot, and his plane, could have stepped right out of the wartime RAF, or indeed the Biggles books of our youth. Our arrival was dramatic, in that we came in on an improvised landing strip cleared of vegetation and surrounded on each corner and on the sides with raised bamboo platforms, duly camouflaged, with an anti-aircraft gun on each but pointed horizontally into the savannah and semi-jungle. It was my first experience of a war zone at firsthand, and the South African Army, as it happened mainly of British ancestry, was certainly a capable outfit.

Out we got, to enter a world of counter-guerrilla war, with maps, borders, penetration points, ambushes and all the rest. This was accompanied by awesome displays of captured weaponry, which was all plainly supplied from the Soviet Union and Eastern Europe. Yugoslavian landmines, for example, and much else was there to be seen. One tit-bit that amused me was that when in trouble, the SWAPO guerrillas would take some performance-enhancing drug and run like mad for miles to make their escape. Their consumption and resulting performance must have rivalled some drug-abusing athletes, but with more urgent cause. The South Africans employed all the techniques used by their Rhodesian counterparts in their day, and it was clear that there was no way that SWAPO would get far until South Africa stood down, which they eventually did as part of the overall settlement

Namibia was of special interest to me as, a few years earlier in 1977, I had been part of a five-strong team, nominated by the annual conference of the Inter-Parliamentary Union, to investigate the Namibian situation and report back. Our chairman was a Finn, with a Russian, a Pakistani, a Zairian and myself completing the team. The South Africans took one look at this assortment, with particular reference to the Russian, and refused entry to Namibia. So we were confined to taking evidence in Tanzania and Zambia, where in particular SWAPO had a main office. They were impressive and we met with everyone from the deputy leader down, their leader, Sam Nujoma, being unable to leave Angola at the time. The investigation was run by the Finn and myself, with the Russian, who was deputy prime minister of Latvia, more intent on visiting every game park within reach. He was not important, as he well knew, as he was accompanied by a KGB interpreter, who turned out to be an expert on all things African. He was busy conducting an enquiry of his own, as the Soviets were very much involved with Africa in 1977, and financed as many freedom fighters as they could find. During the visit a great help to us was Martti Ahtisaari, Finland's Ambassador in Tanzania, who was to go on to high UN office and then the presidency of his country. We turned out a good report for the IPU internationally and for our FCO. This formed the basis of an *Observer* piece I wrote at the time and also a session at a joint meeting on Africa of specialist parliamentarians from the UK, USA and Canada, not to mention the IPU itself, in plenary and committee in Australia. At the time we were told how useful to all concerned it was.

Before this trip, and while I thought we would be admitted into South Africa and Namibia, I somewhat naively made contact with the political section of the South African Embassy in London and asked whether it might be possible for me, without the rest of the mission, to visit the then titular leader of the Namibian independence movement, Herman Toivo ya Toivo, who was firmly incarcerated on Robben Island with the likes of Nelson Mandela. My request was considered and then politely refused. However, very soon afterwards our home in Redington Road, Hampstead, was professionally burgled while we were away in the constituency. On the Friday night the alarm was triggered and the police had to come and switch it off. Then on the Saturday night in they came, but causing minimum damage or mess, and concentrating on my study and any other bureau or whatever that could contain documents. They symbolically stole a clock for effect and even closed the unbroken French windows into the garden when they made their exit. A professional job if ever there was one, and no doubt the work of BOSS, the South African intelligence bureau, who were active in London at the time. I reported it to our own Security Services, but no clue was left and they gained nothing except further knowledge of the activities of BOSS.

South African independence and the parliamentary seminars

My last official connection with South Africa were two visits in October 1993 and January 1994 to help with the training of emerging parliamentarians before their first national elections later in 1994. The meeting was the initiative of both the British Inter-Parliamentary Union and the Commonwealth Parliamentary Association and was part of an overall effort by the then Minister for Africa, Lynda Chalker, with the full blessing of the prime minister, John Major, to contribute to the electoral process. As an ex-chairman of the IPU and on the executive of the CPA, I was asked to lead a small team to set up seminars for candidates from all parties and then to go out to conduct the first seminars. The exploratory visit was most eventful. Because of John Major's endorsement, we were received by the leadership in the form of Prime Minister De Clerk and Foreign Minister Pik Botha and gained their full support. Our meeting with them was very relaxed, and it was clear that having taken the big decisions to give way to majority rule, the pressure was off. There were three of us: Donald Anderson (Labour) and Jim Spicer (Conservative), plus myself. We also had with us an excellent retired army colonel, who worked intermittently for the CPA when needed. At the meeting the ministers agreed for the National Party to attend the seminars and be together with all the black parties, which was a great step forward. We even got around to discussing television programmes, and it turned out that I shared a liking with Mrs De Clerk for *Ballykissangel*. As ever, for progress in great things, it takes events and personalities to come together at the right time. Here we clearly had the personalities on this side, and from the two working visits Nelson Mandela had made to the UK and the Palace of Westminster during the same period, we had the necessary political duet. Mandela was relaxed, very easy to talk to and totally non-aggressive. The result of his moderation and remarkable personality was evident throughout. It was by any assessment one of the most remarkable achievements of leadership in our time.

During the visit we had an important dinner at the Embassy (later the High Commission) which was attended by a cross-section of the ANC leadership. At the dinner, I had a very bad experience for my digestion in the cause of political understanding. I was transported to a different table for each of three courses and altogether spoke to a number of leading ANC figures. Nobody showed any animosity at all about the years of struggle and imprisonment. At one stop I had on my right and on my left future government ministers who had served twelve to fifteen years apiece on Robben Island. One of them who did most of the talking was referred to as 'Tiger', about which the other put me at ease by explaining that this nickname had been earned on the football field and not the battlefield. They explained that over the last years of their captivity Mandela was allowed to preside over regular meetings of his ANC lieutenants, where he conducted seminars on government after independence and, most important, peaceful transition. It had all had a remarkable effect on them, and where there could have been considerable animosity towards anything white, there was instead a practical acceptance of what was best for South Africa and constructive views as to its future. After what they had all been through, it was quite remarkable but it was the reality and has more than proved its worth over the years since.

One of the most memorable visits was to Chief Buthelezi, leader of the Zulus and of their Inkatha Party, to get that party, which had been an arch-rival of the ANC on a largely tribal basis, to attend the seminars. We flew from Durban in a small plane to his capital Ulundi. On the way we passed over the sites of the great battles of the Zulu Wars of the 1870s, and in particular the disastrous battle of Isandlwana, and the gallant stand of the South Wales Borderers at Rorke's Drift. Coming from South Wales my interest had been encouraged by the spectacular film *Zulu* with Stanley Baker and Michael Caine, not to mention Chief Buthelezi himself, who played the part in the film of his ancestor, King Ketchwayo Kapande, and which of course also starred the South Wales Borderers or the 24th Regiment of Foot. On the plane it transpired that our colonel was a former officer of that same regiment and still had a lot to do with its affairs through the Regimental Association. I had a riveting journey learning of the fighting techniques of the Zulus, and not least their use of their shields and stabbing spear. Notwithstanding this bit of history the visit went extremely well, their full cooperation was freely given and gifts were exchanged, theirs being far more impressive than our humble offerings. We then settled down to a full and convivial lunch for some twelve people, including three ministers in the KwaZulu Provincial government, who all were of the chief's close family, and were introduced by their official title and then their family designation. In the later stages I got the conversation gently around to the Zulu Wars and these two great battles in particular. My excuse was to tell the chief that our colonel's great-uncle was an officer in the Borderers and was killed in the battle of Isandlwana. The chief went silent, and then said how sad that was and not least as his grandfather had also been killed in the same battle. There was a pause and then, without a word, the two of them both got up and solemnly toasted each other and their forebears. It was a very poignant moment.

As for the seminars, we divided into two teams with one two-day seminar in Johannesburg and the other in Durban. The FCO could not have been more supportive, and we were all impressed with how able the delegates were. Valuable links were established and it was more than appropriate that the UK should perform this role, which was much appreciated, not least by the soon-to-rule ANC.

East Germany and Cuba

I made these two separate visits as the only guest, and as part of our IPU programme to improve East-West contacts. I had no brief and could raise anything, which pleased our ambassadors no end. Both visits were interesting but trying. East Germany with its controlled society and dull nature of everyday life was depressing. Berlin still had very visible war damage which set the tone for an area still paying the price of defeat. It all appeared as if in black and white, like the depressing Scandinavian films I watched in the 1950s. It was a background for John le Carré and his novels but in no way a place to live. Cuba on the other hand was in a 1950s time warp in which little had changed since the 1958 revolution. Even room service came up with an immaculate period heater to sustain the food, but with no means to turn it on. The best hotels were getting older by the day, and were decorated in their original style. This was like living with history and the film *Godfather 2*, with the thought that the original US Mafia owners might suddenly reappear. The motor cars were a cannibalised treat, again from the 1950s, which I am told is still the case today.

For my own security in East Germany, I took with me my wife and my IPU secretary, Captain Peter Shaw RN, retd. Our host was Horst Sinderman, president of the Volkskammer, a former prime minister and number three in the national hierarchy. The political discussions revealed little but the social programme was something else. The feeling steadily came over me that Germans were first Germans, whether they be Communists, allies of the Soviet Union or anything else. In addition the top echelons lived luxuriously, while those less fortunate could hardly get a decent cut of meat in shops whose shelves were often empty.

Cuban Communism was different. The divisions in society were not so evident. Society was more genuinely egalitarian and whilst it was all a bit faded, life was visible. Hospitality was genuine, and shows like the Tropicana Club offered rum cocktails aplenty. The sad thing was that this beautiful island had lost its very attractive style to that of socialism. Efforts were being made to restore the lovely old city of Havana but money was scarce. I was taken to stay at the beautiful beach of Valaderra, overlooked by the large estate of the once-present Du Pont family, of industrial chemical fame, and now populated by a few tourists from Eastern Europe. All too sad. Efforts have been made since to improve facilities for tourists, but without US investment and patronage it cannot get far. The Cuban revolution has never delivered to the people, and they still cannot wait to get away from it.

I was taken for a shooting expedition, with the Ambassador, of sea birds off a large motor boat. As he said, I shot well for Britain, accompanied by cheers from the Cubans, and was assured in the process that the birds would be sold in the market. All was well until the next day when my legs, exposed to the sun while shooting, became seriously sunburnt. I could hardly walk at the end of the visit, which was poetic justice.

Whilst more formal, the East German visit also had its splendid moments. It included a trip to Potsdam and its palaces. We were conducted around them by the local general secretary, a figure of consequence, and after inspecting their heavy splendour, went for a walk in the town. There we encountered the realities of Communism, by way of an impromptu visit to a butcher also trying to put on a show as a delicatessen. The empty shelves and lack of any choice was embarrassing, by comparison in particular to the West Berlin we were to visit the next day. I sometimes wonder whether they, or someone, caused us to see it.

We then proceeded to lunch, which was a fine affair accompanied by abundant quantities of wine, and a very potent corn spirit, much liked by all. There were only some twelve people present and it was as private an occasion as we might be able to have. On the way that morning, we had passed a large number of Soviet troops on exercises outside the town, and I decided to use this to test the solidarity of the Eastern bloc. When it came to speeches, I made my theme clear in stating how much we missed them in the European Union, where they belonged as Germans. I mentioned the Soviet troops and remarked that it seemed unnatural for them to be on exercise in such a place as Potsdam, although I respected their alliance with the Soviet Union. All this seemed to be sinking home somehow. The general secretary replied warmly but gave nothing away. It was not until we left that he hugged me, clearly moved, and said nothing. His eyes were moist and said it all. At that moment I formed the opinion that a German is a German before he is a Communist, and that the wretched Berlin Wall was coming down, sooner rather than later.

My visit to Cuba ended with me hobbling home, clutching this time two enormous stuffed fish I had somehow acquired along the way. I spent the night at the hotel at Miami airport, and did not know what on earth to do with my fish. Fortunately the manager of the hotel was a Cuban in exile who could not understand what on earth I was doing visiting those 'Bastards over there'. That said he was a fisherman and had no qualms about decorating his boat with Communist fish. They don't have any politics, he remarked as he thanked me.

Our visit to East Germany ended by going through Checkpoint Charlie and learning of all the dramatic escapes of Germans trying to be free in their own country. Then to the Reichstag to see the wall going right through between the main building and the President's residence. After that streets, shops, restaurants, people laughing. It was a different world, soon to be once more part of a united Germany.

The Foreign Office and parliamentary diplomacy

I have always found the Foreign Office first class, and it never fails to help and assist parliamentarians with the many foreign visits those interested undertake. When I arrived at Westminster in 1974 the help was always there, but the contact was more formalised. There were elements in the FCO who thought that Westminster was a place of dangerous contamination from which could only come more problems. It was therefore very difficult to get ambassadors to the House of Commons, or the officials with special knowledge that we needed to hear from. Projects had to be impregnably non-party political to have a chance of securing attendance and this was often difficult to achieve. A good example of the then prevailing mood came in 1979 when one of the new Ministers of State, Peter Blaker MP, a former Foreign Office man himself, decided to invite the backbench Conservative Foreign Affairs Committee to a private party in his room to meet officials. The function was not all-party but it was private and was a great success, enjoyed by both sides. However, such fraternisation was not approved of at the FCO, and any repetition of the event was quietly dropped. It was not until the Falklands War and its aftermath that the light dawned on government that good relations with Westminster could be very useful for both sides, and attitudes became much more relaxed. Geoffrey Howe as Foreign Secretary did a lot to encourage this and could not have made himself more available. By 1987 when I went onto the Foreign Affairs Committee the attitude was most welcoming, and it was appreciated that we could work together for the common cause. The new committee was entertained to a complete morning's tour of the citadel, in all departments, followed by a very agreeable lunch with various luminaries.

Parliamentary diplomacy became an accepted part of the overall picture. As chairman of the British Inter-Parliamentary Union, I was right in the thick of this development. I used the margins of our international conferences, and the opportunities presented, in the joint interest of Parliament and government. This included Ireland, the Soviet Union, the Communist bloc and Argentina after the Falklands War. A small example of the benefit of working together occurred at the IPU Rome conference in 1982. We contrived a vote on the Falklands War and our FCO adviser, an able future Ambassador, Christopher Wilton, and I ticked off the votes, country by country. We then had a virtually complete guide of national voting intentions, to help with the approaching United Nations vote on the same subject in a few weeks time. The vote of the democracies in a parliamentary assembly can go anywhere, but that is not what matters in these exercises. The votes of the rest of the world, anything but democratic, go the way of government policy. Hence you have your guide.

At Geneva in 1984 we judged it the right timing to begin re-establishing relations with Argentina, now that, thanks to our efforts and sacrifice, they were again a parliamentary democracy and back in the Inter-Parliamentary Union. It was a little difficult, but I got the Spanish to act as intermediaries, which was a good example of European co-operation. This led on to a lunch, which was repeated at successive conferences until a full-blown UK parliamentary delegation went over. Naturally this parliamentary contact helped the restoration of diplomatic relations. Our first lunch with the Argentine delegation was a testing lesson in the use of bonhomie and alcohol in good proportion. We invited them to lunch in Geneva and decided on maximum hospitality. This strategy seemed to work until I realised that of the two Argentine Senators present amongst our guests, one was one of the richest men in Argentina and the other was a mere millionaire but one of the most potentially difficult members of their Senate. As a generous host, I was a bit put out when the richest senator decided to order his own private bottle of Champagne to accompany his lunch. He stolidly went through it and more, and I have yet to discover whether we paid for it. However, this left more wine for his senatorial colleague, who drank on undaunted and fortunately got steadily more benevolent as he went along. The main thing was that the lunch went excellently, subject to one small hiccup. After the food we went into speeches around the table, and one of our number, Lord Molloy of Ealing, got into full flow and likened the search for peace to that for the Holy Grail. Around the table we had several interpreters sacrificing their lunch for our benefit. We got used to their almost musical accompaniment, and suddenly it ground to a sudden stop. British and Spanish interpreters alike looked at each other in desperation. ' "Grail" – what is it? How do we say "Grail"?' It was actually very amusing and was never solved, as Lord Molloy, seasoned in the House of Commons, got going again and motored around the problem.

The main vulnerability of the FCO, which I observed over numerous travels, was the danger of ambassadors and others 'going native'. I saw numerous examples of this as a tendency only, and I was told from on high that the powers that be within the system were always on the watch for it. It even struck at ambassadorial level and ironically the more an Ambassador got successfully into the system of his accredited country, and became more influential on behalf of our country, the more vulnerable he became to taking the side of those he was getting on so well with. Normally this was a relatively minor problem which would get back via a good MI6 person on the Embassy staff or whoever. The two major examples of this tendency I encountered are interesting, not least for their importance.

The most glaring example, which caught the whole of the West on the wrong foot, was the Iranian Revolution of 1978–9. The sheer magnitude and scope of the revolutionary change involved completely wrong-footed foreign embassies, and leading Iranians alike, as to the realities of the situation until too late. The serious lesson is never to relax into false security, however comfortable a life you may be living in an agreeable diplomatic community, and never to believe that any system is more powerful than the change that can come from its own weakness. The Iranian regime steadily lost touch with the bounds of reality and its own capacity to govern effectively. Foreign embassies were so busy chasing the many lucrative trade deals, that their eye went right off the proverbial ball. Not for the first time it took the press to get to the realities of the situation first, but even then nothing effective was done to guide the Shah in the right direction before it was too late. The *Financial Times* ran a full supplement on Iran during the summer of 1977, containing a very perceptive contribution from Robert Graham, supported by academics such as Fred Halliday of the LSE, setting out the situation for all to see and giving a clear warning of what could transpire. No doubt our embassies noted it, but it was not taken seriously enough and sadly US leadership from the Carter Administration was abysmal. It was very sad that at a time of utmost need we had perhaps the weakest US Administration in years and a British government going through a bad economic situation without a parliamentary majority. When the Shah needed strong advice he did not get it. Ambassadors and governments were too entrenched in the system and did not believe that the ultimate disaster could possibly happen. The regime was too grand to fall and they would find a way. By the time the West came to appreciate the seriousness of the problem, it was too late. What we could have done is another story, but at more than one stage in the sequence of events, with some strong leadership, we could either have saved the day or limited the damage. However, Western leadership collectively was so bad and disjointed that events were allowed run their course.

The other example, which again I had the chance to observe on the spot, was the 1989 crisis in China that led up to the Tiananmen Square massacre. It so happened that the Commons Foreign Affairs Committee was in Beijing at the time, taking evidence for our enquiry into the future of Hong Kong as part of China. Our official contact with the Chinese was over Hong Kong, but we found ourselves in the midst of a gathering crisis, with marches getting bigger and an increasing occupation of Tiananmen Square by protesters wanting more freedom of expression. Our Ambassador, who conducted our briefings, was a huge man, a rugby player if ever there was one, for whom the Chinese could do no wrong. The sight of him bowing down in greeting to Chinese officials of normal size was a sight to behold. We sensed a crisis, and asked repeatedly for background to alleviate our concerns, only to be told that it would not come to anything and there was nothing to worry about. One evening some of us went out to look at the Square from afar, and saw it getting into a state of gathering tumult, before going to one of the big hotels to meet up with some of the gathering pack of journalists, who had asked to see us. Then, at last, we had a proper briefing from two correspondents of leading UK newspapers, both Chinese-speakers, who had been out with the marchers during the day. They were in no doubt of the seriousness of the situation but stressed that at the present stage it was good-natured. Apparently the student marchers were cheered and waved at by onlookers from their windows and pavements. Sadly, as the square steadily filled up, the authorities had no idea how to deal with the situation. The whole thing was then exacerbated by more radical elements stirring up the crowds amidst mounting tension. Some sort of climax was coming, but was held back by the impending visit of Mr Gorbachev, then leader of the Soviet Union, which was hardly the occasion for a crack down by the authorities. Once his visit was over we were warned to watch out for trouble, and on that note, and with our work done, we left Beijing just before he arrived and in a state of considerable suspense.

We departed with no change in the Embassy's position, which seemed oblivious to what the press were increasingly saying. If they were not, then they had no wish to take parliamentarians, or for that matter the press, into their confidence, which was an unnecessary mistake. There was little as a country we could have done about it and our main national interest was overwhelmingly to get Hong Kong settled as smoothly as possible. That said, we were entitled to a realistic briefing, which we never had from that Embassy. I cannot see that happening had Sir Percy Craddock still been in charge, and I can only hope that at least some private reports going back to Whitehall were more to the point.

Part IV

IRELAND

Ten

THE PEACE
PROCESS AND THE
PARLIAMENTARY ROLE

If one could only teach the English how to talk, and the Irish how to listen, society here would be quite civilised.

Oscar Wilde, *An Ideal Husband*, Act 3, 1895

Background

I have always been drawn towards the affairs of Ireland. Perhaps in some small way I want to try and redeem the considerable historical injustices which have been meted out by the English and Scottish to the Irish. I have no Catholic blood that I know of, and the best I can do by way of background is my maternal grandfather, David Hamilton Thompson, who was a Protestant from Northern Ireland and was of English extraction. He came over to England in the 1890s, married my grandmother and did not return. Many Irish audiences were somewhat bemused as to why an 'English Tory' like me should be so concerned about Ireland. When I explained my Welsh background it was immediately understood. When the British–Irish Inter-Parliamentary Body was launched in 1990 by Geoffrey Howe (MP and deputy prime minister and of a similar heritage to me), sitting next to him it was evident that he was visibly moved by the occasion. Anyone who has seen the camaraderie of British and Irish rugby supporters towards each other, in the same pub, after a match, will get the point.

To this day the average Englishman has little feeling for, or knowledge of, what happened on the island of Ireland. To the Anglo-Saxons, the Irish, and for that matter the Welsh, were something else. However, the Irish and the Welsh were Celts, and different by nature and background from the Anglo-Saxons. Added to this, the Irish stayed loyal to the old religion of Catholicism, which with much historical agony the English discarded, and this left them vulnerable to even greater measures of English repression. Irish Catholics were totally suppressed over hundreds of years and anyone who wanted to play any part in the affairs of Ireland had to be part of the Protestant ascendancy. These were English colonial gentlemen who lived in some style, with their own parliament and peerage, beautiful homes and estates, and who answered to London rather than Dublin. Catholics played no part in it, not even allowed to vote or stand for the Irish Parliament. A prominent example would be the 1st Duke of Wellington, part of the Wellesley family ennobled in the Irish peerage as the Earldom of Mornington, who arrived with his brother at Eton in 1781, and from then on pursued his career and his eventual success in England, but from a privileged Anglo-Irish background.

Wales is an interesting comparison. Smaller, adjacent to England and never seen as desirable enough to have a full-blown ascendancy, it was administered as part of England from the time of Henry VIII. Large tracts of it were given to royal favourites, such as the donation of most of Cardiff, together with its castle, to the Scottish Bute family. This contributed to their vast wealth, going with the Industrial Revolution and the development of Cardiff and its docks into a cosmopolitan city with its own ways and even accent. The development of the coal and steel industries made a huge difference to South Wales, which was something Ireland never had. The emerging professional and commercial classes were educated almost exclusively in England, assuming an Anglo-Welsh identity. The status of Wales increased in recent times with the power of Lloyd George, and disestablishment of the Welsh Anglican Church, together with the creation of Cardiff's Civic Centre and National War Memorial. However, it was not until the Blair government finally introduced devolution that Wales became more its own master in administrative terms. That said, if they have talent, the Welsh, like the Irish, can always succeed in England. Many Irish, such as Terry Wogan, become outstandingly successful by the application of a bit of the old Celtic charm. Politically, Lloyd George was the same. Sadly Neil Kinnock was not; of Scottish ancestry and lacking the Welsh ways, he displayed all the characteristics of the Welsh 'boyo', which the English greatly dislike, and none of the charm to go with it. It was very sad for someone of such warmth and ability.

From the outset of my parliamentary career in February 1974, I followed Irish matters. My chance to contribute came in the spring of 1982, when I became, against traditionalist Conservative opposition, the elected head of the British Group of the Inter-Parliamentary Union. This is a backbench-controlled organisation, largely free of government, which has the responsibility for attending international IPU conferences and events and, importantly, the exchange of bilateral delegations with other parliaments throughout the world, with the exception of the Commonwealth. The opportunities that such an organisation gives for political initiatives at parliamentary level, most effective if they are conducted in cohesion with governments, is manifest. When I took over, the group had become a private club used by the Conservative right to pursue its own travel preferences in alliance with the equally conservative trade union traditionalists of the Labour Party. The chairman had to be a member of a government party and my opponent in the election was Sir Patrick Wall, the well-known neo-colonial MP. Our contest was considerable and they ran out of ballot papers, as the queue to vote stretched down the stairs from the Grand Committee Room and into Westminster Hall. Fortunately I had all-party support and won well.

I soon used the potential of the organisation, and one of my first priorities was to improve our relations with the Irish Parliament. The timing in 1982 was just right, as post-Sunningdale both governments were looking for a way forward and were between the Joint Studies Report and the Anglo-Irish Agreement. I began at the IPU conference in Seoul, South Korea, September 1983. The good thing about these conferences was that there was plenty of time in the margins, and one could take advantage of the fact that many countries chose to send delegates who were senior and influential. I gave a lunch specially for the leaders of the Irish delegation who up to then had only been invited to something we called the 'Commonwealth Lunch'. I had present my future co-chairman of the Inter-Parliamentary Body, Jim Tunney TD, who was the sitting chairman of the Fianna Fáil Parliamentary Party and Kieran Crotty TD, his Fine Gael equivalent. With them was the Irish Ceann Comhairle/ Speaker, Tom Fitzpatrick TD. We all got on well and plans were formed to bring our two delegations closer together, as well as our parliaments. In a short time our conference delegations were having drinks in our respective 'common rooms', we co-operated on agendas and problems and, most important, we arranged golf matches between our respective parliamentary clubs. Next followed a formal exchange of delegations, with the first into London in 1985 being led by Speaker Fitzpatrick. Again it was influential and included Bertie Ahern, then Shadow Labour Minister, and later the Taoiseach/Prime Minister, who delivered the Irish side of the eventual Belfast Agreement, after a long and arduous peace process.

By 1987 a change of government in Dublin led to a delegation to London, headed by David Andrews, Fianna Fáil TD, later Foreign Minister. He was assured and confident, and had clearly been briefed to take matters forward after the successful conclusion of the Anglo-Irish Agreement. He met a ready response from the British side during a series of well-attended meetings and functions. It was the wish of all to create a parliamentary body to give shape to our future exchanges. We were now on our way in the active process of creating the Inter-Parliamentary Body.

The parliamentary role

Political writers are in general preoccupied with executive power. They all too often give insufficient weight to the significance of the activities of the rank and file, who create the situation giving those on high the opportunity to act. One pre-eminent example of this was the overthrow of Margaret Thatcher in the autumn of 1990. This was followed all over the world and not least in Ireland. I never forget the quiet words of the attendant at the entrance to Leinster House when I entered during a Dublin visit in 1990, while I was in the thick of it. 'Good luck, Sir, good luck', he murmured almost without his lips appearing to move. The same is true of the congratulations and good wishes volunteered in a Wicklow pub when the worst was over. Such support of the people, Irish as well, was not fully portrayed by the British media. The all-important build-up to Mrs Thatcher's resignation was dealt with briefly, as page after page went into which minister said what to her during the famous Cabinet meeting, prior to her resignation, when she saw them one by one. This opened the way for individual Cabinet members to speak their minds more personally and frankly than perhaps they would in a full meeting. At the end of a successful battle it is the generals who take the credit, but it is the poor wretched infantry who relentlessly and opportunistically stir the pot and make it happen.

The peace process makes an interesting comparison. The structure, with the historical background, was far more complex than the removal of a leader. The stirring came from the will of the people kept alive by the two Cabinet Offices over the years. The right personalities then dropped into place at the right times as years and agreements went by. The relationship of the British and Irish governments was absolutely crucial and was steadily improving. During the last decade or so from 1987, the parliamentary relationship played a valuable role in establishing confidence amongst those whose support was very necessary. Again the leaders were the right ones. The political demise of Mrs Thatcher helped in Ireland particularly, but also in Britain, in that John Major presented to both sides of the Irish Sea a far more benevolent image which matched that of Albert Reynolds. Albert kept the balls in the air at a difficult political time for Major, and what Major did not move on or complete was brilliantly taken on to its conclusion by Tony Blair and Bertie Ahern, a formidable pair.

In contributing to the political climate the Inter-Parliamentary Body was well endowed with talent. From our foundation in January 1990 until the Belfast Agreement of 1998 we had amongst our membership four past and future Irish Taoiseachs/Prime Ministers in Garret Fitzgerald, John Bruton, Brian Cowen and Enda Kenny; on the British side two former Secretaries of State for Northern Ireland in Tom King and Peter Brooke; and on both sides a string of other ex-ministers and prominent backbenchers. When the five ministers, British and Irish, of the then British–Irish Ministerial Council sat down to meet after the 1992 British General Election, three were former members of the body and Patrick Mayhew had addressed it as Secretary of State. They were at once on first-name terms.

The media exposure was considerable and it became common for British and Irish politicians to appear together on the same programmes. In the UK it was a great help in keeping Ireland on the political agenda. My Irish co-chairman for the post-1992 period was Dermot Ahern TD, and we became regular media partners on both sides of the Irish Sea, in addition to lectures and appearances together. All this represented the changes to come. Dermot later became Justice and then Foreign Minister, posts he filled with considerable ability, before retiring to his law practice in Dundalk. Public recognition in Dublin became such that we were sometimes stopped in the street for friendly words and encouragement. It was a good example of how normal people crave for the peace that politicians cannot always provide. It became noticeable how the UK media, during the almost continuous British wrangles in Europe and over the Maastricht Treaty, often turned to the Irish Foreign Minister for comment. This particularly applied to Dick Spring, not to mention Gerry Collins also. I often paused to wonder how the relationship of our two peoples was allowed to sink into such a historical mess.

Irish ways and personalities

Once the described preliminaries were over I was formally charged by the IPU, with the full support of the Foreign Office and the Clerks of the House of Commons, with the formation, jointly with the Irish, of a Parliamentary Body or Tier. I thus became formally committed to help in bringing Britain and Ireland closer together, which was the worthiest of causes, and where I might make a difference. From the outset this led to heavy media exposure and many public engagements in the Republic, and to a lesser extent in Northern Ireland. The British–Irish Inter-Parliamentary Body was formally launched in January 1990 and my profile within the Republic remained very high. I got to know all the main players in Irish politics and was increasingly trusted by them over the years. On the British side, things were more complicated, in that I had access to everyone, but the closer I got to the Irish the less trusted I was within my own British Conservative Party, not to mention the Ulster Unionists, who treated me as a virtual untouchable. To be seen as 'Green' rather than 'Orange' within my party was not healthy. However, within the Labour Party and the Liberal Democrats, it could not have been more different.

During the two years' work that it took to create the Inter-Parliamentary Body and get it up and running, under the active eye of the two governments, a succession of Irish personalities came forward who all helped to acclimatise me to the ways of Ireland. This included alerting me to the many pitfalls awaiting an innocent Englishman. The first such personality I encountered was Richard Ryan, by 1986 a veteran of the Anglo-Irish Agreement and, as the political Counsellor at the Irish Embassy in London, a born political operator. He rendered his country great service, even if the expenses bill of the Irish Foreign Ministry suffered considerably as a result. His style of entertaining was of the highest standard, be it individually, domestically or with the organisation of embassy dinner parties. He believed in quality and the need to get the right personalities together for whatever occasion or purpose. For serious politics he would always entertain one to one. This was a good lesson to learn. The common mistake is to entertain politicians *en bloc*, and quite miss the point that politicians are both vain and careful when together in company. One to one they will talk far more. Beginning relationships in this way, he developed a wide range of influential friends in London going way beyond politicians. Garret Fitzgerald, the distinguished Taoiseach/Prime Minister, remarked in his autobiography that Richard spent much of his time in London 'dining for Ireland'. He went on to become ambassador in various countries and most particularly Irish Ambassador at the United

Nations and President of the Security Council. Once again his political and social talents were very well used.

The Irish Embassy in London in those important years of the 1980s and 1990s was generally a very level-headed place, whatever the difficulties of the moment. There were private jokes about the security game being played out on the Irish by our zealous Security Services. Bugs going wrong was a favourite, which could lead to such things as the target's voice coming back through items of household equipment such as the television, to his initial shock and later amusement. One more serious episode that got into the press was the fact that every electronically typed letter or document from the Irish Embassy was automatically recorded by the UK Security Services. A few of us rather naive Conservative MPs were concerned and I had a word with the then Irish Ambassador, Noel Dorr, who, charming and at the top of his game, did not seem in the least disturbed. We did not leave it there, as soon afterwards we had Ted Heath at a private meeting of our Conservative Foreign Affairs Committee, and we put this to him as a matter of concern. I never forget the enormous smile that broke out on his large countenance as he gave one of his famous shrugs. He then could not resist saying that during negotiations it was an enormous advantage to have your opponent's brief laid out before you. Rapidly wising up to the ways of the world, I then discovered that the Irish were not put out and all important documents were couriered in any event. They also appeared to know far more than they should have about the inner workings of the British government by the use of more human methods. Probably a score draw all round.

As soon as the Inter-Parliamentary Body was under way Peter Barry TD became a member of our Steering Committee. He served as Foreign Minister under Garret Fitzgerald and negotiated the Anglo-Irish Agreement. He was always a potential leader of Fine Gael, who in my view should have been that and prime minister as well, but a political career has little that is predictable about it. At the beginning I needed someone on the Irish side to help and advise me and Peter opted to fill the bill without any prompting from me. He came from an old and prosperous Cork family and as a major tea importer he was one of Ireland's richer men. A Cork man through and through, he declined to have a Dublin home throughout his political career, and preferred to live in his regular accommodation at one of Dublin's grandest hotels. His late wife, Margaret, brought up their six children from their home in Cork and he ran his business, became Lord Mayor of Cork and pursued a distinguished political career nationally.

My friendship with Peter began at one of the earliest meetings of the Steering Committee when he took me aside and asked whether I would like some guidance over the niceties of Irish politics, and in particular what to watch out for when I presided over meetings of the Inter-Parliamentary Body. I have never forgotten this act of kindness. The basics were then set out for me from the Irish point of view. 'Don't say Ulster', he told me, explaining that only six of the counties of Ulster were included in the creation of Northern Ireland in order to give a Unionist majority in the Province. 'Say Northern Ireland, and you will offend nobody', he continued. By the same token, say 'Ireland or The Republic of Ireland, but not Southern Ireland', and so it went on, as history came to life for invaluable practical use. I then asked about various phrases that seemed to come up in the press such as 'Friend of the Castle', which was translated to me as an English collaborator. How about 'Free Staters'? Supporters of the Treaty with the British which caused the Irish Civil War and the formation of our political parties, I was told. I found all this invaluable in my public life in Ireland and, throughout my period of office, Peter was always on hand to help. A marvellous man.

On the six-strong Steering Committee of the Inter-Parliamentary Body were three Irish TDs and three British MPs. First was my dear friend and co-chairman, the late Jim Tunney, an ex-headmaster who became an Education Minister and then chairman of the Fianna Fáil Parliamentary Party. With his flower in his buttonhole and always ready with a quick riposte, he was in his element as a chairman. He was determined to make the Inter-Parliamentary Body work and was particularly good at keeping his more difficult members in line during the two-year formation period. I felt that when he led the first official Irish parliamentary presence at the Palace of Westminster since 1921, when the Inter-Parliamentary

Body had its formation meeting in January 1990, he was proud that he had achieved something truly worthwhile. From the outset we rigidly imposed the principle of national equality in all things and it worked. Irish miscreants in the chamber were treated by Jim in a friendly but firm headmasterly way and we worked as a close team. Very sadly he lost his seat in Dublin through the swing against Fianna Fáil in 1993, together with adverse boundary changes which caused him to have to compete with another Fianna Fáil member. He remained popular and carried on with his voluntary work. I kept in contact and we visited the Dublin count together during the 1997 elections, before his sad death not long afterwards.

Fine Gael was represented by Peter Barry, as already mentioned, and Labour by its then party leader, Dick Spring TD. Scion of a prominent family, married to an American and a practising barrister, he was an international rugby player to boot. I'll never forget going into the Cardiff County Club for lunch before a rugby international, the day after I had appeared on the television news with Dick, by then Foreign Minister of Ireland. Not a word from members about the subject matter of the television item but rather the exclamation, 'What were you doing with the man who dropped the ball in front of the Welsh posts at the Arms Park? Ireland could have won!' During his tenure of office as Foreign Minister in the coalition government of John Bruton, 1993–7, he was constantly teased in the cartoons of the time by highly imaginative applications of this mishap to the politics of the day. We are never allowed to forget such things!

On the British side I was well supported at the outset by Conservative Andrew Mackay MP, who as Northern Ireland Secretary Tom King's PPS played a considerable role in getting the Inter-Parliamentary Body off the ground. He was far more perceptive of the future worth of the Inter-Parliamentary Body than was his ministerial boss, whom he kept on side on the subject. He was followed by an ex-minister, the late Sir Giles Shaw, an excellent appointment. For Labour the late Sir Stuart Bell MP oversaw all the preparations for the Inter-Parliamentary Body and its early days. He could not have been more supportive, nor could his successor,

David Winnick MP, who succeeded me as co-chairman on the change of government in 1997. Conservatives thought of him as left wing and difficult. In fact he is anything but difficult and politically very practical. An able man, it seems a pity he was never given any government office, which by ability he could have undertaken.

That leaves the all-important public presentation of the Inter-Parliamentary Body and its work. For our press and public relations we appointed Mike Burns. He was a natural for the job and the best appointment we could have made. An experienced journalist, he had been RTÉ Chief Correspondent in London for some years and knew everyone there was to know in both London and Dublin. A popular figure, his leaving party filled to overflowing the largest hall in the Westminster Conference Centre. He worked hard, played hard, had good taste and, rare for anyone, was liked by all.

Differences

These provide a pleasant contrast rather than any difficulty. The reason so many English people like going to Ireland is that they find sufficient similarities in the country to feel at ease but also a far more relaxed lifestyle and general approach to life.

In 1989, Stuart Bell and I were in Leinster House dealing with various administrative matters concerning the emerging Parliamentary Body. Our presence was acknowledged by an invitation to go through to the adjacent government Buildings for tea with the then Taoiseach, Charlie Haughey. He posed for photographs between Stuart and myself; Stuart towered over him and I did not do too badly in an uneven contest. Charlie looked to his left and then to his right and remarked, 'What am I doing here between you two Saxons?' This phrase neatly expressed the constant need to be aware of the differences between the Celtic Irish and the Anglo-Saxons from across the Irish Sea. It necessitated the golden rule in the foundation and operation of the Parliamentary Body, which was that everything should be conducted on the basis of complete equality.

With this, the imbalance of history, and associated chips on shoulders, on both sides, disappeared. Because of this approach it was amazing how well we all got on together from the outset.

Celtic attitudes often confuse the more straightforward Anglo-Saxons. An example of this was the attitude to Charlie Haughey. It was general knowledge that Charlie had amassed a considerable fortune, which had not all come from his wife, herself the daughter of a former Taoiseach, Sean Lemass. He lived in some style in a beautiful classical house on the outskirts of Dublin, he owned an island off the Dingle Peninsula and a yacht, known as the 'Gin Palace', in which he toured the beautiful Irish coast in some splendour. On one occasion the British military impounded the boat in Carlingford Lough, claiming, perhaps mischievously, that it was in British waters. Haughey was not on board at the time and amidst a few smiles the matter was quietly swept under the carpet. He raised a lot of money by way of party contributions; owned racehorses; was involved in various ventures; was known to have an eye for the ladies; and was widely regarded as 'a bit of a lad' who had got away with it and good luck to him. However, this mood prevailed as long as the going was good. Late in his career things got out of hand, owing to the family divisions of one of his major party contributors, Ben Dunne of the supermarket chain, leading to the exposure of large contributions, with little control over them, heading in Haughey's direction. The Moriarty Tribunal into the wider question of political contributions followed, but reached no final conclusion before Charlie Haughey sadly died. It was an unhappy ending to a distinguished career.

I prefer to remember Charlie in the good times. The pride with which he once showed me around the then newly refurbished government buildings is one such instance. This impressive project had much to do with him and he did it in style, displaying Irish craftsmanship along the way and resisting the all-too-usual objections on the grounds of public expenditure. In his private life he openly enjoyed the good things and without any hypocrisy that I could see. My visit to his grand house on the edge of Dublin was an event to be enjoyed. I was taken to see Charlie, after he had left office, by Jim Tunney. It was by way of a private courtesy call, with Jim addressing him as 'Boss' in and out of his presence. The house was in a lovely setting with paddocks and horses on the approach. Charlie greeted us in his shirt-sleeves and open-necked shirt, and ushered us through reception rooms to his private 'bar' overlooking the gardens. It had been specially constructed as a male sanctum with leather furnishings and all the equipment of a real bar. A bottle of Champagne was quickly produced and the three of us settled down to drink and gossip. Outside the entrance to the bar was a corridor with what I call a 'rogues' gallery', namely many photographs from all over the globe of my host with the rich and powerful. I picked out several photos of him with Ronald and Nancy Reagan and in particular one alone with Nancy. 'What did you think of her?' I asked rather innocently. 'She adored me', came the immediate response. The ego was undaunted by the loss of power, but there was also never a hint of self-pity at being out of office. While much of the conversation was about politics and personalities, far more important to him was the approaching Cheltenham Festival and how his horse would do in the Gold Cup. He desperately wanted to win it, which sadly he didn't manage, but it was good to see an ex-leader enjoying real life. I had just been to see the historic Malahide Castle and remarked on the formidable menu framed in the main dining room, which included Chateau Lafite 1945, served for a European summit during an Irish presidency under Charlie's sway. 'Nothing but the best', he said, 'but I also got a new car park for the Castle out of that one!'

The last time I saw him was at the inauguration of the new Irish President, Mary McAleese, at Dublin Castle in 1997. He was subdued but dignified in the face of the financial scandal which by then had broken, and intimated that he would get out of it all intact. His death denied him a final resolution, but had he lived I like to think he would have been 'Up, up and away', in style, and back to concentrating on Cheltenham.

Another illustration of our differences is in the comparatively relaxed Irish attitude towards sexual transgression. One evening in about 1993, after an official function, we were being treated to a nightcap at the smart Shelbourne Hotel, St Stephen's Green, a centre for Dublin society. Our host was Dermot Gallagher, a senior diplomat of the Irish Foreign Ministry, soon to become Ambassador to the United States. I encouraged a discussion about our different attitudes towards sexual adventures, which was provoked by the British tabloid press then having a field day 'exposing' the amorous activities of various junior government ministers, and contrasting them with the misconstrued Major government policy of 'Back to basics'. This was very much a matter for them, their wives and mistresses, and certainly not for the *News of the World*. When I led off by comparing Catholic attitudes in France with our own somewhat puritanical reactions to these things, I got nowhere and a heavy smoke screen descended. It was then time to go and we got up and walked out past various tables to the door. When we got there, Dermot Gallagher stopped me, and whispered in my ear that a friend had recognised me on the way out and would appreciate a word. He was a former government minister, now in opposition, and well known in the Dáil Éireann as a man with a keen interest in the ladies. Gallagher continued by saying that he was back inside, third table on the right, and be aware that he's 'in company'. I got the message immediately, went back in and lo and behold there was my friend with a young lady, considerably younger than himself, sitting in full view of the entire Dublin establishment, who took not a blind bit of notice of him. I was introduced to the lady, had a nice chat about old times and went somewhat enviously on my way.

In the clearest terms I had the answer to my previous questions, and in a far more literal way than in an academic discussion about moral attitudes. This was reinforced sometime afterwards in the same hotel when my host, an Irish Ambassador, suddenly said, 'Peter, come over here and meet Charlie's mistress' and took me over to meet a charming woman, wife of a High Court judge and Charlie Haughey's mistress for some years. It was a world away from London, and having seen various friends struggling to keep their private affairs away from the press, very refreshing indeed.

Politics could be sensitive

As for political pitfalls, they remained abundant for the unwary on our Inter-Parliamentary Body, and ironically it was always British PPS's who were falling into them. This was partly because they were increasingly appointed by the Whips' Office rather than by their ministers as in the old days. We had two glorious examples, when each had to be rescued by their colleagues, British and Irish alike. The first was at the Dublin Plenary of 1991 via Ken Hind MP, the PPS to the then Secretary of State for Northern Ireland, Peter Brooke. He was a barrister from Lancashire who didn't tolerate fools gladly and believed in the direct approach. In Irish politics this was risky and could be fatal, in his case sooner rather than later. He ignored the wise tradition that a PPS kept silent, particularly on matters concerning his own department. He chose to make a speech on the most delicate matter of the moment, cross-border security, at a time when the Irish media would put every word down as the views of his minister. The political and security debate was always in those days the most important and the most sensitive. In his wisdom Hind made a 'robust speech' on cross-border security, in which he lectured the Irish (a fatal mistake) that they were not pulling their weight on their side of the border, by comparison to the magnificent efforts the British were making on theirs. No doubt he was repeating some concern, privately expressed, within the Northern Ireland Office, and thought it needed saying. Whether it needed saying or not, the debate from that moment literally took off. The wilder, more extreme elements on both sides were unleashed, and press pencils accelerated across the pages. I happened to be in the chair as my Irish co-chairman, Jim Tunney TD, had to leave the Chamber, and when he returned it was so hectic that I had to stay in the chair, as to transfer back to Jim in 'mid-flight' could have proved fatal. Speaker after speaker was piling in, and the most encouraging fact was that the official spokesmen on both sides came together at once and united to try and calm things down. This effort particularly included the Labour Shadow Northern Ireland Secretary, Kevin McNamara MP, and his Irish counterpart, Jim O'Keefe TD, of Fine Gael. The day was eventually saved by a bravado performance from Michael Mates MP, winding up for the British side, who, as a former colonel who had served in Northern Ireland, spoke of the many visits he had made to the border, then and now, and how he had witnessed the increasingly close co-operation of the security forces on both sides of it. We all heaved a great sigh of relief, and Ken Hind, who apparently thought he had promoted a great debate, hopefully realised by the end what a close-run thing it was.

This was not the only time Kevin McNamara was a great help. Obviously attached to the land of his ancestors, he did a lot to give the Irish confidence over the peace process. I always recall his good sense when Peter Brooke, then Secretary of State, was caught off-guard in the *Late Late Show* on Irish television, and was persuaded into singing some song on the same day that a number of British soldiers had been blown up in the North. There was a storm of protest and it could have led to his resignation, but McNamara sympathised and saw beyond the immediate situation, with the possibility of losing an excellent minister over an innocent mistake. He so conducted matters from the opposition front bench and Peter Brooke came through intact. Kevin rose to the occasion and many were grateful to him.

The other great faux pas, which caused governmental, not to mention parliamentary, consternation occurred at the Cork Plenary of 1993. The main speaker was Dick Spring, the then Irish Foreign Minister and formally a founder member of the Inter-Parliamentary Body, who took questions after his speech. One of our members was Henry Bellingham MP, then PPS to the Defence Secretary, Malcolm Rifkind. Henry was an agreeable Tory gentleman barrister who had family connections to the Irish ascendancy. He was then a little too inexperienced and eager to please. Once more articulating something he must have heard privately within the Ministry, he was itching to say thank you to the Irish for their kind co-operation in the destruction of an IRA 0.5 inch heavy machinegun by a British military helicopter. The problem was that the machinegun had been operating, as was often the case, from the Irish side of the border and within the Republic, where technically the British had no right to operate. On this and many other 'hot pursuit'-type occasions, the Irish government turned a very helpful blind eye, but this was certainly not for public consumption. Such revelations were acutely embarrassing for them in dealing with their own more Republican elements. These finer points seem to have completely eluded the eager PPS Bellingham.

Dick Spring, caught completely off-guard, gave a suitably Delphic answer, saying absolutely nothing, and we hastily adjourned for lunch. All hell broke loose. The press clamoured for comment; Dick Spring was spirited off to lunch; Graham Archer, the head of the Foreign Office Irish Desk, was in a flat spin as he desperately phoned London and many a meal was disturbed. Dick Spring's very good speech was forgotten and a special press conference had to be called for him to rescue the situation. Such were the perils of British–Irish relations on the road to peace. The key point at the end of it was that both sides kept their heads in difficult moments and worked together to sort it out. Of such stuff was the peace process made.

Not all difficult

Amidst all these difficulties the positive side of our long-standing historical relationship also came out from time to time. One of the most moving moments for me during my active relationship with Ireland occurred in June 1995, when I attended a memorable ceremony celebrating the restoration of the Irish National War Memorial, at Islandbridge on the edge of Dublin, presided over by the then Taoiseach, John Bruton. This memorial raised sensitive issues from 1916 onwards, with Ireland carrying out the uprising against the British and involved in World War I participation with the British, all at the same time. Its restoration was therefore a significant and symbolic event. I was representing the Parliamentary Body and had due pride of place along with Irish government ministers and the Northern Ireland Delegation headed by the Secretary of State, Sir Patrick Mayhew. As our car approached I saw a familiar sight from all the Remembrance Sundays I had attended over the years in my constituency, with members of the Royal British Legion, complete with insignia and banners, walking up to the memorial. This was not a usual sight for Dublin and I was told that these were members of the Royal Dublin Legion. I felt something special was happening. When we arrived there they were, the Dublin Legion, erect men in their seventies, dripping with medals, with their banners, standing in line and side by side with similarly turned-out members of the Royal Belfast Legion. This was a moving sight and I must admit that it brought a lump to my throat.

John Bruton outlined the enormous losses suffered by both North and South during the World Wars, and not least the South during World War II, when many went into British regiments as volunteers. Afterwards the leader of the Dublin Legion came over to talk to me. He was a former Parachute Regiment major, who told me he had gone into France the night before the D-Day landings, on one of the special missions that the Paras carried out so brilliantly. He then said: 'If you think I got there early let me introduce you to him' and he ushered forth a stocky, short, ex-sergeant, saying: 'This sergeant was a frogman who got there ahead of all of us to help clear, as far as was possible, the beaches of mines and obstacles.' The major added that he had been a member of the British Special Forces, 'which was something I could not admit to around here for so many years'. The spirit of togetherness was finally added to by my last meeting with Senator Gordon Wilson, the marvellous father from Northern Ireland who lost his daughter in the outrageous bombing of the Enniskillen Remembrance Day Parade in 1987, and whose Christian example of forgiveness in the cause of peace set a way for us all to follow.

Mrs Thatcher

The attitudes and leadership by individuals on both sides was crucial in bringing about the peace process and then pursuing it through to realisation. The motivation for it on the Irish side was natural and understandable, and involved along the way keeping Ireland on the British agenda, which was easier said than done. The only defence the British had, when some appalling happening in Northern Ireland came up on the news, was to moan, go off and make the tea and try to ignore the whole ghastly business. But leaders persevered in spite of many difficulties along the way, such as the eventual failure of the admirable 1973 Sunningdale Agreement; the violence of the IRA; and the difficulties created by the Unionist parties. The main thing was that the agenda was always moved forward, bit by bit. One early example was the play by Irish Taoiseach Charlie Haughey in 1980 to woo Mrs Thatcher, the new British prime minister. The full charms of Charlie were deployed, a present of Irish silver was given and we were told that the Prime Minister was very impressed. She later became furious when the very same Charlie let her down with a great thump by declining to support her over the Falklands War. Peter Mandelson tells a lovely story of one of the very few conversations he had with her, when their paths crossed just after he had been appointed Secretary of State for Northern Ireland. She came up to him in true Thatcher style and said: 'Young man, I only have one bit of advice for you. Never trust the Irish. They are all liars. They are all liars.' After which comment she turned on her heel and marched off without another word. However, the Haughey–Thatcher contact led to the Anglo-Irish Studies Report of 1981 which continued the momentum towards the Anglo-Irish Agreement of 1985 and incidentally established the idea, if the Parliaments so wished, of establishing a 'Parliamentary Tier' to any agreement.

Mrs Thatcher's somewhat basic view was not typical of her fellow countrymen, and certainly not of the many who have a love for Ireland and Irish ways. The ministers and particularly the senior civil servants from both sides who dealt with the 1985 Anglo-Irish Agreement, and associated matters, were crucial. In Ireland we had a moderate Fine Gael-led government under Garret Fitzgerald, with Peter Barry as his Foreign Minister, and backed up by excellent support from their Cabinet Office, under its Secretary Dermot Nally, which itself had a close relationship with our own Cabinet Office. So many journalists and others wonder how Mrs Thatcher ever agreed to the Anglo-Irish Agreement. The answer is that in addition to having the right Irish players, we had within the top ranks of the British Civil Service, from Cabinet Secretary Sir Robert Armstrong down, a deep desire to sort it all out, once and for all. These were people who understood and manipulated the wheels of power, as well as getting on well with their Irish counterparts, who were of the same mind. The British side also had the right ministers in the right place: Geoffrey Howe was Foreign Secretary and Douglas Hurd Northern Ireland Secretary, and both saw the chance of future peace and went for it. Mrs Thatcher was carried along with the tide and advisers such as Ian Gow MP, with strong pro-Unionist views on the subject, were no longer in place. She expressed reservations about the Agreement years after, but it was too late.

The Inter-Parliamentary Body: Creation, 1990

With the right ministers in place it still took two years to establish the British–Irish Inter-Parliamentary Body. The key once again was Geoffrey Howe as Foreign Secretary, who was supportive throughout. Under him was the then Northern Ireland Secretary, Tom King, who lacked enthusiasm and seemed doubtful about it all, reiterating views that saw the whole thing as possibly yet more trouble. He never encouraged our efforts but as Northern Ireland Secretary he was not directly responsible for us. He in no way obstructed us and in any event was skilfully kept on side by his Parliamentary Private Secretary, Andrew Mackay MP, who was a great help in the whole endeavour. The other key minister was the Leader of the House, John Wakeham, who gradually took over responsibility from the Foreign Office as we got closer to realisation as a parliamentary entity. So into the hands of John Wakeham we went, and capable as they were, we never quite knew where we stood. He was always pleasant, laid-back and avuncular, perhaps too much so. Our two meetings were trying as Wakeham had seldom read or mastered his brief, with the almost comical result that it would become a race for him to get on top of the facts, as the meeting progressed, in time to make the necessary decision, which to give him his due he always accomplished. The good side was that in the true manner of a former chief whip, he always had complete confidence that if there was a problem, it could be fixed or managed.

The contrast with Geoffrey Howe was striking. In July 1989 he lost the Foreign Office, after difficulties with Mrs Thatcher over the ERM at the Madrid European Council, and became deputy prime minister (even if Mrs Thatcher never referred to him as such) and Leader of the House of Commons. He immediately took over our matter, as it was still with the Leader of the House, and saw it through to a rapid conclusion. I saw Geoffrey Howe for the first time about the Inter-Parliamentary Body shortly after the fateful reshuffle. Understandably he looked battered and down, but in no way did he let his feelings interfere with his work. He produced his Civil Service brief for the meeting and what a contrast it was to his predecessor. Sitting opposite him and looking at his file upside down, I could clearly see that rather than looking at a series of virgin pages, undisturbed by ministerial hand or mind, his pages were scored, underlined and minuted. He had clearly done his homework and I got every decision I needed virtually straightaway.

Launch

We proceeded to the launch of the Inter-Parliamentary Body at the beginning of February 1990 in Committee Room 14 of the Commons. It was a Parliamentary occasion but conducted at Deputy Prime Ministerial level, with me as first British co-chairman presiding. Geoffrey Howe represented our government with Roy Hattersley, deputy leader of the opposition, and Paddy Ashdown, leader of the Liberal Democrats, in support. On the Irish side Brian Lenihan, Deputy Prime Minister, or Tanaiste, led the team supported by Peter Barry, ex-Foreign Minister for Fine Gael, and Dick Spring, the leader of the Irish Labour Party. It was a historic occasion, and the first official visit to Westminster of Irish parliamentarians since 1919.

During the launch Geoffrey Howe was sitting on my right. As he spoke I could not help noticing that he clearly felt the emotional side of the occasion, as well as the obvious political significance of it all. I have never asked him but I put this down to his coming from South Wales, as I do myself. The Welsh, like the Irish, are Celts and have a certain sympathy with the historical situation of the Irish, having been effectively governed by England for hundreds of years.

So now we were launched. In session we were facing a galaxy of talent on both sides, and not least Garret Fitzgerald, the former Taoiseach/Prime Minister, who had presided on the Irish side in the achievement of the Anglo-Irish Agreement of 1985. The problem from the chair was that he spoke so fast that it was an agony to keep up, and not miss the pearls, as they fell out amidst the eloquent torrent. As virtually the first item on the agenda on came David Andrews TD, with a motion on the Birmingham Six, then still languishing in prison. David was a Dublin barrister and Fianna Fáil TD from outer Dublin, on the coast, including the desirable Dalkey area. He had informed the press of his efforts on behalf of the Six, but handled it all immaculately, and so much so that our initial rule of having sensitive matters dealt with *in camera* went rapidly out of the window. David was his own man and not always popular with his peers, but with his electorate he amassed formidable majorities. He was left out of the incoming government of his party in 1997, and led from the back-benches the important incoming Irish delegation to London in 1988 that laid foundations for the creation of the Inter-Parliamentary Body. Tall and confident, the talent was there, and he became Foreign Minister in 1991.

Brian Cowen I remember for drinking innumerable cups of coffee in the chamber, but very sharp and quick on the ball over any issue involving our freedom of speech. He led the way to abolishing our *in camera* rule for sensitive matters. From the outset it had become apparent that we did not need it. As for Enda Kenny, he presented as the chief whip he later became. Taciturn, excellent company and loving a good joke, but a listener rather than an extrovert performer. However, nothing passed him by, and his later success proves his obvious ability. My favourite memory of Enda is his appreciation of Peter Brooke's somewhat antique stories. Out would come Peter with something direct from the days of the good Queen Victoria, to be greeted with great guffaws from Enda, and for that matter the rest of us.

John Bruton appeared to me as the Irish version of the English country gentleman. In session his great booming voice dominated his audience and made him a daunting prospect to interrupt in mid-flow. Relaxed and friendly, he was all too ready, in and out of office, to listen to people like me and get our views. His period as Taoiseach/Prime Minister was limited by the electability of his coalition government, but he had three years in the post and certainly proved well capable of the office. As I mentioned earlier, my best memory of him was when he presided over the reopening of the Irish National War Memorial at Islandbridge, after renovation. He spoke movingly of the sacrifices in both World Wars of his compatriots and not least in the Second, when they joined British regiments as volunteers from a neutral country.

There were many others of note on the Inter-Parliamentary Body. On the British side we had at various times both Tom King and Peter Brooke, former Secretaries of State for Northern Ireland; Alex Salmond, later First Minister of Scotland and doing his best not to be British; and on the wilder side of things Denis Canavan MP, a well-known Labour firebrand from Scotland. He left our Irish members spellbound in Edinburgh, when we took them to see the Castle and the Scottish crown jewels. Standing in the throne room he delivered an impromptu speech, pointing dramatically at the jewels, which was so nationalistic that our Irish friends must have thought how moderate they were in gaining their independence. However, on historical and constitutional matters this Scottish influence was well balanced by the distinguished Irish academic, Senator Dr Maurice Manning, former TD and now Chancellor of the National University of Ireland. As for the continuation of the quality of the Inter-Parliamentary Body, over time we were well served by the appointment of Michael O' Kennedy TD, former Cabinet minister and European Commissioner, who became a distinguished co-chairman in 1997. Similarly from Fine Gael we were well blessed with John Bruton's appointments of Paul Bradford TD as my agreeable co-chairman from 1994 to 1997 and Charlie Flanagan TD, who rose to become Minister for Foreign Affairs and Trade under Enda Kenny.

Our lighter side was well served by our perennial European flag debate. This was always moved by Hugh Dykes MP, now Lord Dykes, veteran

European of the House of Commons and chairman of the European Movement in the UK, who felt it his duty to assert that we should meet under a fluttering European flag, in addition to our national flags. This caused horror and fury in the ranks of the Tory right, as we were in the midst of the divisive Maastricht debates.

The more serious side was always there. In 1994, at our meeting in Bath, Patrick Mayhew, then Northern Ireland Secretary, came to address us and was with us for the better part of two days. He took questions and out of the blue came the old and mutually sensitive question of the burning down of the British Embassy in Dublin in 1972. One of our members was Des O'Malley TD, ex-Fianna Fáil and later founding father and leader of the Progressive Democrats, who was Minister of Justice at the fatal time. There was a tense exchange as to what the Irish government did to ameliorate or prevent the situation. Mayhew stood up to it but I don't think he expected to have to deal with the still raw feelings around that sad event. However, that was what our Inter-Parliamentary Body was for.

From the outset, our first and foremost woman was Nora Owen TD, of Fine Gael, who went on to become Justice Minister under John Bruton. As a local government member, in addition to her work at the Dáil, she got considerable credit for exposing a cosy deal on land owned for profitable development by none other than Charlie Haughey. The problem was that all sorts of public utilities were laid down before there was full planning permission. An *Irish Times* cartoon of the time featured a field in which various pipes and cables ended up in a quite empty space at the centre.

Westminster attitudes

Attitudes towards the Irish within the House of Commons varied enormously. This made the peace process much more tortuous than it need have been. Put broadly the Conservative Party was known as the 'Conservative and Unionist Party' and even the 'Unionist Party' for a period after the Liberal Unionists came over to the Conservatives at the turn of the twentieth century. Ireland had been ruled by a succession of Tory or Whig/Liberal grandees for many years and they had left their mark on Irish history. During the 1990s I often entertained the Inter-Parliamentary Body Steering Committee, at London meetings, in the Carlton Club. On the first such occasion the Irish members were all grouped together at one end of the room and I made some joke about them being unsociable. Peter Barry immediately replied: 'It's not you. It's them we don't like!', pointing to the Tory grandees who in all their glory were hanging from the walls of the room.

All this helped to add some historical colour to our relationship and we could make a joke of such things as at the Cavalry and Guards Club on Piccadilly. Those familiar with this splendid club will know that much of the wall of a bar and reception area is or was taken up with a formidable painting of a cavalry charge during the Crimean War. It comes straight at the viewer with swords outstretched and is enough to give any pacifist a nightmare. Some fragile diplomat in the Irish Embassy told the Foreign Office that it might be too much for his apparently sensitive members. This came straight to me and I had a quiet word with my Irish co-chairman. He could not understand what they were fussing about and when we all arrived and had a drink in the face of this cavalry charge, with a later dinner in the similarly decorated Waterloo Room, it drew nothing but admiration from our Irish guests, who included a Sinn Féin member. Since independence the Irish may have been officially neutral but their fighting spirit remains undaunted.

For much of the nineteenth century it was the Conservative Party which repeatedly played the 'Orange card' and stifled Gladstone's attempts to establish Home Rule, thus facilitating the eventual exit of Ireland from the United Kingdom. These attitudes remained with traditional Conservatives, who in many cases were one and the same as the Euro-sceptics who gave John Major's administration such a hard time. In this context John Major was brave to take up the issue and to carry it on, both overtly and covertly, as best he could, given his reducing parliamentary majority. That said, his government and their

Unionist allies very nearly broke the peace process, and might well have done so had it not been for the constant support of the Labour opposition and the Liberal Party. Major himself acknowledged this in an interview with Lord Hennessy (BBC Radio 4, 13 August 2014), when he said he was never able to feel sure of his party or even his Cabinet on the issue. It is both significant and generous that Labour never blamed Major for the near-debacle of the process, which, thanks to Tony Blair, was brilliantly recovered and led to the renewal of the IRA ceasefire in 1997.

Labour was very different over Irish matters. They had no Unionist traditions as a party, with many more MPs of Irish descent, plus Scottish Catholics with close Irish connections. This led them to sympathise with the Irish much more readily than did their Conservative counterparts. One interesting illustration of this occurred during our early efforts to get the Parliamentary Body off the ground. The BBC in association with RTÉ made a mainstream half-hour programme on efforts being made for peace, with particular reference to our parliamentary side. It was a good programme, filmed in Dublin, and many MPs remarked on it to me and were very complimentary. My problem was that they were nearly all Labour and Liberal MPs. I hardly got a word of encouragement from the powers that be on my side, and even some resentment from a few for stirring it up and making life with the Unionists more difficult. On the Labour side it could not have been more different. One evening in the Commons, as I emerged from the Conservative Lobby after a vote, the leader of the Labour Party, Neil Kinnock, coming in to vote on the other side, came over to me specially to wish me well. His sincerity was obvious.

As for the Liberal Democrats, the history of the Liberal Party over many years in trying to settle the Irish question meant they could not have been more supportive. The irony was that the weakest link, the Conservatives under John Major, triggered the final stage of the peace process without the party support or government majority to sustain it. One might ask why, with a large overall majority for the peace process, it could not have proceeded with all-party support. Sadly parliamentary democracy under our system makes the obvious very difficult. For a weak government to be seen governing by leave of the opposition is potentially fatal for both the government and party concerned. It was not on under conventional circumstances. John Major, for better or worse, decided not to be exceptional.

Eleven
POLITICAL DIFFICULTIES

This is not the time for soundbites. I can feel the hand of history on our shoulder.

Tony Blair on Northern Ireland peace talks, *Daily Telegraph*,
8 April 1998

Introduction

T he Troubles beginning in the late 1960s led to continuous efforts by many to establish the necessary structures for peace. The first major breakthrough was the Sunningdale Agreement of 1973, between the Conservative government of Edward Heath and the Fine Gael/Labour Coalition government of Liam Cosgrave, with Garret Fitzgerald as Foreign Minister. From there on in, and through to the Anglo-Irish Agreement of 1985, Garret Fitzgerald played a central role on the Irish side, first as Foreign Minister, responsible directly, under the Taoiseach, for Northern Ireland, and later as Taoiseach himself. Sunningdale was the first success story but collapsed in 1975 under the second Harold Wilson government, which had not the will or inclination to stand up to the quite ruthless strikes by Protestant workers in Northern Ireland. However, the work went on in the two Cabinet Offices, and in particular by the two men who came to head them, namely Sir Robert Armstrong and Dermot Nally. They and other officials, and here I might mention Sir David Goodall of the FCO and our Cabinet Office, were a tremendous influence for good over many years. Without them the Anglo-Irish Agreement would have been even more difficult and vulnerable than it was. The negotiations for the Anglo-Irish Agreement of 1985 were intensely difficult, and at every stage it was the initial negotiations between Sir Robert and Dermot Nally that formed the foundation for later ministerial negotiation and agreement. Without good ministers on both sides, senior civil servants mainly in the two Cabinet Offices and many dedicated people in support, the story could have been different.

Also very relevant are the Secret Intelligence Services (SIS), who kept it all going through good times and bad. After the Troubles began in the late 1960s it did not take long before back channels were opened to the Provisional IRA via SIS operator Frank Steele, an old colonial hand. This led to the meeting in London of Secretary of State Willie Whitelaw with PIRA leaders, including the young Martin McGuinness, in 1972. Steele retired and was replaced by another SIS man, in preference to a straight MI5 operative, namely Michael Oatley, who served continuously, if intermittently according to demand and opportunity, between May 1973 and 1991. He was known in PIRA circles as 'the mountain climber' and his contribution was outstanding. Whatever has to be said publicly, governments and those opposing them need these channels if they are to deliver peace. Michael Oatley retained his concern for peace on the island of Ireland after he retired, and when the Parliamentary Body was up and running, he came to see me. I found him, what he had to say and the encouragement he gave very valuable indeed.

The relationship between the two governments was crucial. Steadily the blocks of an eventual settlement were put in place and governments delivered, including the Thatcher and Major governments. Sunningdale was a good try; contacts did not lapse and Fianna Fáil continued the process with the Joint Studies Report of 1981; then comes the Anglo-Irish Agreement of 1985, after which we were into serious business. Important groundwork to follow it up was accomplished by Secretary of State Peter Brooke, who has received too little credit for getting the last stages of the process under way. In 1991 he made it clear that the United Kingdom had no 'selfish, strategic or economic interest in Northern Ireland'. This became the fundamental statement to establish our credibility with our partners in the Republic of Ireland, and was repeated in the Downing Street Declaration of 1993. These few simple words played an important part in getting it all under way. The Declaration continued the peace process by making the considerable commitment from the Irish that there would be no united Ireland without the consent of the people of Northern Ireland. This went against the Irish Constitution, which enshrined the right of the people of Ireland to exist in one united country, Unionists or no Unionists. However, as the process develops, while the British could deliver on agreements and declarations, it was not so easy for them to do what logically followed. This was filling in the details, or quite simply negotiating with the Provisional IRA and keeping the Unionists on side at the same time. They were seriously needed to sustain Major's disappearing parliamentary majority and this was the fundamental British problem. The Irish one, epitomised by the formidable efforts of Albert Reynolds, the Taoiseach, was to keep some appearance of progress going, so as not to lose the momentum vital for success. Albert Reynolds was Taoiseach from 1992 to 1994, when his coalition government unexpectedly fell apart over the appointment of his Attorney-General as President of the Supreme Court, having been involved in a controversial extradition matter concerning an alleged paedophile priest. As a previous Finance Minister he had met John Major at various ministerial meetings and the two got on well together. This helped and Albert did his utmost to keep the process alive and well, whilst Major was hidebound by his difficulties at Westminster. Without the British government and the Unionists, it was *Hamlet* without the Prince, but Albert did as much as anyone could. Amidst constant activity he opened public and private discussions with the Northern Ireland political parties and not least Sinn Féin, entertained John Hume and Gerry Adams together in Dublin and began the setting up, with all-party consent, of the Forum for Peace and Reconciliation at Dublin Castle. He deserves much credit for the eventual outcome.

The fundamental problem

I became close to most of the main players on the Irish side of things, but had difficulties with the British side. The closer I was to the Irish, the more difficult it all became with the British Conservative Party and with the Conservative government. They found my proximity to the Irish of no help in their tactics of delay to placate the Unionists.

In 1992 John Major was, surprisingly, elected, but with a small majority. Great and controversial projects need a strong majority to sustain them. Major, coming to power in his own right, was advised that now was the time to have a serious push towards peace on the island of Ireland. He started off this last stage of the endeavour in earnest, but underestimating the parliamentary perils ahead. As his party tore itself apart over Europe, he became more and more dependent on Unionist votes to sustain him in office. This made the maintenance of the peace process appallingly difficult.

To have it both ways, which meant displaying good intentions, but without delivery on those intentions, could only last so long. The fact that the process under Major lasted as long as it did was a tribute to the many on both sides of the Irish Sea who wanted it to work. Major had to keep the Irish happy and the process alive, but also had to look after his diminishing UK parliamentary base. This was a virtually impossible double act to keep up for long. As soon as there was progress, particularly on the Irish/Sinn Féin side, which is what it should have been about, there was a frantic effort on the British side to modify the impact or simply to play for time. This was necessary to keep their Unionist allies, together with their sympathisers within the Conservative Party, on board to provide the government's majority. An early example came just before the Downing Street Declaration of 1993, when Patrick Mayhew, Secretary of State, made it clear in the Commons that the role of the British government was not to persuade the parties but rather to facilitate, encourage and effectively to retire into the position of being a referee. Given the history of Britain as the major player on this issue, this was insufficient. After the Downing Street

Declaration I attended a lunch at the Irish Embassy and did a joint broadcast with Albert Reynolds, when this obvious question was put first to me. To keep the answer within the bounds of reason I said that our involvement in the peace process made us all, whatever else was said, 'Persuaders for Peace'. Albert followed me with support for the phrase, and later used it himself in a speech in Dublin Castle, and which he kindly attributed to me. It became part of Irish policy.

Enter IRA/Sinn Féin

During 1993 and 1994 intense contact continued between the British government and the IRA through intermediaries, as well as a profound dialogue which took place between John Hume and Gerry Adams. Throughout the peace process John Hume was in the thick of it, engaged, as was Albert Reynolds, in keeping up the momentum. A warm and emotional man, he gave his all in the cause of peace. At this time there was still considerable violence, which included the huge Bishopsgate bomb in 1993 and a mortar attack on Heathrow in 1994, but then suddenly an IRA truce was declared over Easter 1994. Then came the most dramatic event thus far. On 31 August 1994 came the IRA statement announcing the first ceasefire. This really put the British government, with its narrow majority, on the spot. Until then what had been going on involved talks and contacts, common aspirations and the important Downing Street Declaration of the two governments. But until the IRA/Sinn Féin came on board as a public part of the process, we were dealing with governmental agreements and aspirations: in essence roadmaps, but not involving any traffic. Now suddenly all this changed and along came the first fruits of what it was all about. Once the IRA responded and called a ceasefire, the ball not only landed in John Major's court, it positively left a crater in it. I often wonder, when John Major was advised to launch the peace process as his initiative, how deeply he had thought through the prospects of success. For the sake of his majority he had struggled nobly to keep all the balls in the air, but now they had started to land.

What a time it was. The Conservative Party was busy tearing itself apart over Europe, with the Maastricht debates in full and perpetual flow. The Unionists were playing the situation to their advantage and being very difficult about any moves in Northern Ireland which involved progress with IRA/Sinn Féin. They were supported by some twenty to thirty Conservative MPs who were mainly the same people who, as Euro-sceptics, were causing such trouble over Europe. They maintained good relations with David Trimble and saw the party as very much the 'Conservative AND Unionist Party'. At a private ministerial briefing I attended, with both Secretary of State Patrick Mayhew and his Minister of State Michael Ancram in attendance, several members became somewhat over-excited and 'throwing their gauntlets on the floor', declared to the ministers that if David Trimble was not happy with the situation, then they were not happy either. This reflected the extreme end of the Unionist tendency within the Conservative Party, and in a tight situation of a virtual minority government, all votes were vital. The government itself did little to resist all these pressures and at no time offered strong leadership. Some thought that a little more firmness could have limited internal dissent but that was not to be.

The British play for time

The British government's reaction to the ceasefire was to conduct a tactical retreat, while lobbing all sorts of questions at the IRA to play for time. The IRA statement made it clear that as of midnight of 31 August 1994, 'there will be a complete cessation of military operations'. It further said: 'We believe that an opportunity to secure a just and lasting settlement has been created' and later 'a solution will only be found as a result of inclusive negotiations [...] in our desire to significantly contribute to the creation of a climate which will encourage this, we urge everybody to approach this new situation with determination and patience.' There should have been no doubt at the time, let alone since, that this ceasefire was genuine and represented a momentous development in historical terms. The fact that it

193

lasted for over sixteen months, with little or no progress from the British side to show for it, was good proof of this. As for the Irish government, they made every effort to preserve momentum and keep the peace process alive, while the British government was doing exactly the opposite. The British chose to ignore the fundamental point that a ceasefire is only a ceasefire. It is not an agreed armistice, and certainly not any form of surrender or by definition permanent. The guns fell silent so that the talking could begin. Sadly, and because of the British, it did not.

We can begin with the reactions of John Major and his Secretary of State, Patrick Mayhew, on the evening of the ceasefire announcement itself, 31 August. John Major appeared uneasy and even surprised, as did his Secretary of State. There was no warmth of welcome, bearing in mind the obvious difficulties the Republicans would have had to get sufficient consent on their side to make the statement in the first place. There was no effort from the outset to focus the public mind on the realities of what had occurred, namely that we had a ceasefire per se and an opportunity to talk about terms for peace. Instead we had the first obstacle created to slow down this new vehicle for possible peace. This was: 'We welcome it, but is it permanent?' This was unreal, as manifestly, and by definition, a ceasefire is not permanent. It is an opportunity and an invitation to talk about peace, no more and no less.

I went on the *Today* programme the next morning, to find a barrage of doubt and objection from Unionists in Northern Ireland. As I said on the programme, and John Humphrys repeated the phrase in questions to others later, it was almost as if 'they were afraid of peace'. The British government did little or nothing to alleviate these fears, or show any kind of leadership. Rather they continued to ask the question 'Is it permanent?' for a full six months, without entering any formal negotiations to find out. Encouraged by the Irish government, the IRA/Sinn Féin side made it clear that the statement was 'unconditional and open-ended'. Martin McGuinness said it represented the opportunity for the 'end of violence in all circumstances' and Gerry Adams even said that the Nationalist leader John Hume's assumption that 'it was permanent' was correct. All to no avail.

Soon after the ceasefire, the Taoiseach, Albert Reynolds, received John Hume and Gerry Adams at government Buildings in Dublin and emerged onto the courtyard for a historic photograph. Both Adams and Hume came up with the phrase that they were 'all totally committed to democratic and peaceful methods of resolving our political problems'. This was important as it brought them within the Downing Street Declaration, to which the British government was a party. Again to no avail.

The Forum for Peace and Reconciliation

Positively one of the best things the Irish government did to maintain momentum was to establish the 'Forum for Peace and Reconciliation' on 28 October 1994. It met regularly at Dublin Castle. This was intended to bring Sinn Féin into the fold and succeeded in doing so. As ever the Unionists refused to attend, and called it 'just another talking-shop'. The British government appeared tormented in its reaction, and could not even agree to send its Ambassador, or a representative, to the opening ceremony. British representation was left entirely to the British–Irish Inter-Parliamentary Body, which was outside government control, and as co-chairman I had a permanent seat on the Forum. This kept me in close touch with all the players on the Irish side, most of whom I knew personally and was on good terms with. This came in very handy. The Irish government played a full part, as did the Nationalists and many other organisations from Northern Ireland. As for Sinn Féin, they fielded a full delegation, played a very constructive part in the proceedings and clearly were ready for wider democratic participation.

While all this went on, the British were rendered ineffective by their political difficulties. The overwhelming reality was that the response to the IRA had to be delivered by the British government, who were the other party to the prospective peace. Movement had to be from them, with the Unionists, towards the Irish and the Nationalists. The inability of the Major government to deliver this meant that the peace process was flawed at its core. For six months after the ceasefire the British government prevaricated over whether the ceasefire was permanent. This stance eventually became too hard to sustain, and John Major, in his wisdom, decided at last that he would make a 'working assumption' that it was permanent. However, another obstacle was immediately set up in the form of 'Decommissioning'. In the face of a real offer to talk about permanent peace, all this made it hard for the Republicans to sustain the process. There had still been no start to formal negotiations, and at last the Clinton Administration responded to appeals from the Irish government and others and began actively pushing for some progress. The American Ambassador in Dublin was no less a figure than Jean Kennedy Smith. She had the ear of the President and was a natural ally for the Irish.

Enter the Americans

In May 1995 there was an economic conference in Washington which Gerry Adams on the one hand and British ministers on the other were due to attend. The British had to come up with something and this they did by refining the decommissioning argument and their requirements in relation to it. They now defined this as a willingness by the PIRA to disarm progressively; a common practical understanding of the modalities of decommissioning; and the actual decommissioning of some arms as a tangible confidence-building measure and to signal the start of a process. From behind this shield of rectitude, and still not having talked officially to IRA/Sinn Féin as a result of the ceasefire, the British government surveyed their adversaries, who could not possibly deliver on decommissioning without some actual negotiation. They gained time, plus something to say to the Americans; the support of the Unionists for Major's government was preserved.

Throughout this period I had good relations with the Americans in Dublin and social contact with their Ambassador Jean Kennedy Smith, sister of the late President Kennedy. The Americans were marvellous in keeping things moving with a bit of appropriate pressure, and their role throughout the peace process deserves nothing but credit. Indeed they kept it up right to the end to ensure the completion of the Belfast Good Friday Agreement of 1998. One of the worst examples of the British atti-tude, in trying to keep the Unionists happy at all costs, occurred over the attendance of Gerry Adams at an economic conference which was to be held under the auspices of the White House. The battle of Gerry Adams's visa ensued, with Jean Kennedy Smith having recommended that it be granted. From the British point of view to oppose this was bad politics. The British Embassy in Washington was placed in the invidious position of having to pull whatever strings it could find to get the visa refused. This was trying to resist the inevitable, which should have been seen as the lost cause it was from the outset. The unfortunate Michael Mates MP, by then an ex-Northern Ireland Minister, was dispatched from London to go over to New York and broadcast with Gerry Adams from there. A spe-cial *Newsnight* programme was made and beamed back to London for UK consumption. The whole thing was almost totally unwatched in the United States, made the British government look petty and did not help our relations with the White House.

During the first half of 1995 talks about talks took place at the offi-cial level with Sinn Féin, but these never got to the actual issues involved at all. Apart from an arranged 'encounter' between Secretary of State Mayhew and Gerry Adams in the margins of the White House confer-ence, there was no ministerial contact at all. By July it was nearly a year since the ceasefire announcement, and as far as the IRA were concerned they had nothing at all to show for it. It was fast becoming a question of how long this fragile ceasefire could last.

The messenger

In mid-July I attended a Friday meeting of the Forum for Peace and Reconciliation at Dublin Castle and found myself in considerable demand. Something important was being discussed and everyone who was anyone in Irish politics was present. I first got called out of the cham-ber for a private meeting with the then Taoiseach, John Bruton, who voiced his serious concerns about the lack of progress on the British side. He spoke very deliberately and said that unless the whole thing gathered momentum the ceasefire would collapse. He had obviously considered the matter very seriously and meant every word that he said. Would I please take the message back and say it loud and clear?

No sooner had I returned and sat down, than I was again called out and had a long private talk with the Irish Foreign Minister, Dick Spring, whom I had known well for some years through the Inter-Parliamentary Body. We walked slowly through the gallery of the castle, and settled ourselves alone on a large antique settee in a deserted throne room. The same message came through: the British had to act or it was all over. As for the IRA's timing of a resumption of violence, he considered that they would want to be sure that the negative situation would not change. So he thought the visit of President Clinton to the UK and Ireland in the autumn would delay a recurrence of violence, and after that the publication of the Mitchell Report in the New Year could delay it further. No action in response to either from the British government would cause the PIRA to register their frustration by some act of violence. The situation was therefore very urgent and the establishment of some momentum in the peace process was critically necessary. In the light of subsequent events all this was sadly and accurately prophetic

I next saw John Hume, who was at a very low ebb about the future for similar reasons. For a man who had driven himself to the point of exhaustion to get the peace process under way his unhappiness was manifest. I then met with Bertie Ahern, opposition leader and later Taoiseach, and his principal adviser, Martin Mansergh, both well known to me. Again they did not mince their words, and asked me to take back a strong message to John Major as to the seriousness of the situation. Ahern served as Taoiseach from 1997 until 2008, and played a leading part, in close partnership with Tony Blair, in delivering the peace process and the Belfast Agreement. We have a lot to thank him for. As for Martin Mansergh, one could not ask for a sounder or more loyal political adviser. He served Albert Reynolds and Bertie Ahern in that capacity and was intimately connected to all stages of the peace process up to and beyond the Belfast Agreement. When Albert

Reynolds went out of office in 1994 he was offered his job back serving John Bruton, but politely declined and continued with Bertie Ahern as leader of the opposition until 1997, when he went back into government and his old post. Like other officials, such as Dermot Nally, he is one of the comparatively unsung heroes of the Process.

Adams and McGuinness

All this left one key element outstanding, and sure enough I received a request that afternoon to meet Gerry Adams and Martin McGuinness in the Sinn Féin offices at the Forum. I had met both of them individually on various previous occasions, but it was interesting to meet them privately and at the same time. Adams did most of the talking and gave the impression of being in charge, although McGuinness listened very carefully and made very relevant interjections at appropriate moments. The two of them appeared in complete harmony, and there was absolutely no tension evident between them. Their simple message was that the ceasefire would not hold for much longer and there was absolutely nothing they could do to keep it in place without real progress. We even discussed the weakening of their own position, and I queried at one point the possibility of one or other of them being in some form of physical danger. Adams replied immediately that they had chosen to do what they did, and how they lived, and therefore they had to abide by the rules and customs of their situation. He said it with considerable dignity, with McGuinness concurring, and it made quite an impression on me at the time.

Rejection by the British government

I wondered how best I should feed all this through to John Major. He knew well my interest in Ireland, and close relationship with many Irish politicians, but he saw me, as most of the Conservative Party did, as being 'too Green for comfort'. I decided to set everything out in writing for him, listing the people I had seen, what they said and so on. I then sent it through to Number 10, expressing a willingness to come and see him about it. Bearing in mind the importance of the messages I was carrying, I fully expected that he would want to see me about it. That was not to be. A personal but bland reply came back, thanking me for what I had said and telling me that Michael Ancram, then Minister of State in the Northern Ireland Office, would be in touch to arrange a meeting with me. He would then take me through 'the Policy'. That was all I heard from him, and like everything else it seemed that I was to be stalled, and the pleas of virtually all the main players on the Irish side were to be ignored, as were the dangers involved in the overall situation. It is therefore quite wrong to say, as some have, that the British government had no warning of the recurrence of violence that was just around the corner. I am sure I was not the only means through which the Irish gave warning. Indeed I had been given chapter and verse, even as to probable timing, which proved accurate, and all was ignored. The fact has to be that Major gambled that he could hold the situation until the General Election and at least stay in government, with his party intact, until then. Thereafter he must have realised that four terms of power were about the democratic limit, and he could then pass the mantle on to Tony Blair, who, unencumbered by the Unionists, could complete the job.

Michael Ancram's office duly arranged the meeting and we had a friendly but excruciating discussion for an hour or so with both of us well aware that this was just an exercise. I left the Northern Ireland Office even more aware than I was before that, other than playing for time, the government had no immediate 'Policy'.

Violence inevitable

The final months of the ceasefire were played out with awesome predictability and followed precisely Dick Spring's forecast of events expressed to me at Dublin Castle the previous July. President Clinton's visit came and went and was a great success in Britain and Ireland alike. As for the Mitchell Report, it was presented in Belfast on 24 January 1996 and made it quite clear that the decommissioning of arms before negotiations was never on offer, was not on, and had it been demanded before the ceasefire, there would have been no ceasefire. A process for negotiations to proceed was suggested and, had the British government so wished, the whole process could have got under way at last.

John Major once more played for time, and in the direction of the Unionists, by extracting the somewhat obscure Paragraph 56 from the report, which said that in certain circumstances 'an elective process could contribute to the building of confidence'. Northern Ireland was to be destined to have an election to create a constitutional body, out of which, at some future stage, would hopefully come negotiations with Sinn Féin. The Unionists liked this as it gave them a better control of the situation. In fact it was a recipe for another delay of some length and which would have got Major beyond the approaching election. This was not on from the Republican point of view. IRA/Sinn Féin wanted no more delay and least of all some remote elections, which could eventually lead to negotiations they considered they should already be having anyway. They were also primarily and obviously interested in talking to British government ministers and not directly to Unionists. Had there been a constructive reply to the Mitchell Report I have no doubt that the Canary Wharf bomb would have been aborted. As it was the wretched bomb duly blew on Friday, 9 February 1996. Violence had resumed as anticipated and with a vengeance.

Enter Tony Blair and a Labour government

All that could be done now was to await the probability of a Labour government under Tony Blair. Mo Mowlem took over as Shadow Northern Ireland Secretary in early 1996. We had always got on well and from an early stage she chose to consult me, as co-chairman of the Inter-Parliamentary Body, usually involving meetings in her office over a cup of tea. She was refreshingly non-partisan in her approach, open and inclusive. Compared to my own party I found this very welcome indeed. I was also on close terms with Clive Soley, then chairman of the Northern Ireland Select Committee, later chairman of the PLP, and now a colleague in the House of Lords. In May 1996, both he and Mo asked me if I would be prepared to participate in a private briefing afternoon Tony Blair was holding in his Commons office as leader of the opposition. I agreed and was given a half-hour slot, with others such as John Hume given similar individual slots. Both Mo and Clive also attended. From the outset the meeting was relaxed and constructive, and at the time I was quite struck by a leader who sat back, listened and questioned, rather than having to battle through the constant interruptions of Mrs Thatcher.

What he was most interested to hear about from me concerned the situation over Ireland within the Conservative Party. What were the chances were of Conservative co-operation in a bipartisan policy under a Labour government and, most particularly, if that government had a small majority? I told him that interest in Northern Ireland on the Conservative side was limited, and tended to be dominated by a few who had strong Unionist sympathies. I thought that the Conservative Party in opposition to a Labour government with a small majority could not be trusted and certainly could not be relied upon. They were so divided in government that in opposition they were unpredictable and unlikely to be rational. It amused me at the time that the Labour Party, having been out of power for so long, could not see themselves back in power with other than a small majority. As we now know the eventual majority was of astronomic proportions and gave them the backing and power to act decisively. The Unionists could be firmly dealt with. At the end of the meeting I asked Tony Blair whether, in addition to his bipartisan policy of supporting Major's Northern Irish initiative, he had at any stage offered to help Major out over Northern Ireland, should he be in real difficulty with his party and the Unionists in carrying matters forward. He said he had done so, and his offer was politely received but he heard no more about it. Such things seem like common sense, but, as stated, for Major, weak enough already, to be seen as governing, albeit in the national interest, with the help of Labour, at the end of a long period in power, would have had effects way beyond Ireland. It could have split his party and ended his government. It was a risky and perilous course, which he chose not to take. Perhaps he could hold on until the General Election without a resumption of violence. As he had been warned, that was a vain hope.

Twelve

TONY BLAIR AND THE
BELFAST AGREEMENT

After the General Election of 1997 we were free to make progress. This time, we had a strong and committed prime minister and government with a large majority. It is unnecessary to go over the detailed negotiations that followed which are well set out in Jonathan Powell's book, *Great Hatred, Little Room* (Bodley Head, 2008). Once in power Tony Blair wisely chose to keep control of Northern Ireland firmly in Number 10. This had to be done, as the Northern Ireland Office had too many Unionist sympathisers within it and traditionally leaked like a sieve. This had always been a problem, and throughout the troubles repeated efforts had to be made by the Westminster departments, particularly the FCO, to oversee matters. Tight control by Number 10 directly was the most effective thing, particularly over the delicate negotiations that now had to take place. So Jonathan Powell, ex-FCO and Tony Blair's Political Secretary in opposition and throughout his period of government, was put in charge of the detail under the direct control of his prime minister. In the longer term this added to the cumulative strain upon Mo Mowlem.

From the outset the day-to-day conduct of affairs was in her hands, and she was a breath of fresh air for Northern Ireland and an excellent appointment. At the time she took over in government it was also necessary to give the Nationalist side confidence after their frustrations with the Conservatives, and this she soon accomplished. She was close to Number 10 and to the Prime Minister. She made a change, and the Unionists realised they had something different to deal with. She was bold, brazen and unhesitating in doing what she considered the best thing for peace. That included a brave visit to the IRA prisoners in the Maze, which quite took them by surprise. For the Unionists, dealing with Mo, who took her medically necessary wig off in their presence and was capable of colourful language, was a little too much. They then intimated that they would not talk to her and wanted to deal with Number 10 directly. Enter Jonathan Powell. This was not easy for Mo or anyone, but it was a decision Blair had to take for the sake of the peace process. As for the Unionists, they used to joke that during talks they would send Mo out to make the tea (John Taylor, Deputy Leader Ulster Unionists, to me, 1998), which summed up the attitude.

As for Mo Mowlem herself, sadly she was diagnosed with cancer at the very time that Labour took power in 1997. At the beginning she managed, but it was all too clear that it was a great strain on her. Her husband supported her as much as anyone could, but her strength was waning and she would on occasion run out of steam at Irish Embassy dinners and so forth. After doing so much she eventually had to be moved. This was not just on health grounds, but also because having rung the changes in Northern Ireland, it was necessary to have someone who could relate better to the Unionists. Initially she was not prepared to go, and as one of the most popular figures in the Labour government expected a job to match, but had not the health to endure it. She eventually went to the Cabinet Office.

I first got to know Mo when she was a junior Shadow Minister in the Northern Ireland Office in 1989. By the time she was appointed Shadow Secretary in 1994 I was the established British co-chairman of the Inter-Parliamentary Body, and she sought me out and suggested a chat. This led on to various such talks and of course the meeting with Tony Blair already mentioned. She was a natural and fun to be with, but on the many practical matters she had to deal with, and also in formulating her likely policy when in government, she was straight, thorough and down to earth. Once Secretary of State she took me out of a reception to an adjacent room and suggested that I should put myself forward for the chairmanship of the Northern Ireland Select Committee, which was an opposition position. This I did, but was promptly vetoed by my own whips, as described elsewhere. Throughout my long passage into the Labour Party we kept on close terms. She knew it was a difficult time for me and, quite unprompted, she made a point of occasionally phoning to speak to me or my wife and ask how I was. Similarly her Political Adviser, Anna Healy, now Baroness Healy of Primrose Hill, could not have been more understanding. My last official contact with Mo was when the government whips asked us both to greet a nervous Shaun Woodward on his arrival at the Commons after defecting to Labour. She was not enamoured with our task but put duty first. We all miss her. She was one of the best.

Peter Mandelson then took over her role, knowing that he had to make it up to the Unionists. He did this so well that the Nationalists got unhappy, but he kept the show on the road, with Number 10 always there, which must have frustrated him. Sadly he got into yet another difficulty over the Hinduja passport issue in January 2001 and for the second time was obliged to resign Cabinet office. A succession of Secretaries of State followed, all carefully chosen and working in close harmony with Number 10. As negotiations followed negotiations, John Reid was followed by Paul Murphy, with Peter Hain coming in for the finale in May 2007. It is worth considering the timescale involved with the whole thing. Decommissioning was not finally delivered until September 2006. Final agreement on institutions and power sharing was achieved in May 2007. This was a full twenty-two years after the Anglo-Irish Agreement of 1985, and nine years after the Belfast Agreement of 1998. It was a road of hard work and constant frustration for all concerned, maddening at times, and a tribute to all who had the stamina to stay the course. Some did not politically survive, at least at the same level. John Hume and David Trimble won the Nobel Peace Prize, and thoroughly deserved it. John Hume's great contribution had helped blaze the trail, which task he did well, knowing that his party, the SDLP, would thereafter take second place on the nationalist side to Sinn Féin. Similarly David Trimble ended up losing his Westminster seat at Upper Bann to the DUP by a majority of over 5,000. His party was supplanted by the DUP and it was for Ian Paisley to deliver the peace and final agreement. To his credit Paisley did just that, and coming from him and the DUP the whole thing was thus much more solid than it otherwise would have been. Trimble became a Conservative peer in 2006 and Hume is a Freeman of Derry and has numerous honorary US degrees, but strangely neither has received a UK honour appropriate to his service and political sacrifice.

The historical significance of all this effort is very considerable. There are still problems but the worst is surely over. Ireland over hundreds of years has suffered continuous injustice. From Elizabethan invasion to the sword of Cromwell and beyond, the Irish in general, and the Catholics in particular, suffered the repression of the English and eventually of a Protestant ascendancy. At long last the scars of history have been overcome. Wandering around in Dublin, or for that matter in rural Ireland, it is difficult to imagine how awful life had been for many in the not too distant past. In spite of it all we can get on with each other very well indeed, and once more are doing so.

So it was that many factors came together to deliver peace in Northern Ireland, and most major contributors have been mentioned earlier. However, it must be emphasised that Gerry Adams and Martin McGuinness took far more than political risks and showed real courage along the way. Last, but certainly not least, come Tony Blair and his counterpart Bertie Ahern. I don't think any other British prime minister would have given this, however important it was, the priority in time, effort and dedication that Tony Blair did over his entire ten-year premiership. Indeed before, as leader of the opposition, he had decided that something should be done. He, and John Major before him, were greatly helped by successive Taoiseachs: Albert Reynolds, John Bruton and of course Bertie Ahern. Blair fully lived up to the responsibilities of the great office he held and we all have reason to be profoundly grateful to him. From a British perspective the achievement of Tony Blair in Ireland amounts to a lasting tribute to a man of outstanding talent and determination.

Part V

THE ANATOMY OF A DEFECTION

People have to know that we will run from the centre and govern from the centre.

Tony Blair, speech to the Newspaper Society, London,
16 March 1997

The reasonable man adapts himself to the world: the unreasonable one persists in trying to adapt the world to himself. Therefore all progress depends on the unreasonable man.

George Bernard Shaw, *Man and Superman*, 'Maxims for revolutionists', 1903

Part V

THE ANATOMY OF A

DEFECTION

Thirteen

EVENTS AND DISILLUSION

I have never found, in a long experience of politics, that criticism is ever inhibited by ignorance.

Harold Macmillan, *Wall Street Journal*, 13 August 1963

After one of our meetings Alastair Campbell asked me how long the process of leaving my party and joining Labour had been going on. I replied: 'Ever since Margaret Thatcher became Leader of the Conservative Party.' 'My God', he replied, 'slow burn, Peter, slow burn!'

Such comments can represent the basis of the truth. For me Edward Heath, elected in 1965, was the natural leader to bring a less class-conscious Conservative Party up to date. He had all the attributes to lead a modern, progressive, pro-European party but sadly lacked the common touch, that vital ingredient in the new television age, of being attractive to the people he aspired to lead. Had he even been moderately so, he could have won the February 1974 election and consolidated his industrial and domestic reforms and our presence in Europe. There would have been no need to go through the period of 1974–9 which created a need for Mrs Thatcher, who became the leader chosen to deal with the economy, trade union power, privatisation issues and related problems, ignored or postponed for too long.

From the moment she took over, the climate within the Conservative Party began to change. At election after election out went the moderates and in came the Thatcherites. The party steadily became more nationalistic

211

and less European in sympathy. While all this was going on after 1975 for us Conservatives, from 1979 Labour became more and more convulsed by internal crisis and dissension. Thanks to Neil Kinnock, via John Smith, this ended well for Labour with the advent of Tony Blair and New Labour. I then found myself a member of a Conservative Party less and less like the one I joined and a Labour Party travelling strongly in my political direction.

It was a difficult period in which I was actively engaged in the losing cause of moderate and pro-European Conservatism. The internal conflict during the Major years of 1992–7 was soul-destroying and did lasting damage to the party. I was very unhappy. By 1995 the tension for me got worse, for a variety of reasons, including the defection in September 1995 of Alan Howarth, the Conservative MP for Stratford-upon-Avon, to Labour. I was deeply unsettled myself, but I was more exposed on the left of the party than he was, in that I was the chairman, and chief creator, of the Macleod Group, which we named after the late Ian Macleod, the political hero of my generation of progressive and moderate Tory MPs. Our brand of Tory had been steadily shrinking within the Commons since 1974 and comprised, by 1992, the remaining elements of the old, moderate, pro-European Conservative Party. When Alan defected he wrote us a letter which I had to read to a full meeting. The effect of personal loss, and political loss on the issues, came to the fore in the expressions on the faces of our membership, as I continued to read his all-too-appropriate letter in total silence.

I soldiered on under constant media speculation and newspaper pictures of 'the usual suspects' as if on the sheriff's wall in a Western film, along the lines of 'will they defect or won't they?'. In almost everything I said publicly I had to restrain myself. When you get out of step with your party it gets worse and worse, not least because much of it is self-induced in reaction to events. One small example will suffice. Just after Alan left us I had to do a '*Newsnight* Special' from Blackpool on the evening before the 1995 conference began. It was chaired by Peter Snow, and was on the subject of the future direction of the Conservative Party. As ever I was on the left, with John Redwood on the right and the late John Maples in the centre. We put on a show of a unity that just was not there in reality. The next day I was with John Maples at the conference when we found ourselves being congratulated by the right for having kept the lid on our differences. We on the centre-left of the party, including John Maples, who liked to think of ourselves as moderate and gentle Tories, generally tried to do this, but were not generally matched in our benevolence by the Euro-sceptic right. In our case we had to pick and choose when we had to go into internal conflict for the sake of party unity overall. We had no wish to bring the whole house down. The right had no such scruples.

During 1996 it all deteriorated. I had a very unsettling time with the constant party divisions over Europe, but even more so over Ireland. My exposed position on the left of the party caused never-ending pressure from the media. When Senator Mitchell's report on progressing the peace process in Northern Ireland came out in January 1996, as related in my Irish chapters, I attended a private briefing meeting for Conservative MPs conducted by the Secretary of State, Sir Patrick Mayhew, with Michael Ancram, his Minister of State, in attendance. For me it was a difficult meeting and came on top of my earlier experiences with John Major's response to the clear warning I transmitted to him after my meeting in Dublin Castle the previous autumn (see p. 193). Mayhew was dismissive of the Mitchell Report, which was in fact an impressive document, pointing the way ahead to make progress towards peace. Sadly, and as usual, this was in the direction that the Unionists wanted and the meeting was with them in support of their views and position. I was the only person in a room of some twenty to twenty-five MPs to say anything good about it at all. One or two potential allies kept their heads down and I was on my own. Several members present declared outright, even aggressive, Unionist sympathies, and one even said that he would only accept our line if David Trimble agreed with it. I then got openly attacked by the inimitable Nicholas Winterton, who, as his face reddened with self-induced anger, accused me of being the 'Leader of the Nationalists at Westminster'. I suppose he meant those within the Conservative Party who were sympathetic to the Irish cause, but it came out as if he was confusing me with John Hume, the leader of the SDLP.

This was yet another example of the Prime Minister, John Major, having to safeguard his parliamentary position as he played once more to the Unionists. The result was that the government ignored the main recommendations of the Mitchell Report and the resumption of violence was virtually inevitable. It duly came soon after with the Canary Wharf bomb on Friday, 9 February 1996. On Sunday, 11 February I was invited to contribute to a feature for the *Guardian* as to what had happened and why. This I did with various others, to discover that, on the same day, the *Daily Telegraph* had run a leading article with a personal attack on me alleging that I was unfit to be a Conservative and Unionist, note the last two words, MP. Odd quotations were dredged up and my Leominster Conservative Association was indirectly invited to express no confidence in me. In the event they did no such thing.

A few weeks later I went over to Dublin for a long weekend. During it the Irish journalist Frank Connolly did a profile piece on me for the *Sunday Business Post*, which included a detailed section on the course of British party politics over recent years. In explaining how the parties had changed I said that if I had my time again I would not, if it were 1996, automatically be a Conservative and indeed I could even be New Labour. The comparison was with 1958, when I felt that I had little alternative but to follow a family line and be a Conservative. There was no way that I, or many others, felt inclined to join a Socialist and trade union-dominated Labour Party. Tony Blair and a Labour Party heading in a Social Democratic direction, as New Labour, was something else entirely. As for the Liberals in 1958, they were too much on the sidelines of national politics, and anyway the Conservative Party then presented a broad and attractive church, with a progressive and influential One Nation wing.

This led to further attacks in the *Daily Telegraph*. First a front-page piece headed 'Senior Tory supports Blair', followed a few days later by a Diary piece lampooning my white hair and the Trumpers hair tonic they discovered I used. Two old friends, seen as being on different wings of the Conservative Party, tried to help. Norman Fowler, an ex-party chairman, and the late Nick Budgen, a senior Euro-sceptic, wrote a letter to the

Telegraph defending me. The paper held this letter for several days while they procured a letter from another ex-chairman, one Norman Tebbit, and then gave that letter, a much longer one, priority over that of my defenders. They drew attention to these letters with a piece on the front page under the headline: 'Ex-Tory chairmen fall out over MP who supports Blair'.

The next thing, with a timing that often seems to occur in politics, was my constituency AGM. It was not easy, but I retained the support of the great majority of those present in spite of the efforts of a small group, led by a retired naval officer and master in a preparatory school, who did their best to be difficult. Despite this, and with the help of deft handling of the meeting by my constituency chairman, Henry Moore, no vote was even asked for. It was another example of the support I received in difficult times from officers and members of our association. They made it very difficult for me to leave the Conservative Party and it was with a heavy heart that I eventually did so.

My exposure to the media was continuous, but another major adventure occurred in early October, just before the Party Conference. I attended a high table dinner at Wadham College, Oxford, as guest of a Persian friend, Professor Reza Sheikh al-Islami, and it was a great evening. For the second placement another guest, Will Hutton, then editor of the *Observer*, and I were placed on either side of the Warden and unsurprisingly a vigorous discussion started up as to the state and future of the Conservative Party, with every don within earshot listening with rapt attention. In particular we discussed Europe and the Conservative left, and Will Hutton made it clear that his paper was doing something on the Conservative left on Sunday, which was two days away. After the dinner he again mentioned it to me and said afterwards he was trying, as far as he could, to warn me.

The next day Patrick Wintour of the *Observer* telephoned me at home in Hereford and went over the ground with me. I made the same basic point on Europe that I had made to Hutton, namely that the pro-Europeans on the Tory side would be likely to support Labour in power on a key European vote, as indeed the Labour Party rebels had done for us back in 1971. At 11 o'clock that evening I was phoned from London by Justin Powell-Tuck, Director of the Macleod Group, to warn me that the Conservative left and I were the lead story in the *Observer*, concentrating on our support for Labour, and with a picture of myself on the front page to boot. We also managed to get a fax through to Number 10 to tell the PM that he could deny the story, as he was due to go on *Breakfast with Frost* that Sunday morning, which was just before the start of the party conference. Major told me later that he only got the message at the last minute as he was about to get into his car. He then denied the story most effectively and blamed it on Labour. It was in fact an *Observer* effort to help Labour, and destabilise the Conservatives in the week of their conference. My problem was that I had become the fall guy. A lot of media calls came through that Sunday and having told the journalist Tony Bevins how fed up I was with the whole thing, who should call me ten minutes later but Alastair Campbell. He was extremely nice about it and assured me that what had gone into the *Observer* was not a 'Campbell operation' and he appreciated how I must feel about it. I accepted this, even if Labour sources had been used for part of the piece. From my earlier encounter with Will Hutton, it was clearly an *Observer* effort to help Labour by emphasising the divisions within the Tory Party. What riled me was that having been the victim of the right-wing press, on this occasion I had been used as the tool of the left-wing press.

The 1997 General Election was a rather miserable affair as far as I was concerned. It was a campaign in which I increasingly felt I was on the wrong side. I decided to keep my head down in the constituency for this my tenth and last General Election as a candidate. The only exception would have been if John Major had been pressured to reject the objective of a single currency in Europe. To this end a group of us went privately to see the Chancellor, Ken Clarke, and told him that if some crisis should occur over this issue during the campaign, we were ready and willing to air our views on the media. He did not have to say anything, but we wanted him to know we were there and indeed we discreetly let it be known that any caving-in on this issue, would cause the party to publicly split in the middle of a campaign. During this campaign there was enormous pressure on John Major over Europe from the Referendum Party, plus multi-millionaires offering money to the campaign funds of Conservative candidates who publicly declared themselves Euro-sceptics as listed in *The Times* and other newspapers but there was no giving in over the single currency. With that currency in such difficulty subsequently it seems strange that it was so important to us, but at that time it was in a very significant way a central symbolic issue.

During the entire campaign I only 'lost it' once. A quite dreadful Conservative poster appeared featuring Helmut Kohl, with Tony Blair on his knee. I had steadfastly been refusing constant media invitations so as not to rock the boat but I could not let this pass. That morning my whip, Jacqui Lait, phoned to find out how the campaign was going. Regrettably, I exploded at her, not that it was her fault in the least. The rather amusing result was that later that day the phone rang and it was none other than Michael Heseltine. The great man had been wheeled out to calm me down. It was pleasant to hear how much I was needed back at Westminster after the election. To give him his due Michael was frank enough to say that the poster had been his idea. That a pro-European like him should suggest such a thing does give an example of how desperate things must have been getting at the top of the campaign. The result of the election spoke for itself, and I was pleased that my majority of 8,835 was some way better than my Euro-sceptic, and more right wing, neighbours. There was then but a short break before I was off back to Westminster as one of the Conservative survivors of the considerable 1997 Labour victory, and intent on assisting the campaign to make Ken Clarke Leader of the Conservative Party.

Any hope that I had was soon dashed. We went straight into the leadership contest, with me as a member of the Clarke team. The campaign was conducted from the offices of the Macleod Group and Mainstream, which I had set up with Justin Powell-Tuck, our director. We had put together a complete list of the parliamentary party, with each member on a scale of one to five. One denoted a good guy, being One Nation, pro-European, and at the other end five indicated a bad guy, being Euro-sceptic and right wing. It was quite a lesson to look at it, to see how the party had changed over the years. From being tolerant Tories, we had gone to being rather aggressive, self-made, right-wing Thatcherites. Our numbers before the election had been severely culled and what was left was sad to see. It was obvious from the outset that Ken could not win and in the circumstances he did well. Our campaign had its bizarre moments for me, which added to my general political discontent. The first one was the Clarke–Redwood pact at the end of the campaign, which was an exercise in desperate futility and was aptly described on the floor of the House by the Labour MP Rhodri Morgan as something the like of which had never been seen since the Molotov–Ribbentrop Pact of 1939. The second was the sight of Mrs Thatcher arriving at the St Stephen's entrance of the Commons to be greeted by William Hague and his cohorts, and taken into the Tea Room, where in full cry she assailed any available Conservative who might have been seeking quiet teatime refreshment.

Things then went from bad to worse. The reality came home to me that I was far more acceptable to the incoming Labour government than I was to my own side. The chairmanship of two select committees was to be given to the Conservative opposition and I was asked to put myself forward for both of them by Labour ministers rather than by my own side. First George Foulkes, the new Under-Secretary at International Development, and then, more central to my political activities, Mo Mowlem, Secretary for Northern Ireland, took me aside at a party given by the number two at the Irish Embassy, Philip McDonagh, and urged me to go for the chairmanship of the Northern Ireland Select Committee. I was not naive in appreciating why I would be acceptable to Labour, but it was flattering and I decided to go for the Northern Ireland position. I saw the Conservative deputy chief whip, Andrew Mackay, and registered my interest but, polite as he was, it became clear to me that I would not be welcome in that position because of the Unionists.

Word of the possibility of my getting this chairmanship got out, and one or two on the Labour side joked with me that I was not to worry about the Tories as the Labour majority on the committee would vote me in anyway. Needless to say, this thought had not escaped the Conservative Whips' Office. They decided to trump the situation by not nominating me to the committee in the first place so that I could not be a candidate for the chairmanship. All this caused a hiatus while a chairman had to be found who would be acceptable, and that, after delay, turned out to be the admirable Peter Brooke.

So there I was in July 1997 firmly beached within a right-wing Conservative Party and with nowhere to go. I had been offered membership of the Council of Europe via the whips, with the original invitation coming from our opposition leader on that body, David Atkinson MP. It would have kept me out of the way from the whips' point of view, but I had no great wish to spend much of my life in hotel rooms and on aeroplanes, so I refused. That left me to face four years at least under William Hague, and as a member of a party from which I felt alienated. If Ken Clarke had become leader I could have stayed in post with real hope for our future. As it was, I began to seriously consider defection, although I knew it would be a rough ride.

Fourteen
THE BEST-LAID PLANS

Finality is not the language of politics.

Benjamin Disraeli, Commons speech, 1859

The approach road to my defection was made much easier by the many friends I had within the Parliamentary Labour Party. As related in my chapters dealing with Ireland I had regular contact with Mo Mowlem, when Shadow Northern Ireland Secretary, and through her my first direct contact with Tony Blair (see p. 202). After Mrs Thatcher, it was a pleasure, and even surprise, to encounter a leader who did not interrupt, listened and followed up with questions based on what you had said. The encounter also gave me the opportunity of meeting up with Jonathan Powell, Blair's Political Secretary, whom I had already met briefly when he was still at the Washington Embassy, and from where Blair recruited him. Also present at the Blair briefing session was Clive Soley, then the Labour chairman of the Northern Ireland Select Committee. We had much in common over Ireland and kept in close touch during 1996, with, in particular, a series of lunch meetings at the not entirely inappropriate People's Palace at the Royal Festival Hall. I realised that he was quite properly 'marking' me as a possible recruit for Labour, but it was good to have someone like him to talk to from my point of view. I made it clear that I was not coming over, much as I might have liked to. I did air my frustrations, so that after the *Telegraph*

220

episode, Alan Howarth phoned me at home to test the water. At that point there was no way I could make the break. Above all I had to see my Constituency Association through a difficult General Election.

One lunch meeting was set up by Clive Soley, on behalf of Jonathan Powell, in June 1996, which I remember with some amusement. It was essentially to continue the discussion with Tony Blair but to apply it to Europe. In other words could the Conservative Party in opposition be relied upon, in whole or in part, to assist a new Labour government with a narrow majority on key votes over Europe? I had given advice under the same heading over Ireland and now we continued with Europe. Our rather conspiratorial threesome had to meet somewhere private outside Westminster and Clive came up with a small Chinese restaurant in Lisle Street, China Town, and easy to get to. Clive and I met Jonathan there and we secreted ourselves as anonymously as possible on the top floor. I advised that the Conservative Party in defeat, and opposition, was likely to be even more Euro-sceptic and difficult to rely on.

I realised that after the 1997 election, and in the mood described, I was completely at ease with Tony Blair and those around him. I had for example known Alastair Campbell since his journalistic days and various others within and outside government. By the end of July I felt I was coming to some sort of watershed, the agonising had to stop and a decision had to be made. I could not face the prospect of having to obey a Conservative whip which would oblige me to vote against my views and conscience, not only on Europe, but on the constitutional agenda as a whole, possibly including Ireland, not to mention a load of other matters that could come up over the next four years or so. It was a prospect I just could not tolerate. I thought the best course would be to leave the House altogether, return to the law and join the New Labour Party in the hope that I could make some contribution in the public sector along the way. So I made the fateful call to Jonathan Powell and at 10 a.m. precisely I passed through the famous door of Number 10 to be received by Jonathan.

The first Powell meeting

Inside Number 10 is always interesting in itself, as different occupants seem to create their own image. Under Blair it was unusually natural and relaxed. For our meeting we could not find an office. This may seem strange, but the house, for its many duties, is a comparatively small one. We ended up in one of the adjoining drawing-rooms used for receptions. I outlined the situation to Jonathan: I was utterly fed up and wanted out, being minded to leave the Commons but wanting to join the Labour Party from outside the House and to be of some service to it. I was very keen to support the Blair government but I made it clear that I could not face a full-frontal defection within the House of Commons. Jonathan said he would think about it and get back to me, which he did at the beginning of the following week. He asked if I could come over for a private chat with Tony Blair the day before he was due to take off for his Italian holiday. For better or worse I was now involved in a defection process.

The first Blair meeting

Tony Blair at the time worked out of a small sitting-room near the Cabinet Office which had traditionally been used as a waiting-room. Comfortable enough, it was not what I expected, which was the upstairs study where Mrs Thatcher's spirit still lurked. John Major, her successor, tended to avoid it, preferring to work in the somewhat impersonal Cabinet Room. I gather Tony later moved to the study, but at that time he sat in this small room on a settee with a coffee-table in front of him on which sat a dictation machine and one or two personal items. I went in and sat down with Jonathan and after a minute or two in came Tony in his shirt-sleeves, explaining that the place was chaotic as everyone was trying to finish things off before he went on holiday. We had a cup of coffee and talked for thirty to forty minutes. Considering the year Blair had just gone through, he appeared surprisingly fresh, although he said he needed his holiday as the election had 'gone on for ever' and the need, under the British system, for a new government to 'hit the ground running' had given him no let-up at all.

I explained the basic situation, with Jonathan chiming in to the effect that he was trying to find ways to help. I made it clear that on my main interests of Europe and Ireland I would not suffer any strain within his Labour Party. He said some nice things about my efforts in Ireland and we digressed into what had happened to the Labour Party during the 1970s and 1980s. He agreed that things had gone politically wild, but that he had always believed that sense would prevail at the end of the day. I replied that he was lucky to be young enough during those times, but for my part, with the Conservative Party beginning a not dissimilar phase, I had fought the good fight from within for long enough and wanted peace of mind. On this we readily agreed that the Conservative Party had lost its political balance and in this regard he counted himself lucky that he faced William Hague as leader of the opposition rather than Ken Clarke. He said this quite naturally, and it was clear that he had high regard for Clarke. The whole meeting was friendly and relaxed. Jonathan and I agreed to meet up once we all returned to Westminster in early September.

The second Powell meeting

Jonathan telephoned on Tuesday, 9 September and a meeting of the two of us was arranged for 10 a.m. on Friday, 12 September to discuss ways of taking things forward. I was by now a little apprehensive of marching into Number 10 through the front door as things were going past a simple visit and were getting more regular and potentially more serious. So it was agreed that I should come in through the Cabinet Office with its Whitehall entrance, and a secretary would meet me and take me through the various corridors and security doors, eventually emerging into Number 10. It is a fascinating walk as one passes through part of what remains of the old Tudor Whitehall

Palace with the medieval brickwork vividly contrasting with the more modern additions. I did three such journeys before I again qualified for the front door.

Jonathan and I settled once more in Tony Blair's sitting-room in his absence on a normal Friday, and with the whole place comparatively quiet as a result. The presence of a Prime Minister causes frenetic activity wherever he might be, and his absence from Number 10, in his constituency or wherever, delivers to the staff who remain a deserved opportunity to work in comparative peace. Jonathan concentrated the discussion on where, if I came out of the House of Commons, I would want to go. I didn't want to go to the European Parliament and it was not a runner. The Welsh Assembly was open for me to go for, but with my South Wales Conservative background, and given the tribal nature of Welsh politics, I really felt happier in the Commons, whatever the circumstances. In any event if I went back to the law, being both a qualified barrister and solicitor, I'd would want to stay in London. The House of Lords came up then, and in other discussions, but always negatively, as we all agreed that to come out of the Commons and into the Lords would give me no credibility at all with the press. One or two fringe things were touched upon such as the soon-to-be-appointed Electoral Reform Commission under Roy Jenkins, which would have been agreeable but something I could almost have done as a Conservative. As we went through the options, it became increasingly clear that I had to make up my mind as to whether I was prepared to face the daunting task of defecting within the House of Commons.

I was due to go away for a week, and we agreed to meet again when I returned, with Jonathan still trying to help on the basis that I was leaving the Commons. The party conference season then took over and Jonathan phoned me during week beginning 13 October, when it was arranged that I would go to Number 10 on Friday, 17 October. It was apparent to me that we were moving towards 'action stations', when it was mentioned that Alastair Campbell would also attend the meeting. I was obviously well aware that I was moving towards decision time and that the heavy cavalry were now approaching to assist the process.

224

Enter Alastair Campbell

The three of us met in the Cabinet Room, and at an early stage Alastair took over the lead role and asked me directly, but nicely, whether a defection over to Labour in the Commons was really not an option, as 'naturally we would love that'. I still admire the direct nature of the question and the frank way it was put. In effect, it brought me round to face up to what I had started, and I replied that it was not now completely out of the question but must depend on having a very good excuse to leave the Conservative Party and cross the floor of the Commons. I had come to terms with it all and the best thing had to be to do the 'Full monty'. I was still cautious as to what I could stand up to within the Commons, and said I could not guarantee how long I would remain in the House, bearing in mind the pressures there, and of course my constituency, where a by-election would be demanded as we were at the beginning of a Parliament. As far as the Commons was concerned, Alastair underlined the fact that I would receive considerable support from the Parliamentary Labour Party, which would make life much easier. As for the constituency, he said that Alan Howarth had found it surprisingly normal after his own defection and from my own experience subsequently I can say that both these observations proved to be correct. Everybody involved in the tribal side of British politics assumes that if you defect then somehow everyone will turn against you, but this is far from the reality of the situation. For my part I had always conducted my representative career on the basis of being there for everyone, and over the years that message got home and for me paid off locally and nationally.

We then got down to the real business, which meant considering the grounds upon which I might defect. Jonathan mentioned the two areas to consider, which were Europe and Ireland, in terms of the Conservative opposition ending any pretence at a bipartisan approach. I entirely agreed with this and we went on to the details of how my defection might be handled. Alan Howarth then came up as the obvious recent example to be considered, although in his case mistakes were made from which I benefited. For Alan, the journalist Anthony Bevins, then with the *Observer*, was sworn to secrecy and brought in to write a tailor-made piece for his newspaper. The defection would then become public news in the mid-evening of the Saturday and Alan would go on *Breakfast with Frost* on the Sunday morning and the *Today* programme on the Monday morning. Alan was to handle the other interviews as they came up. This sounds easy to the uninitiated, but the reality for him was unforeseen in the amount of media attention it generated. Alan had a chaotic few days.

We were now in business and I had committed myself. My mind was settled and a determination to see it through took over. The whole thing had progressed over several months, from wanting to get out and do something for the Labour government outside the Commons to a full-scale defection within the Commons to Labour, for whatever period I chose to remain there. Quite rightly we all agreed that I had to come over on a matter of principle and there could be no question of me being seen as getting anything in return. From my point of view this was paramount, as when the story hit the media, I had to be able to completely deny that I had done any deal for my own benefit. In the result this worked out perfectly, as it was the truth of the matter.

The scene is set

The meeting ended in pleasant mood, with Alastair intending to walk me right through to Whitehall, Jonathan protesting in horror that this could not happen as we would be seen together. So Alastair took me only to the first door of the back route through to Whitehall and, during that brief walk, made a remark that proved to be both perceptive and true. He said that he felt that my reason to defect might come sooner than we all thought.

Indeed it did. On the following Thursday, 23 October, the Conservative Shadow Cabinet met and came up with its policy of Britain not going into a single currency for ten years, which meant that the party would campaign against a single currency at the next General Election. It was an unnecessary policy to burden oneself with in opposition, and those Conservatives who were in favour of a single currency were given a free vote on the issue and the liberty of expressing their views on the subject at any future referendum. This reflected the internal strains of the party, but it gave me my excuse. There was no way I could campaign as a Conservative at the next election on the basis of that policy and supporting a party which would effectively take us out of the centre of power within Europe. Soon after I heard about the decision the Press Association phoned me in the constituency and I came out publicly against the policy. I followed that up with an open letter to my constituency chairman, John Stone, making my position clear.

Alastair Campbell phoned that Friday en route to Scotland, where he was attending Tony Blair's first Commonwealth Heads of government Conference as prime minister. We agreed that I had my grounds to move and the only condition I made was that I needed to be happy with the statement Gordon Brown as Chancellor was due to make on the single currency on the next Monday, 27 October, which was the first day the House was back after the recess. Alastair said they were confident I would be content with the statement and over several phone calls we arranged for me to see the Prime Minister at Number 10 immediately after the Chancellor's statement.

A simple but near-fatal mistake

On the morning of Saturday, 25 October Alastair phoned from Scotland to ask whether I was agreeable to him mentioning at his press briefing that morning that I had written to my constituency chairman expressing my opposition to the Shadow Cabinet decision on the single currency. As this was already in the public domain I saw no harm and agreed. What we both overlooked was that something about me, still a Conservative MP, and coming from Alastair Campbell, of all people, at a Number 10 Lobby briefing up in Scotland, was something very different from some utterance I might make on a radio programme while sitting in my constituency. Whilst there was nothing special in what Alastair said, in merely referring to my discontent, one might have hoped that the remark would be left at that but it was not to be.

With hindsight it was a serious mistake against a background where a defection, like a covert military operation, has to be conducted at all stages with maximum secrecy. The incongruous nature of the statement was picked up by an observant journalist on the *Sunday Telegraph* and appeared in that paper the next day, 26 October. It was reported that Temple-Morris's thoughts and movements seemed to be known to Alastair Campbell and that could only mean that he was in contact with Labour. That did it. If I had wished to turn my then constituency residence into something resembling BBC Television Centre I easily could have done so. As it was I had to play off numerous approaches without giving anything away. Phillip Webster of *The Times*, whom I knew well, was particularly persistent, and whilst I did not give anything additional away, a further piece, hinting at the possibility of defection, appeared in *The Times* on Monday, 27 October. I now found myself committed, subject only to the Chancellor's statement, to a highly organised defection the next Sunday on the *Frost* programme. This had to be secret, but now had to be conducted against a mounting background of press publicity. It developed into a nightmare, with me as the pig in the middle.

The build-up of tension that had been growing throughout the summer was now coming to a head. Apart from the press interest, everything was going smoothly, including, and most important, the issue of Europe, which meant I could depart on a matter of principle. We got back to London in time for the Chancellor's statement, which my wife and I watched together in my Westminster office. I could not stand facing the press in the Lobby or going into the Chamber. It had been arranged for me to see the Prime Minister as soon as he got back from the statement, so over to Number 10 I went to discuss the details.

The second Blair meeting

We gathered in the little sitting-room: me, Tony Blair, Alastair and Jonathan. I told them I was happy with the statement as being in favour of the single currency in principle, while being practical on the political side

228

and keeping options open. We were to go ahead on the Howarth model but with some improvements. The chosen paper was again the *Observer* and as Tony Bevins was no longer with that paper, Patrick Wintour was the chosen journalist with whom I was to do a full-scale interview the following Wednesday or Thursday, for publication on Sunday. He was to be sworn to secrecy, even with his own newspaper. I was to do the *Frost* programme and other interviews and then proceed to Dublin, where in any event I was due to speak at the Institute of European Affairs. By coincidence but extremely appropriately, Robin Cook, Foreign Secretary, was due to speak at the same gathering. I would do the *Today* programme from Dublin that morning and the rest would hopefully fall into place.

The main improvement on Alan Howarth's defection, where the media attention had been underestimated, was that a Labour Party press officer, Ian Austin of the West Midlands, now a Labour MP, would be assigned to me throughout. He would accompany us to Dublin and I would have help in handling the media scramble. The meeting was generally as cheerful and informal as previously and we parted with Tony Blair thanking me and wishing me all good luck with what had to follow. I then went back into the Cabinet Room to retrieve my coat, only to bump into Blair again with some young staff members. His wife, Cherie, had just phoned wanting him to go to the cinema that evening, and he was cheerfully complaining that he needed to get over the rigours of Edinburgh. The film was *The Full Monty* and all the staff thought it would do him good to get out.

With hindsight the interesting thing about this meeting was that we all thought that we could proceed as planned, in spite of the media leak of the weekend. We might have got away with it but Michael Heseltine was still to come.

The countdown: Enter reality

I then had to pick up various pieces and leave my Conservative political life in as orderly a state as possible. On that evening of Monday,

27 October I took the chair, as usual, of the Executive Committee of the Society of Conservative Lawyers. I managed to back out of chairing the dinner that followed, for none other than John Redwood, but the entreaties to stay within the party began to come in. Everyone had read the press, where it was being increasingly discussed, and my secret week was rapidly becoming a public event. Chairing this meeting was not easy for the committee or me, but generally most of them did their best to ignore the situation, perhaps for fear that a mention of it might cause me to up sticks and leave the party on the spot! Old friends like Jonathan Evans, who had just lost his seat at Brecon and Radnor, plus his ministerial office, did say, with a smile, 'You are not going to leave us, Peter, are you?' I made some bland comment, but these approaches were due to increase as the days passed slowly by. I was rapidly coming to the conclusion that things were turning into rather a mess.

On the morning of Tuesday, 28 October at 10.30 I had the first of two meetings with the Conservative chief whip, James Arbuthnot. It is an odd fact that when you are going to do something like defect you live your old life to the last moment, even when you are actively on the road to the new one. That said, I wanted to set out for him my main differences with Conservative policy, which I saw as an honourable thing to do. He listened to me carefully and said I was all right on the issue of the single currency because of the free vote, although he did not seem at all enthusiastic about my voting against Conservative positions on the constitutional agenda. He seemed to indicate that some abstentions would be tolerated.

That day I arranged, for obvious reasons, to meet with Alan Howarth. For reasons of security, my room, which was comfortable for the task, was chosen as the best venue. He arrived somewhat furtively and once secure could not have been more helpful. Having gone through it all himself he knew exactly what my feelings would be. He took me through his experiences, explaining how the main thing that had gone wrong for him was what Number 10 was trying to correct in my case, namely the handling of the media. It had somehow been assumed that all would settle down after he had done *Breakfast with Frost* on the Sunday morning.

So he went off alone to collect his daughter from university. He arrived at his Warwickshire home to find some fifty or sixty members of the media camping on his doorstep. He gave them a photo opportunity but they stayed there for several hours. His phone was incessantly ringing, while at the same time he was trying to write articles promised for Monday's newspapers.

At a more profound level he reassured me that the worst time was right now, at the last stages before the final act. Once I 'pushed the button' and things took their course it would be much easier. I felt better for that.

Enter the Lib-Dems

That afternoon a strong Lib-Dem approach got under way and I had a meeting with my Herefordshire colleague, Paul Keetch, in his room. I had already been told by Richard Holme, the Lord Holme of Cheltenham, that Paddy Ashdown would be delighted to talk to me at any time, and this was repeated at a chance meeting the day before with Menzies Campbell. That said, Ashdown had already guessed that I was going to Labour even if there was no way I could say this at that time. So Paul Keetch gave me a strong and persuasive last-ditch argument for joining the Liberal Democrats with local angles about holding my seat as a Lib-Dem, which he was sure I could do. It was all a bit exhausting, not least because I had firmly decided that there was no way I would fight my own seat as a Lib-Dem against all those of my association and others who had been of such help to me over many years. I could not defect in that way. Labour was not a competitor in my constituency, and therefore to go that way caused no local grief with my former supporters.

On Wednesday I had one more difficult meeting that had been arranged some time previously. It was the important translation of the Macleod Group into Conservative Mainstream. I had set it all up during the recess by securing new officers prepared to serve. I chaired the meeting at the outset and got Tony Baldry into the chair. The atmosphere was difficult and I made excuses for having to leave for another meeting. Before

I did so Robert Jackson got up and thanked me for all I had done for the centre-left interest in the Conservative Party. He then made an appeal for me to stay within the Conservative Party which the meeting supported. I found the whole thing, flattering as it was, emotionally exhausting, and I backed out with what dignity I could muster. As I left the room, out through the other door burst Quentin Davies, who had arrived late and wanted to make a personal appeal of his own. He forcefully told me that I was playing into the hands of Alan Duncan and the rest of those who wanted to salami-slice us all off so that the party could devote itself to the true line. By this time I could not say very much. In retrospect it is interesting to note that, some years later, both Robert Jackson and Quentin Davies joined me as members of the Labour Party.

From there I proceeded to my last task for the Conservative Party, which was to finalise the finances of Conservative Mainstream with Sir Trevor Smith, soon to become Lord Smith of Clifton, via the Rowntree Trust, of which he was chairman. He had been invaluable in financing the Macleod Group and this was effectively a transfer to Mainstream in the same cause. As the left of the Conservative Party got into difficulty it says a lot for the Rowntree Trust that they saw us as representing liberal values within the Tory Party. We agreed the transfer without difficulty, and Trevor offered wise counsel over my all-too-public difficulties.

Transfer without difficulty was not to be my lot, however. After dinner the calls started to come in and each amounted to a somewhat agonising conversation for me in speaking to old friends. I remember Geoffrey Howe, Norman Fowler and Alastair Goodlad in particular. Each in his own way urged me to stay in the party, and for my part I was not going to lie to them. I tried to block by admitting my difficulties over the single currency and giving the true impression that I was in a state about it. However, there was no way I could go on to tell them that I was defecting this coming Sunday. I eventually got to bed to emerge in time for the 8 a.m. news on the *Today* programme. Michael Heseltine came on straight after the news, all guns blazing, for this prime-time interview. I sat on the side of the bed and listened, as he opposed the Shadow Cabinet decision on the single currency outright, started a campaign within the Conservative Party to oppose it, referred to a recent sympathetic speech by Kenneth Clarke on the same subject and called on all sensible Conservatives to join up in doing the same thing. What could I say or do after that? I was politically stunned.

Heseltine kills it

Thus started the most difficult day in the saga so far. I was a known member of the Heseltine camp, and had played a very public role in his successful 1990 campaign to remove Mrs Thatcher. There was absolutely no way I now had credibility in leaving the party over this issue, when he himself was becoming the champion of my cause. I would be murdered by the press should I try and my motivation in going would look very bad, as if personal ambition was the order of the day. Michael Heseltine knew perfectly well what he was doing. After the meeting to establish Mainstream the day before, Michael Mates, Heseltine's ADC over the 1990 campaign, had called Heseltine and told him that he had to do something as I was obviously about to join Labour. He also mentioned Ian Taylor, who was very exercised over the same subject, although had no plans to defect. Apparently Heseltine at first grumbled that he was beyond this sort of thing, but Mates persisted. Heseltine then decided on action, and action it was. It is an amusing comment in retrospect that he did not let me know in advance. He knew that would make no difference and so he decided to just make my position quite impossible at one stroke. The *Today* programme was contacted and the means of delivery after the 8 a.m. news secured. I was effectively blown out of the water.

My wife and I agreed that there was no way I could defect as planned. I went straight into my office and called Alastair Campbell. I told him that Heseltine had effectively ruined my case and credibility for defection. I would be expected to stay with him and fight the issue within the Conservative Party. To Alastair's great credit he said he understood completely and made no effort to try and change my mind. I then told him that in view of all the circumstances and the matter being already partly in the public domain I intended to call a press conference later that day and come out with the whole thing, chapter and verse. I said that certain newspapers would go on digging for details and the last thing I wanted was for a drip, drip, drip of information which would be highly prejudicial to me. Alastair accepted that but immediately said that the only thing that would worry him would be if it was to come out that I was the one that got away. In other words, that Tony had in any way been chasing me and had not been successful. I made it plain that that had never been the position and, indeed, everything that had happened had been at my request. I would make this utterly clear at my press conference. I agreed to send him a copy of my statement to be made at the conference, which was set for 4 o'clock that afternoon. The conversation ended with Alastair saying he would help where he could.

Justin Powell-Tuck, who was a great help to me over this period, arranged the press conference. The only room he could get at short notice was a small room in 1 Parliament Street, which, when I arrived, was absolutely packed with journalists and cameras. It was the Westminster circus looking for a story. I read my statement and answered questions. My main memory looking back is their reaction to my frankness, which gave them less to write about. They seemed disappointed. I then went upstairs to Bellamy's Restaurant to finish the job. I went through the whole sequence blow by blow with the political correspondents of the *Sunday Times* and *Sunday Telegraph* right down to whether we drank tea or coffee at the Blair meetings. I then had to repeat the whole thing for Stephen Castle of the *Independent on Sunday* and Patrick Wintour of the *Observer*, who because of all this had missed his story of the moment. It all appeared in the media over the next few days, ending on Sunday, 2 November. Apart from my local press it was all over, and I had been proved right in that they eased off, as there was nothing left for them. Tony Blair issued a statement saying that they would indeed have liked to have me in the Labour Party but understood the position and there was now a need for me to fight the good fight within the Conservative Party. That ended this particular scene, but the drama was far from over. I now had to face life back in the Conservative Party, which, had things gone to plan, I should have left by now. One way and another I was completely neutered, without any political role to play and having to contemplate standing down from my constituency before the next election.

Consequences

After my press conference and related events, it was hardly surprising that I received an urgent message to see the Conservative chief whip, James Arbuthnot. At 6 p.m. I presented myself and felt immediately that James did not like the situation one little bit. He told me that both the leader, William Hague, and he had received various strong approaches that I should be disciplined and the party whip withdrawn from me. However, they had decided that no disciplinary action would be taken. He then tried to widen my differences with the Conservative Party, no doubt in the hope that I might resign and go away, which would be a much neater solution from their point of view. This was directly the opposite to the spirit of the meeting of the previous Tuesday, when we had tried to narrow differences. He even brought Ireland up as a major point of difference in that I was 'more Republican' than was traditional in the Conservative and Unionist Party. I weathered all this as I had nowhere else to go but to try and remain within my party, at least for the moment, although I realised that I had no lives left and my position was very weak, to say the least. Our meeting ended with James saying that perhaps he should have conducted the meeting in a somewhat angrier mode, but that was not his style.

What a mess

So there I was on the evening of Thursday, 30 October, with all my efforts to leave the Conservative Party absolutely shattered. Had I gone ahead after Heseltine's intervention my credibility would have been severely undermined. To make the point, Heseltine kept up the media pressure

235

throughout the week and even appeared on the same *Frost* programme I had been destined to defect on! What a farce it would have been had I appeared on the same programme announcing my defection over the same issue that he was campaigning on within the party.

I may have made some mistakes in my political life but to hold that press conference and come completely clean over the matter was not one of them. I did not, all things considered, get that bad a press and there was even a little sympathy from one or two papers. The main thing was that it had largely blown over by the following Monday.

I spent the Friday mending fences, not least within my constituency. My chairman, John Stone, was an absolute rock throughout this difficult period, when apart from everything else he emerged as a media star, however reluctant he may have been. He made no bones about the fact that we had to go through a very difficult period but felt he could keep the balance within the association. With all the tribulations perhaps there was an element of relief that he did not have to go through a full defection and, however damaged I was, I was back.

There remained my long-standing engagement in Dublin and out we went on Sunday, 2 November. It was a relief to get away from London for a few days. The seminar at the Institute of European Affairs went well, although not quite as dramatically as might have been the case. As Robin Cook entered I was talking to Ruairí Quinn, then leader of the Irish Labour Party. Robin gripped my shoulder and as I turned around remarked that he hoped that if we shook hands it would not cause an international incident. Most important, he looked me in the eye and wished me well.

Fifteen

THE WITHDRAWAL OF
THE WHIP

Well, Sir, you never can tell. That's a principle in life with me, Sir, if
you'll excuse my saying such a thing, Sir.

George Bernard Shaw, *You Never Can Tell*, Act 2, 1896

On the beach

A difficult period ensued when I was still a Conservative but with
nowhere to go. I had to try and pick up the pieces until things
settled and then plan my wider future outside the House. I was
finished within it.

The interim

First I had to secure my position on the British–Irish Inter-Parliamentary
Body, where with the change of government I was now opposition deputy chairman designate. The new Labour leadership, David Winnick and
Kevin McNamara, wanted me to do this while they played themselves
in and normally this would not have been a problem. I now needed the
approval of my Conservative colleagues, whereas before it would have
passed on the nod. At a meeting of the Conservative membership which
I chaired I asked for views. David Wilshire directly and politely said I
should not undertake any representative role as a Conservative. Two

237

others, Andrew Robathan and David Tredinnick, made relatively mild comments that life could not quite be the same after what had happened, but took it no further than that. A number of MPs spoke in support, but the *coup de grâce* was delivered by the Northern Ireland peer Hugh Rathcavan, who spoke in an Irish context as to how much I was respected north and south of the border. This did the trick and without further ado I was approved as the Conservative vice-chairman designate of the reconstituted Inter-Parliamentary Body

I then went straight on to a meeting of the Positive European Group, which had been greatly reduced in numbers by the General Election, and with about a quarter of the barely twenty present being old members, now in the Lords. We had to discuss how we were going to vote on the Amsterdam Bill and all the old difficulties immediately reappeared. We should stick together, not rock the boat, and if we could, we should find a way to support the opposition line and vote against Amsterdam. I spoke twice, saying that I was hardly in a strong position but thought we should abstain. At least one other agreed, and Ken Clarke, who kept silent, did not look happy. So we ended up supportive, if possible, the only caveat being that we could not support some anti-European amendment that could possibly be tabled by our spokesman, Michael Howard.

I was due to return to Dublin for a major debate at University College on Friday, 7 November with Henry Mount Charles (then the Earl of Mount Charles) but had to cancel in order to attend an important Leominster Conservative function. My chairman, John Stone, thought rightly that the sooner I broke the ice the better. This was not an easy evening, but my president, Philip Verdin, and officers, could not have been more helpful in sticking by my side and being seen to support me. It was the first step in a concerted effort by John Stone and his officers to calm things down and avoid any deselection meetings or unnecessary drama.

My final duty on a constituency weekend in the aftermath of crisis was Remembrance Sunday, a full public event and wreath-laying at Ledbury. Here I was exposed to the wider public and the result was absolutely fine. Mine is a Conservative constituency but moderately so, and it is amazing, if you come out of the tribe, how little those of the wider world care. As long as your actions in office are in accord with what they see as the greater good then they could not care less about political parties, and appreciate the limitations of democracy. So, on the street, to and from the church, I was stopped repeatedly and with sympathy. It was good for my morale to be back with my own people. That said, I was about to encounter the reality of the political machine. It was not pretty.

The set-up

My final days as a Conservative began with a lunch with a journalist from *The Times* on Thursday, 13 November. What happened was my fault, but it is difficult to deal with the media when you are under pressure and have no organisation behind you to help. So I thought I could benefit from his attentions, which was a naive mistake. He was particularly interested in my constituency and what my position there was. I told him I had written a position paper for my chairman and constituency officers, which I was making available to the local press but it was not intended for the nationals. He asked for a copy of it and said he virtually controlled the Saturday political input to *The Times* and would write a sympathetic piece in which I would star and which would be helpful to me. I gave him a copy of my constituency position paper and hoped for the best.

My paper was intended to make life easier for my constituency association and set out my position for the rest of the Parliament, which was likely to be my last. First I made it clear that if Conservative policy on Europe and the single currency did not change by the time of the next General Election I would find it impossible to stand as a Conservative and would stand down. Secondly, if during the course of this Parliament I could no longer accept Conservative policy then I would honourably resign the whip, and serve out the rest of the Parliament as a One Nation Independent Conservative. This was not phrased aggressively in any way and on receipt of it my chairman wrote to thank me and say it was very helpful to him.

On Friday, 14 November the journalist phoned to say that his piece would not be in on the Saturday, despite his alleged control of input to *The Times*. On Monday he phoned again to apologise for it still not being in, but to say that it would be in *The Times* the next day, Tuesday, 18 November. It was about as unhelpful as any such piece could be. The headline was 'Tory rebel renews threat on Hague', in heavy type throughout. The purport was that my paper for my constituency constituted a threat to the leader, William Hague.

That evening Archie Hamilton, the chairman of the 1922 Committee, asked for a copy of my paper, which I duly sent him. He circulated it to all the members of the 1922 Committee before their meeting on Wednesday, 19 November. After some discussion it was decided to take no action. They also had a copy of the reaction of my chairman, John Stone, and I think it was realised that this position paper represented no change to the situation prevailing when the chief whip and the leader decided to take no disciplinary action against me. However, the leadership had decided to withdraw the whip from me at the behest of the right wing, who had been protesting at the lack of action against me. My final minutes as a Conservative ticked by on that Wednesday and Thursday. On the Wednesday I did a programme with Ken Livingstone on Talk Radio and he made one glorious comment to me after the show: 'For Christ's sake, Peter, don't join us. We've got quite enough of you on our side already!' That evening I had a drink with my old friend Stuart Bell, Labour MP for Middlesbrough, who told me that I was absolutely finished within the Conservative Party and, being dead in the political water, I should go where I would be welcome, which was the Labour Party. On the following evening I met with a prominent constituent and supporter, Dennis Sampson. He gave a positive view of the constituency reaction and wanted to help in any way he could. During our talk Tristan Garel-Jones, former Conservative minister and now peer, came up and warmly congratulated me on choosing to stay within the party. Indeed the whole talk with Dennis was to that end. It was to no avail, as the leadership had made its decision.

The withdrawal of the Whip

At about 8.35 a.m. the telephone rang in our London flat and it turned out to be Shana, the Conservative chief whip's secretary. Apparently the chief whip wanted to send me a fax and she had been asked to find out my fax number. I gave her my fax number, which was in my office at the Commons, and told her I would receive it when I got in a little later on. As soon as I put down the phone I said to Taheré that they could well be taking the whip away and, if they were, it would be a blessing. Effectively it would end my isolation and let me back into the game.

Five minutes later Shana phoned back to say that, as I was not in the House, the chief whip had asked her to read the faxed letter to me. The letter removed the parliamentary whip from me, and as soon as she had finished reading it, I told Shana that of course this meant that I would be resigning from the Conservative Party. I thanked her for the kindness and courtesy she had shown throughout these events. She was a very nice woman, well known to many of us, and she seemed a little upset to be used as an instrument of communication in this way. She finally said that from now on events would take their normal course, which meant that a press release was imminent. In fact it had been embargoed for 9 a.m., so they were cutting it fairly fine.

Enter Labour

Immediately after 9 a.m. the phone started to ring. The first call was from the Central Television political correspondent Simon Mares, and all credit to him. An interview was arranged, and as soon as I put down the phone it rang again and it was Jonathan Powell from Number 10, wanting to know the situation so that they could react accordingly. I told him I had just resigned from the Conservative Party and in effect was on my way. He asked for a couple of minutes so that he could get Alastair Campbell on for a three-way conversation and we paused. This presents a good example of how well tuned and quick on the ball Tony Blair's Number 10 was, and even ahead of the mass of the media.

On came Alastair Campbell from Luxembourg, where he was with the Prime Minister for a European summit. What was I going to do? Was I coming over? How was I going to play it? They would help me out if they could. I had already made a basic plan and told them that I could not come over straight away because of my constituency statement, which made it clear that in these circumstances I would resign as a Conservative and sit as a One Nation Independent. I would have to stick to that, but I said I would make the big gesture as soon as we agreed and publicly cross the floor to sit with Labour. It would then be very clear where I was eventually heading. Alastair said he would deal with the matter at his approaching briefing session with British journalists in Luxembourg. Jonathan became the point of contact over the next few days, as necessary, and for the moment that was that.

Then all hell broke loose, with media call after media call. I decided that there was nothing for it but to go to the Millbank studios and just broadcast away until everyone had had enough of me. I began broadcasting at about 10.50 a.m. and the session ended at 1.20 p.m. It was two and a half hours solid to just about every British news programme that existed, with Ireland thrown in for good measure. The results of the Winchester and Beckenham by-elections had come out overnight and were very bad for the Conservative Party. No doubt the Conservative leadership thought it could dilute this a bit by doing some strong-arm stuff on me, or at least kill two birds with one stone. However, all it did was to compound the message and it came out as if the way they had treated me was an example of why they were so unpopular.

Back in my Commons office during that morning there occurred a welcome bit of light relief. Taheré was my main secretary and took a call from, of all people, an official from Conservative Central Office. In full flow he asked whether I could help them out over a visit they had on their hands with some South Africans. Taheré's voice never changed when she asked if the young man realised that I had now left the Conservative Party. There was a shocked pause followed by silence on the other end of the line. Eventually out came: 'Oh, my God ... I

242

should have listened to the news. I will go and check it out.' End of call. It was most amusing.

Media activity continued throughout Friday and then lifted. The main thing I did at the weekend was the *Target* programme for Sky on Sunday morning, when I was given an easy run by David Mellor and Charles Kennedy, who were presenting the programme. Press coverage generally was good and even the *Daily Telegraph* and *The Times* were fair in their news coverage, even if they were critical in leading articles.

Half-time comment

I sometimes ponder whether the Conservative Party was right to take the whip from me at that particular moment. From my side they did me a great favour in that they liberated me from a period of unhappy limbo which would have lasted for the rest of my time in politics and brought my career to a premature end. Having almost defected to Labour and being obliged to draw back at the last moment, in full public view, I was a busted flush with little credibility left. As it was they gave me a second chance to complete the job and go over to Labour and, from the moment the whip was withdrawn on that Friday morning, no horse could have galloped out of the stable faster. I learnt afterwards that the decision resulted from continued pressure from the right that I should be disciplined and the leadership then had to manufacture the set-up in *The Times*. The announcement was to distract from the by-elections, but none of this strategy really worked for them.

In the aftermath I received a surprising amount of sympathy from those well placed within my former party. I was, for example, told that the Shadow Cabinet were not consulted over the decision, and one prominent member was only told via his pager as he was broadcasting about the dreadful by-election results. In retrospect I would not like ever to have to go through that Friday again, but it ended on a pleasing note. Out came Michael Heseltine again, on various programmes, to denounce the decision to remove the whip as the wrong one and over in Luxembourg Tony Blair was saying nice things about me and sounding incredulous about the decision. I had the Tory leadership in a unique and effective cross-fire and I had my first good night's sleep for some long time.

Sixteen

LIFE AS AN INDEPENDENT

We know what happens to people who stay in the middle of the road. They get run over.

Aneurin Bevan, Observer, 9 December 1953

I was not a genuine Independent, but in House of Commons terms, that was my official status. I had indeed crossed the floor and sat with the government, but as an Independent as I had not yet formally joined Labour. I was immediately contacted by the Liberal Whips' Office, who had the responsibility of looking after Independents. They offered help, but I already had the full weight of the government Whips' Office behind me as needed. I also had some amusing exchanges with Martin Bell, the only Independent in the House, who went around telling everyone that his party had the largest increase in numbers of any party as, with me, we had increased by no less than 100 per cent. He, of course, was well aware that I was actually in political transit.

I was now beginning the final journey on my extended route towards defection to Labour. It would take nearly a year, ending with the 1998 Labour Party conference. The unpleasant side of it all came home to me after only a day or two. I had a curt note from the opposition deputy chief whip, Peter Ainsworth, saying that as I occupied my Commons office as a Conservative and was no longer such, I should vacate my room immediately. The Sergeant-at-Arms had been informed and a number of removal baskets had been placed outside my door to emphasise the demand. The rooms available to each party are negotiated by their accommodation whips, which they then allocate. I was expecting this because of what had happened to both Alan Howarth and Emma Nicholson in the last Parliament and, at our recent lunch, Alan Howarth had specifically warned me about it. I was determined not to submit to this as I was very attached to my room and had been in the same building for some years. I was expected to go to the Liberal whips to get them to offer me some alternative but I had other ideas. That evening I went straight to the government chief whip, Nick Brown, and his deputy, George Mudie, in the Lobby and told them the situation. They had already offered me any assistance and immediately their Accommodation Whip, Janet Anderson, was called in to take charge. She dealt with the whole thing immaculately.

Although essentially controlled by the Whips' Offices, decisions on accommodation have to go through the Accommodation Committee, which is all-party and which at that time was chaired by the Conservative Sir Sydney Chapman, but with a large Labour majority prevailing amongst its membership. Both Sir Sydney and Sir Patrick Cormack, Conservative MP and Shadow Deputy Leader of the House, and on the committee in that capacity, were old friends of mine and not unsympathetic. The Liberal Democrat representative was fully on my side and if called upon the Labour membership would have out-voted the Conservatives and put the whips in their place. Janet Anderson convinced the Conservative whips that their position was hopeless. They were informed that the government would take no responsibility for accommodating me and that I already had a perfectly good room which the opposition did not need. They were also tactfully reminded that the government had been generous to the opposition in the overall allocation of rooms. This included providing John Major with an admirable office that was within the government's allocation rather than the opposition's. No vote took place – I was told to stay put, and the offending baskets were rapidly removed from my door. Shortly before Christmas a further letter arrived from Peter Ainsworth saying that as the government refused to find me alternative accommodation, and as it was Christmas, I could stay where I was.

Life in the House

A difficult side of defection within the House of Commons is who to greet and who not to greet. In the Commons you are continually bumping into each other. From the outset I put into operation my 'No Greet' policy, which meant I would not greet until greeted, although I would look people straight in the eye on the approach. Very quickly it became clear who the few awkward ones were and the rest were fine.

Everyone at the time was asking me about the Conservative reaction to my leaving them, which was understandable but actually not the most important thing. They were now my past and represented for me the 'Departure Lounge', whereas far more important was the 'Arrivals Area', namely the Parliamentary Labour Party, which was where I had to make my mark and live my parliamentary life. I was particularly careful with Old Labour, who, to be fair, were generally good to me. That said, I was conscious of the fact that walking through their Lobby to vote made me a very live example of New Labour, which might not instil feelings of instant happiness into all and sundry. I had few problems, but it was nice to know that the powers that be were keeping a wary eye open, just in case. One evening, when about to vote, I was having a genuinely jocular exchange which involved me being addressed as 'Comrade'. Suddenly the formidable brooding presence of Donald Dewar loomed over us and shut the whole thing down with one curt comment and look.

The public reaction

If you have any difficulties within the House of Commons it is no bad thing to get outside it. When the whip was withdrawn and I left the Conservatives it was reassuring to have a very sympathetic public reaction. In fact it surprised me how substantial it was. Letters poured in from the constituency, from across the country and beyond, and it is no exaggeration to say that they were 90 per cent in favour, which at the time was a great boost for me.

As for the world outside Parliament, I had nothing to fear, and for two weeks after I crossed the floor I was warmly greeted wherever I went. An amusing example was the day after I crossed, returning to the Commons from a nearby meeting with Justin Powell-Tuck, Director of the Macleod Group and Conservative Mainstream, when I was stopped by a lady who introduced herself as an area-level officer of the Conservative Party who had just had lunch with her own MP, somewhat ironically the deputy chief whip, Peter Ainsworth. She had told him straight that it was quite wrong to remove the whip from me and invite defection. She was very sorry about it. No sooner had I expressed my thanks than two young men in overalls passed by and recognised me. They shouted out at full blast 'Well done, mate, we're not Tories anymore either!' The lady concerned enjoyed this comment as much as I did. I now had to put matters to the test in my constituency.

In the constituency

My first exposure in the constituency was on Friday, 28 November at a private charity function. It was a pleasant occasion with a cross-section of the county present. I made a point of going around the room and, to my relief, received general sympathy, including from several known Conservatives. The following day involved an engagement switching on the Bromyard Christmas lights, which exposed me on the street for some three hours. It was a worthy occasion, involving the lights plus a shop-front competition and Victorian costumes. During the entire time only two people politely disagreed with what I had done. I was aware that I was now an Independent, and people like that, but I had very publicly crossed the floor to sit with Labour in a moderate but Conservative constituency. I returned to London on Sunday, 30 November, feeling much stronger.

Back to Westminster

It was now a short haul to the Christmas recess, during which I was deluged by all the correspondence that kept coming in. In early December

I made what I called my 'Second maiden speech', which was my first from the Labour benches and naturally enough was on Europe. This was another of the many hurdles I had to take and it went well, with Robin Cook, the Foreign Secretary, giving me a warm welcome from the front bench. The only bit of unpleasantness in the Chamber then, or over the next three years, came from the Conservative MP Patrick Nicholls, from whom, if trouble had to come, I would have expected it. From a sedentary position while Robin Cook was speaking about me he exclaimed 'You're welcome to him', which drew no support from other Conservatives present, who made entirely reasonable interventions when I spoke. I came out feeling that my new place was now an accepted fact and it was to rub this in that I made a point of speaking in the House.

The final thing I had to do at Westminster before Christmas was to meet with Nick Brown, the government chief whip, which I did at 12 Downing Street on the morning of 23 December. As far as my defection saga was concerned, I had passed out of the hands of Number 10, although remained free to contact them at any time, and I needed to go over the ground with the chief whip to formalise an interim and rather unusual relationship. I wanted to set out the situation for the chief whip so there was no misunderstanding. He had already been very kind over my room and I wanted that spirit to continue. I made it clear that I would join Labour as soon as the situation was right, but I had to take a bit of time to 'serve out' my undertaking to sit for a period as an Independent. He was particularly interested to know what I thought of the present atmosphere of No. 12, which was now in Labour hands. My reply that the atmosphere of the Whips' Office hardly changes, whoever is in power, amused him. We had a wide-ranging talk during which I told him how impressed I had been with the New Labour members, and he readily agreed that they were very pro-Blair and seemed not the least bit factional about it. He told me he had agreed to my taking a Labour place on the British–Irish Inter-Parliamentary Body, where a Labour member, Nick Ainger, had generously made way for me. Brown would ensure I got the Labour whip each week and we would stay in touch. It was a cheerful meeting and we parted with me feeling happy to be on my way to Labour. It was only a matter of time and I just had to pick the right moment.

Back home for Christmas and with decisions taken, and much of the drama behind us, it was for me, and my wife and family, the most settled time we had had for some months.

Seventeen

1998 AND THE
FINAL PUSH

I no longer desire happiness: life is nobler than that.

George Bernard Shaw, *Candida*, Act 3, 1895

The early months of 1998 found me marking time. I had no intention of settling down as an Independent at Westminster, which was not my scene. I concentrated on preparing the way for my defection to Labour. At Westminster as well as in the constituency I needed to settle things with various personalities who would be relevant when the time came. One obvious example in the Commons was my old friend Clive Soley, now chairman of the Parliamentary Labour Party, who said it was up to me when I came over but the sooner the better. It should be when the Commons was in session so that I could be formally received within the PLP, and be seen to be part of it. As for the future, he said the Lords would be best for me and provide more opportunities for me to be useful with Lords Reform, foreign affairs and Ireland. Over the same period I had a similar meeting with Martin Bell. I did not want him to feel in any way let down by my impending departure, as he had been supportive and played a great role as a genuine Independent. Far from being let down, he told me to go for it with Labour.

I was taking soundings in the various departments of my life, and there seemed to be no obstacle in the way and little expectancy that I should remain an Independent. I went to my then Livery Company, the Barber Surgeons; the governing body of my old school, Malvern College,

251

of which I had been a member for years; and various other connections and all seemed well. At Westminster I seemed to be regarded already as a Labour supporter and accepted as such. One evening I had been at a dinner for EU international representatives addressed by Peter Mandelson, who made nice references to me in his speech and gave me a lift back to the Commons in his official car. As we pulled up at the members' entrance and I got out, who should be waiting there but Diane Abbott, a staunch representative of the Labour left. The Tory defector getting out Mandelson's car seemed to put a momentary strain on Labour unity as her face took on a deeply suspicious look. Despite this she did say hello to me.

Back to the constituency

The last phase began with the constituency. Very important for me there were the local Labour parties of Leominster and Hereford. At a Hereford City Council Freedom ceremony two local Labour leaders, Councillor Chris Chappell, chairman of the Herefordshire Labour Party, whom I had known for years and who fought me in the 1992 election, and David Hallam, our sitting Labour MEP, approached me needing an urgent word. They needed to know exactly what was happening and were important players as far as I was concerned. From there on in we were in regular contact. Locally as nationally, I had to deal with two major elements, namely the departure lounge of my local Conservative Association, and by this time, even more important, the arrivals area of the local Labour Party. I was always far more worried about having a happy landing with the Labour Party at large and the Leominster and Hereford Labour parties in particular. I was put on my guard when in the Commons a senior West Midlands Labour MP, Bruce Grocott, soon to become PPS to Tony Blair, told me, partly as a joke, that the Leominster Labour Party was, in the Blairite sense, one of the most unreconstructed Labour parties in the whole region. In fact I need not have worried as my local party was under the chairmanship of Richard Westwood, a long-standing journalist on my local newspaper who had fought me in 1997. He made a good job of welcoming me in the local media when the time came.

After Easter I began a series of key meetings to explain myself and prepare the ground for my passage to Labour. It is ironic in retrospect that throughout these sensitive days we were staying with Henry and Cessa Moore, old friends who had been prominent supporters of mine, with Henry as my association chairman and later its president. Wednesday, 15 April was the first of three days of concentrated meetings; first meeting two of my oldest Conservative political friends in the constituency, namely John Arnett and Don Preece. John Arnett was like me, a left-wing Conservative who had been chairman of the old Herefordshire County Council and then of its successor authority, the Hereford and Worcester County Council. Don Preece was the secretary and agent of the Leominster Conservative Association when I arrived in 1973 and continued to serve them and me until he retired after the 1992 General Election. I owed them both an explanation and I needed their comments and advice. I told them I regarded the association as the injured party in all this, but that I could not go backwards and had the choice of staying as an Independent or going to New Labour, which would suit me much better. I had no intention of becoming a Liberal Democrat, which in practice would mean that they would want and expect me to stay on and fight the seat as a Lib-Dem against all my old friends. In any event I would stand down at the next election.

The first point they made in response was that the association was now progressing without me, and facing the future in looking to select a new candidate. In the words of John Arnett, 'Many of them still love you as ever but they have gone beyond you now.' My decision not to consider joining the Lib-Dems was obviously welcome, as was my decision to stand down at the next election. It made life easier for the association to settle down and get on with life with a new candidate. They both accepted my going to Labour, although I felt that John Arnett might have preferred me as an Independent. For both of them the main relief was that I had no intention of becoming a Liberal Democrat.

Over the next two days I completed two further important meetings with my leading Conservative officers. Henry and Cessa Moore took the whole thing in their stride. First I had to see my long-standing president, the late Philip Verdin, subsequently patron of the association. The great thing about true Tory grandees, when it comes to politics, is that they do not take it too seriously, in the sense that they are primarily both practical and pragmatic. A candidate comes, a candidate goes, but they remain, to ensure that the whole operation carries on. Their concerns involved getting the association up and running and a new candidate in place to become the Member in due course. If I was New Labour and not standing again then that was for the best, allied to the fact that I was not going to become a Liberal Democrat, which would have caused problems for them in that I would doubtless be asked to seek re-election as such. He was a great support and we remained friends for the rest of his life. I will always miss him.

The other Conservative I had to see was my long-suffering current chairman, John Stone. We met, went over it all and remain good friends to this day. For a chairman of a local association to suddenly get propelled onto the national media again and again is quite something, and way beyond the normal job description. He did it all magnificently.

After that came a succession of others to whom I owed an explanation, and who would play a role in the eventual final defection when it came. These included the editor of the *Hereford Times*, Stewart Gilbert, who later kept quiet when things threatened to break prematurely and never let me down; the editor of the *Malvern Gazette*, John Murphy, who was most sympathetic because of my work in Ireland and with the Parliamentary Body; and the chairman of our County National Farmers Union, Stuart Thomas, who saw it as in the NFU interest to have me in the Labour Party, with it in government. I ended with a cup of tea with Sir Simon Gourlay, former NFU president, whom I had had to defend before Mrs Thatcher some years before (see p. 57). He had by then joined the Labour Party, which gave me encouragement.

I returned to London all set to go but wanting to delay until after the Three Counties Show in Malvern on 16 June. The reason was that the president of the show that year was none other than Philip Verdin, and I didn't want to defect and then straight after cause him any embarrassment when I turned up at the show, which was a time when we were all on parade. This was fine when I took the decision but in the weeks that followed the word began to slip out. Michael White of the *Guardian* did a full profile of me and various other bits and pieces about possible defection to Labour began to creep into the newspapers. The lid was kept on it locally by the very helpful editors whom I had fully briefed, but it threatened to get out of hand. Having been caught out once before on the point of defection by the press, I was doubly sensitive this time. The fact that I was about to join Labour seemed to develop a momentum of its own, both locally and nationally. As it was, it was timed for soon after the Three Counties Show in June.

The final defection to Labour

The final sequence began with the 1998 Three Counties Show. The show is very much an occasion when 'the County' comes on parade. Everyone is there: lord lieutenants, bishops, high sheriffs, landowners and local government in force.

The presidential luncheon is given in a great marquee for over 200 people, and is preceded by a reception. I had received my itinerary for the occasion about a week before and was pleased to see that I had been placed on table 1, the president's table, together with the Lord Lieutenant and others. At the reception I again checked where I was sitting and my place was unchanged. That morning I was told that William Hague, then leader of the opposition, was attending the show and lunch, together with his ADC, Sebastian Coe, and had been placed on table 2. We proceeded in for lunch, and the ladies at our table sat down and I was drawing out my chair, when up came the Hereford organiser of the show and told me I was 'wrongly parked'. Taking me by the arm he led me down through the assembled luncheon saying he would find another place for me. This was in view of everyone, and I was rescued by table 14, full of Hereford City Lib-Dem Councillors, who called me over and adopted me for the occasion, having seen what had happened. Fortunately Hague was late and saw nothing of this and I am sure could not have cared less where I happened to be sitting. It all got into the local newspapers and nobody was more distressed than the president, Philip Verdin, who, together with others, wrote a generous letter of apology.

Immediately after lunch events took over, as back to Westminster I drove, with the then Lib-Dem MP for Hereford, Paul Keetch, as my passenger. It was good to have someone to talk to but it all suddenly got dramatic. Alastair Campbell phoned me in the car to say there was an emergency developing, as the Downing Street press office was getting too many enquiries for comfort about my defection and we had to move quickly. One or two other calls came in, and Paul Keetch must have realised what was happening but gave nothing away at any time as matters proceeded over the next few days. That evening, with me back in London, Alastair and I decided that I should defect on the following weekend, with my first declaration that I was joining Labour taking place on the *Frost* programme on the Sunday morning. I expected an easy media run, as I had already defected in all but name six months before, but I was not to be so lucky. Away we went on another merry-go-round, which was summed up well in the middle of it all by a harassed Conservative spokesman who, when asked for comment, somewhat desperately asked, 'How many times can anyone defect from the same party?' Understandable, but the media has its own agenda.

In the midst of defection I had to fulfil my normal agenda. This involved going to The Hague the next day to lead a delegation of the British–Netherlands Group, of which I was chairman. However, nothing could keep me away from events in progress and sure enough on arrival at Schiphol airport our Embassy turned up with our Dutch parliamentary hosts. The Embassy official seemed unduly formal and stiff as he announced to all and sundry that he had a message for me from Number 10, and no less a personage than Alastair Campbell needed to talk to me. He handed the message over with a flourish and, had I not been fortunate with my companions, we could have had a press leak just at the wrong time. I was lucky in the two MPs who witnessed this and they both rapidly gathered what it was all about. Robert Jackson, the Conservative, was a long-standing friend and Charles Clarke, the future Labour Cabinet minister, had seen it all before in running the office of Neil Kinnock when leader of the opposition. Both smiled and held their peace.

The next day, Friday, and for that matter Saturday, were for preparation in that many people, such as the Leominster Labour Party, had to be prepared for my defection, as they would be asked to comment. It was also for me constant media dodging as the gentlemen of the press pursued me in the hope that I would come out with it, which was impossible before the *Frost* programme on the Sunday morning. That said, they announced my defection to Labour on the BBC's *PM* programme on Saturday, come what may, and thereafter on the evening news generally. After the event we were all delighted in that I had several bites of the cherry for the second time around. As it happened, on Saturday evening I had to host a dinner at the House of Commons, as chairman of the Spanish Group, and to meet them at the St Stephen's entrance to the House. The police and Commons staff were marvellous in dealing with the press calls and telling them they thought I was at the Portcullis House entrance, which was safely away on the Embankment, not at the St Stephen's. By the time the press arrived panting and complete with heavy cameras and equipment I was safely inside. It was a close shave.

Announcement and aftermath

At last I got onto the *Frost* programme on the Sunday morning to formally announce my defection to Labour, preceded by such public speculation that an announcement was hardly necessary. I led the programme after the news, and admired the Frost technique, which involved all the right questions but giving you ample opportunity to answer, which sadly is often not the case these days. I had to miss the traditional breakfast after the show as I had many other interviews. I went straight over to the Adam Boulton show on Sky, where I was to be interviewed with the pro-European Conservative Ian Taylor. I had an easy ride, but the unfortunate Taylor had to suffer a string of questions as to whether he was going to defect as well. When it came to the issues, we agreed with each other on virtually everything, probably to the disappointment of the show's producer. There followed a series of interviews which lasted all day and ended at about 4 p.m. I got back to Dolphin Square to meet my neighbour, Tom Pendry MP, who shouted out 'well done' from his car as we both arrived. He had heard me on his car radio and felt, as a friend, that there was no longer a place for me within the Conservative Party. More phone calls and messages and the odd broadcast on the Monday, but the pressure was off. I was now a Labour MP, which had immediate consequences, in that I had to be accepted within the ranks of the Parliamentary Labour Party and the wider party. The whole process would take about another six months.

One hurdle after another

People are apt to think that a defection is just that and, once the deed is done, that is that. Far from it. I now had to be accepted at all levels by the party I had chosen to join. First came the Parliamentary Labour Party on the following Wednesday, 24 June 1998. In this I was greatly helped by the fact that the chairman was Clive Soley, who had been privy to so much of my frustration over the last few years and gave me a warm welcome. That evening I was to attend a reception at Number 10 for the West Midlands Labour Party at the invitation of Tony and Cherie Blair and was taken along by the two senior officers of the West Midlands Parliamentary Party, MPs Dennis Turner and Peter Snape. We had a memorable photo outside the door of Number 10, and in we went. I was taken in hand by officials and in particular by Martin Angus of the West Midlands, who was detailed to stay at my side just in case and to help with introductions. I was well aware that it could be a little testy as I was entering the realm of the established, long-standing party workers. Much to my relief, and even more that of the powers that be, there was absolutely no problem. As soon as I entered the reception an old Labour hand from Birmingham came up to me and said quite simply: 'Peter, what took you so long?' and that set the tone on the whole evening. Tony Blair was able to mention me in his speech to warm applause and I ended up in Whitehall after the event waving farewell to the departing coaches. My publicly expressed political independence over the years and the very open nature of my defection paid dividends. It was very rewarding.

On Friday, 26 June I had an Irish interlude over at the summer school in Gorey, Co. Wexford, where I was due to make a keynote speech together with John Bruton, former Taoiseach/Prime Minister, and now leader of the opposition. As often in Ireland it ended in the local pub, where I had terrific support, with everyone wondering why I had remained a Tory for so long. The amusing thing was the police guard watching over us, which John Bruton understandably thought was for him. When they didn't follow him he enquired about it, only to discover that they were in fact there to safeguard my welfare and not his. For my part I was well aware that my special status was not to last for very long.

Back to the constituency

My first test back home was a very public one in that the *Any Questions* programme was going out on Radio 4 from Ledbury on Friday, 10 July in the context of the Ledbury Poetry Festival. I was familiar with the programme, having done it several times before and knew that it was not their practice to invite MPs within their own constituencies. I was invited to go on and it was explained that my circumstances were rather special and they would very much like me on it. I agreed without hesitation, and saw it as a good opportunity to kill a few birds with one stone, in that I would make myself available in my own patch in a high-profile way and could be got at by all and sundry. I was far from relaxed about the prospect, but do it I must and do it I did. The Labour Party was very supportive locally and nationally. The briefing was every bit as thorough as the equivalent from Conservative Central Office and locally all allocated places were taken up by potential supporters, should I be in need.

I was perhaps lucky in the panel chosen. My Conservative 'opponent' was Nigel Evans MP, later a Deputy Speaker, who was relaxed and entertaining at the traditional supper beforehand, plus Rabbi Julia Neuberger, later Baroness Neuberger, and the one and only Brian Sewell of the *Evening Standard*. One third of the programme concentrated on my situation and in came the questions, in particular as to whether I should resign and cause a by-election. Jonathan Dimbleby was scrupulously fair, but the answers of the rest of the panel were crucial to how I came out if it. Had it been relevant to the majority situation in the Commons I made it clear that I would have given a by-election, but in the circumstances of the vast Labour majority I saw no need to do so. Julia Neuberger followed me and to my relief said that as a card-carrying Liberal Democrat she completely defended my right to do what I had done. Brian Sewell followed and completely ended any tension over the issue by reducing the audience to fits of laughter, saying the whole thing was really about my not wishing to have dinner anymore with all those ghastly old Tories in the Members' Dining Room. Ironically, and with exceptions, this was very true! The fact that he also said there should be a by-election, as did Nigel Evans, got completely lost in the general mirth. After that the general verdict was that the programme had gone well for me. This was all to the good, as I learnt afterwards that an awful lot of constituents were listening to it.

The local Labour Party

I now came to the most important part of my initiation, which was my local party. I had always maintained good relations with Labour locally and been helpful where I could, which was my policy with friend and foe over the years. It now paid off and they welcomed me into the fold. They had kept the Labour flag flying in a Tory seat without any hope of winning but suddenly one early summer morning they switched on their radios to discover that, for the first time in history, their constituency now had a Labour MP. Chris Chappell, a leading Labour Councillor, whose father had been a Church of England canon, exclaimed what a feeling it was: 'Peter, we woke up and there it was. It was our Epiphany.' Perhaps they all did not all see it like that, but their reception was generous. After a successful warm-up at a barbecue in Hereford where I was very well received, I got to the Leominster Labour Party itself. They sent a deputation to see me by appointment and I took them over the whole saga. They seemed to have made up their minds and got straight down to how they might best introduce me to their local party. They thought something social was best and they were organising a barbecue for the whole membership and proposed proceeding, with me there as the guest of honour. I readily agreed, and it was a very relaxed and enjoyable evening at which I spoke and presented a long-service award for fifty years' service to the party to Emilio Ponti, a well-known Ledbury character with whom I had previously shared many laughs. At the height of my troubles with Mrs Thatcher he even sent me a signed application for membership of the Labour Party, telling me that one day I might like to fill it in and send it back to him so he could propose me. Sadly by the time I eventually joined it was all done centrally so he could not propose me, but my presentation of the award made up for it. From then on I related to them as any other MP: attending their management committees where appropriate, functions and the annual dinner. Geraint Thomas, the young solicitor son of a leading Labour Councillor, became my constituency secretary, an old Conservative supporter fixed me up with an office and I was away. As far as my constituents were concerned it was business as usual.

The Labour Party conference

The annual Labour conference was my last hurdle, and it was important to me that it went smoothly, not least because there was still the remains of a media spotlight upon me. I decided to attend the whole thing and really make a go of it. I was also interested to see if there were any differences with the Conservative conference and much to my amusement there were very few. The whole thing was immaculately organised, the fringe meetings interesting and the overall atmosphere surprisingly good and much better than I expected, having viewed some fairly raucous Labour conferences from afar over the years. It became very clear what a difference Tony Blair and New Labour had made. It was indeed ironic that the squabbling over those same years was left to the divided Conservative Party.

At the beginning of the conference I entered my hotel to affectionate shouts of 'Hello, Comrade', also heard later on in the street, which I used to my advantage, with my confidence growing, when I addressed the fringe meeting of the 'Agreed Ireland' movement. I began my speech with a resounding greeting: 'Hello, Comrades!' It went down well and I had arrived. There remained the probability that I would be called on to speak on the conference floor. I was quietly hoping that I would get away without any major appearance but that was not to be. The message came through from on high on the Wednesday morning that they would like me to speak on Ireland. I raced back to my hotel and composed a little speech. Short speeches are always more difficult to prepare. I got in early after lunch in the front row of the reserved parliamentary section, near the podium. Fellow Labour MPs helpfully advised me to wave my arms and look suitably expectant, in order to get called. This was alien to me, in that at Tory conferences there is no pretence about being called from the floor, you are just called. Labour at least does preserve a modicum of democracy with its grassroots.

I was duly called and set about my final challenge. I had only given one speech before to the Conservative Party conference, and a handful of others, to audiences of more than, say, a thousand. It is a totally different skill and involves courting the audience for approval and applause, with comparatively short and general comments. I began with a stirring cry that I addressed them as the Labour, repeat Labour, Member for Leominster. This went down very well and so it continued, with my precious minutes ticking away and I ran way over time. The chairman of the session was the redoubtable Clare Short, who eventually had to interrupt me. The problem was that the Winter Gardens amplification system was so bad that, on the dais, I could not hear a word said from the chair, just a big booming sound. Possible panic, but I divined what was happening and without demur brought my speech to an end. All was well.

After my speech a lot of people came up to me over the final days of the conference. Much of my more personal contact occurred when I called in to share a coffee break with various delegates near the hall. I ended up on the last day with two retired trade unionists, who told me that in their early days they had both been members of the Communist Party. They were thoroughly enjoying themselves and reflected for me the fact, little acknowledged, that the Labour Party, and its 1945 victory, played a major part in preserving the United Kingdom from Communism or perhaps worse. In many ways that election represented a peaceful revolution. Out I came and bumped straight into a formidable woman who congratulated me on my speech. She then added that people like me should be given not only four minutes' speaking time but four minutes' 'confessional' time in addition. The humour and sympathy of this remark added to my most pleasant conference ever and I leave it there. At last I could resume a normal life.

Part VI
REFLECTIONS

Eighteen
AT THE TIME, WHY DID
I DEFECT?

Swift was the race, but short the time to run.

John Dryden, *Absolom and Architophel*, Part I, 1681

In spite of a Tory background I have never felt I was a natural Conservative. That said, for me and many like me the Conservative Party was our natural home and there was little appeal for us in Labour and Liberal. My father had been a Conservative MP, although primarily a lawyer, and my family were entirely Conservative. To align myself with any form of Socialism in 1958, within a trade union-backed Labour Party, was unthinkable and the Liberal Party was reduced by that time to being a non-starter. On the positive side the broad church of the Conservative Party of Macmillan and Butler, tolerant; benevolent and patrician as it was, was just right and I was happy to be part of it.

As a young and contented candidate and general aspirant I inherited Ted Heath as my leader. Acceptable as his views were to me, he was rather underwhelming as a leader. He was the chosen face of modern Conservatism, and had he been just a little bit more attractive to the people he would have won the February 1974 election. Tough going as it undoubtedly would have been, we could then have modernised the country, without the wasted period of 1974–9 which led to Mrs Thatcher.

The advent of Mrs Thatcher in 1975, let alone her assumption of power in 1979, was the end of my enthusiasm for being part of the Conservative Party. I had enough contact with her, in part as related earlier, and found

267

it just too much. I had an almost chemical reaction to her, and could not stand being lectured and hectored by someone who would not let you get a word in edgeways, unless you powered it through, and who had few redeeming social graces. The first part of Chapter 4, on Mrs Thatcher and the way she operated, gives detail on this.

In politics I always had the law behind me as an alternative to return to, and when I arrived in the Commons I had the perhaps misguided idea that being an MP had something to do with controlling the executive. I also enjoyed the life as such, without ambition. Many of my friends made no such mistake and got on with their careers, on the basis that ambition and place came first, and that was why they were there. I view their approach as the more mature, given our system, and mine as understandable and in many ways the more enjoyable.

Events, dear boy, events. As the years went by, and the reforms of the economy and industrial relations were put through, Thatcher's necessary work was largely done. Apart from the odd rebellion over the 1981 Budget fuel tax and in particular over the poll tax in 1988–9, I was much more engaged in foreign affairs than the domestic agenda. This was my principal area of interest, plus of course Ireland, in which I was much involved from 1988 onwards. In both these areas Mrs Thatcher's views were limited and added to my general frustration. On foreign affairs she placed herself again and again on the 'Little England' side of things, whether Europe, South Africa, German reunification, European enlargement or whatever. The Americans never noticed these traits as much as they should have done as she was always on their side on the macro issues of the Soviet Union, expanding the EU to include Eastern Europe and Turkey and the attitude to problems of the 'good guys versus the bad guys'. They thought the world of her. On Ireland it was the same: an insufficient awareness of the historical relevance of past British behaviour towards the problems of today or any sympathy with those who strove to secure some freedom from that past.

The political and social make-up of the Conservative Party was steadily changed under Mrs Thatcher. Election by election from 1979 onwards the traditional country Tory was replaced by career-minded politicians of a different background, character and of a generally more right-wing disposition.

When I was increasingly finding myself on the outside it certainly did not help to have a media campaign waged against me over Ireland in the run-up to my defection. Ironically everyone thinks I defected over Europe, but it was also the very rough time I had over Ireland at the hands of the Conservative supporters of Ulster Unionism in the right-wing press. I did not belong any more and more welcoming hosts in the Labour Party were beckoning.

The advent of Tony Blair was an essential element in my departure. The changing nature of the Conservative Party created the mood and situation. However, the essential part of defection for me was to be happy with what I might be going to. Tony Blair presented a new face, a social democratic face, of Labour, New Labour to be precise, which, together with Peter Mandelson and the entourage, was a considerable attraction and I felt instinctively on the same side. On Europe, constitutional reform, Ireland and social affairs we were on the same page. Once William Hague became leader of the Conservative Party rather than Kenneth Clarke, I realised that my future in the Conservative Party was untenable.

The final stage is personal. Years of struggle within for the values of the old party had got me nowhere. I was getting older and less restrained, and my sympathies were on the move. My Labour friends of many years in the House made it plain that they were ready for me to join them and I would be happier with them. In contrast my Conservative friends had become comparatively few with the passage of time and elections. My state of mind developed and it was all too easy to finally press the button.

Nineteen

REFLECTIONS, SEVENTEEN YEARS LATER

Politicians neither love nor hate.
John Dryden, *Absolom and Architophel*, Part I, 1681

A defection within the House, whilst the House is sitting, is one of the most dramatic events that can happen in a political career. Next would be a defection from a sitting member but during a recess. A change of parties *en bloc*, as with the Labour defection to form the SDP in the early 1980s, is certainly special but it is a different thing. Similarly a change of parties announced outside the House involving a former Member without a seat is different again. Also in a different category would be former ministers or members fighting their way back under a different flag at a by-election, as with Roy Jenkins and Shirley Williams, and much later the Ukip defections.

In my time in Parliament, there was a group of Labour members who joined the SDP and ended up losing their seats, leaving politics or continuing with the Liberal Democrats, or the Conservatives in the case of John Horam. A number were elevated to the Lords. Post-1979, the first Conservative defection, and the only one to the SDP, was Christopher Brocklebank-Fowler in 1982. He lost his seat in 1983 and never returned to Parliament. The more recent crop of political refugees began with Alan Howarth in 1995. Originally a member of the Thatcherite No Turning Back Group, he had a very genuine conversion and settled well into

Labour, first as a junior minister and then in the House of Lords. Next came Emma Nicholson in 1996, from Conservative to Liberal Democrat. Her departure caused more ill-feeling on the Conservative side than I ever expected. She had a very difficult time of it, but Paddy Ashdown gave her a warm welcome, with a seat in the European Parliament and a peerage. Hugh Dykes, a prominent pro-European Conservative lost his seat in 1997, and then went over to the Liberal Democrats, where he was made welcome and was given a seat in the Lords. I came next in the sequence in 1997–8, as already described. There followed in December 1999 a great surprise, with the departure of Shaun Woodward from Conservative to Labour. He had run the Conservative media operation for the 1992 General Election, appeared part of the party establishment and until the time of defection was a very vociferous member of the Shadow Environment team, dealing with London. As a Labour backbencher I was well placed to register the shock of most of my Labour colleagues, and I had to spend a considerable amount of time trying to explain the situation. He was humbly born, intellectually gifted and married into the Sainsbury family, with access through his wife to considerable wealth and a lifestyle to go with it. As a result he had a terrible time from the Conservative press, who turned on him and his own family with a vengeance. By the time I turned out with Mo Mowlem, officially to welcome him back to the House to take his Labour seat, he had had about as much as he could take. We took him into the Chamber before prayers, at his request, so that he could already be in his place when the actual sitting began, rather than 'crossing the floor', and he made himself as scarce as possible for some months after that, until he got his balance back. Sometime afterwards in 2007 there arrived Quentin Davies, who joined Gordon Brown on his accession as prime minister. At the time it, and the justification for it, was a complete surprise, but being Quentin he carried it all off with such style and panache that the past just seemed to look after itself. He had an enjoyable period at Defence as a junior minister and is now active in the House of Lords.

I often reflect as to whether I would do the same thing again. My direct answer is emphatically 'no'. But this is based on hindsight and how

I would have conducted my career with another chance. The answer is that I would not have been a rebel but rather a team player, stayed longer at the bar and then used the Commons for advancement as the opportunity arose. This would have meant a totally different life, and probably a less enjoyable one, even if I had gained high office. Had that happened then, like others, I would have been insulated from the day-to-day divisive pressures that prevailed on the backbenches. As part of the government with a job to do it is easier to conform without the daily pressures from the media and discontented colleagues.

As for Parliament I spent three years as a Labour backbencher in the Commons and it added much to my life. Politically my Labour colleagues were all very kind, and I concentrated on issues I knew about and more importantly on which Labour appreciated my assistance. Ireland and constitutional issues were the obvious ones for me to focus on. However, the social front is more interesting. How could I, from my background, which the press saw as grander than it was, commit myself socially to Labour? Was it not a strain, they asked. It certainly was not and within the House of Commons I much enjoyed myself with Labour. I dined regularly in the Members' Dining Room and was always received as one of the party and a friend. In addition I was more than useful as someone they trusted, to give them views as to what on earth was going on in the Conservative Party at the time. I dined with all sorts, from Glaswegian hardmen to Cabinet ministers, some of whom made no secret that they came from Conservative, middle-class backgrounds, which under Tony Blair became quite normal as part of New Labour. Out onto the terrace I went, and to a different life from the Smoking Room I had been used to. My role was advisory and I was very conscious to play to my strength in this regard. In my case there was no way that I could have influence with a purely Labour Party issue. That said, I was listened to and even if I failed with such things as fox hunting and the choice of a Speaker, I always kept my end up and was accepted for myself.

As to the Conservatives, I have always been very careful since defection. Politically I have never attacked my old party as such and as distinct from dealing with the issues. This has helped me to normalise my relationships over the years, although it has to be said that back in the Commons my old friends were the same as ever, all the way through. Once I was in the Lords it all became much easier and much less party political in atmosphere. In general when I arrived the more distinguished the Conservative peer the easier they were with me. Only in a very few cases did I have any difficulty and these were foreseeable. I have renewed various relationships again and all is normal. As I am still very much the same person I have always been, this is a great relief to me.

There is a fundamental difficulty about defection. With the passage of time comes perspective and there remains a factor that is more difficult to get around than the others. When one defects one travels over the great divide for reasons relevant then, and similarly to personalities to whom one is sympathetically disposed. In my case I agreed with the concept of New Labour, respected the leadership of Tony Blair, and what he stood for, together with the excellent team he had gathered around him, particularly Peter Mandelson. New Labour meant something to me and signalled an effort to move towards Labour becoming a social democratic party, free of the unions as an internal force. The problem for the defector is that the party you join is as susceptible to change as the one that you left. As that change happens it is not necessarily to your taste but you must basically accept it. In my old party I had the right, when in it, to object to anything but in my new one I have to accept the direction of travel. Perhaps if I was younger, and had my career ahead of me, it could be different, but I would still feel that I was intruding and some would undoubtedly resent it. It is also an awkward position generally. Should I come out against a Labour policy, my former colleagues on the Conservative side would notice, smile and say 'Here he goes again'. There is no way I want this to happen. The Labour Party gives me a generous base for any activity other than internal politics. The practical result is that I accept change in my new party, but still live in hope that it will not stray too far from the social democratic style and values of Tony Blair. My situation comes as the baggage of defection.

Historically, defection is not an easy road. Examples are often quoted at me and particularly that of Winston Churchill. I myself have absolutely no intention of moving back to the Conservatives, if indeed they would have me, and the fact that Churchill twice crossed the floor is a factor of his times and of doubtful relevance today. In any event he was somewhat unique, and on the second occasion the Liberal Party was falling apart, and I doubt whether he felt sufficiently a part of it to want to remain in a faction. He saw himself as a major player and ever the Tory when the chips were down. However, the really relevant factor is that after his varied career, he was never really trusted by the Conservative Party and when out of office increasingly isolated within it. He did not make life easier over the India Bill and the Abdication and were it not for the 'gathering storm' his effective political career would have been largely over.

Roy Jenkins is another interesting example. Despite a distinguished career and a formidable personality, he was somehow never quite trusted by his party, in spite of his eminent Labour roots. Had Labour lost in February 1974 he would have been a candidate for the leadership, but that was not to be. Perhaps his undoubted grandeur, and associated social life, denied him enough of the common touch to get on with Labour generally in that era. After he left he had a difficult time leading the SDP as a minority party in opposition. He belonged, if anyone did, to the government front bench. He said once, visibly uncomfortable, as he struggled at Question Time, that he was much more used to answering questions than asking them. Had he succeeded in changing the face of British politics, and I believe he was nearer to this than he is given credit for, he would have ended as a sort of peacetime Churchill. As it was he had to settle for Labour jeers and constant internal difficulties within the Liberal/Social Democratic Alliance.

A very different and less high-profile example is Reg Prentice, in my view a fine Labour man and an excellent Cabinet minister under Harold Wilson. He was the first to be targeted by the hard left and he would not put up with it. He left Labour in October 1977 and joined Mrs Thatcher's Conservatives, serving as a Minister of State in her governments until, duly knighted, he left the House in 1987. John Major made him a life peer in 1992.He dealt with social security as a minister and there was no doubting his competence, even if he was serving at a lower rank than before. The question was whether he was happy as a Conservative. I observed him constantly over the years and he never seemed as relaxed and confident as he had been when he graced the very impressive front bench that Harold Wilson returned to power with in 1974.

I had the nicest of constituencies, which I preserved for the Conservatives in difficult times, and represented for a total of over twenty-seven years. My Constituency Association stood by me when necessary, and I like to think that I repaid them by preserving the seat as Conservative over the difficulties, local and national, of the two 1974 elections and later on handing them back a solid majority after the massive national defeat of 1997. That said, I never forget the expressions of sadness, rather than enmity, of my former County Councillors when I visited the Council officially, but no longer as a Conservative MP, in 1998. I now have no formal contact with my former association, which is a sad loss for me. There are redeeming features and the split is not so bad as some might imagine. During the selection of my successor I was privately sent the selection committee's comments and markings of the various contenders, which was very courteous in the circumstances. I have been made Chief Steward of the City of Hereford, my county town, but not in the Constituency, which gives me a local role and retains my link with the area.

I am fortunate in that my defection caused no difference to my life outside politics. My one big worry was my Cambridge Conservative political circle – 'the Cambridge mafia' – referred to in this book. I need not have worried. I now attend all our gatherings that are, as we get older, on an annual basis, and find that I am not the only non-Conservative amongst us. It gives it a very refreshing aspect that I think the public would appreciate.

Does the defector feel accepted in another party? My experience has been 'yes', with due recognition of all the kindness I received from Labour, at all levels. However, there is the question of one's own confidence and this has to be earned at all levels of the party. I tried just to be myself and found that nobody could be more welcoming than the Labour Party.

On confidence and acceptance, the best story I can tell goes back to the Labour Party unleashing me to canvass for them in the Monmouth

Constituency in 2000, during the Welsh Assembly elections. My first outing with Labour, to face the realities of the actual electorate, was quite an experience. I met up with a very nice crowd of people who adopted me as one of their number immediately, and after a coffee and a speech from me, out we went to face the multitude. Later we devised a plan to give me an experience of the rough and the smooth of canvassing from the Labour side. This itself was an adjustment for me as when I was taken to an area, and later through many such visits, it was always the most Tory area in town so that I, as a former Tory, might make a little difference. I would arrive and after years of doing it from the other side would think 'this is an easy area for us', and then, like lightning, the thought would strike home that I was canvassing as Labour, and not as a Conservative. In Monmouth the plan was to show me, and let me canvass in, the most politically different areas we could find, which meant a very prosperous new housing development and then down the road for a mile to a dreary, dull, overgrown 1960s council estate.

We started with the plush housing. This was a small private development occupied by professional and financial-sector people wanting access across the Severn Bridge to Bristol and its growing financial district. The houses were very expensive and the forecourts had two and even three cars on them. I did it alone, with the others watching intently, and the local branch secretary marking down the canvass. At that time I was recognised by most residents and my message was well received. Then came the responses, and the plain fact was that these potential Tory voters, with one polite exception, all thought the world of Tony Blair, admired what he was doing and had little sympathy with William Hague or his party. The branch secretary could hardly believe it, and with her in a state of politically induced delirium we then departed to the council estate.

Into it we went. Into another world. Everything was unkempt and overgrown, with signs of poverty plain to see. Our first main call was to a corner council house with a large, untended garden. We called out and before I could register anything a formidable old woman, with a stick which she waved when she could, came rushing towards us, and me, shouting 'Get out, get out.' At that moment I thought my brief Labour canvassing career was coming to an all-too-abrupt end. To my partial relief she was chased down the garden by her forty-something-year-old daughter, trying desperately to restrain her. She came straight for me and the others took up firm positions behind me. She arrived and shouted: 'Get out of here. We don't want you.' At that moment I expected a full attack on defecting Tories, which would have been an ignominious end to my visit. Far from it! 'We don't want you here. You're Michael's man. We want Rhodri here. We want Rhodri!' At that time there was a major dispute within Welsh Labour about the leadership of Tony Blair's nominee, Alan Michael MP, AM, in the Welsh Assembly or the preferred local option, which was eventually accepted, of Rhodri Morgan MP, AM. From that great moment I felt I was accepted. Here I was being addressed by a Labour woman, in full cry, as if I represented something within the Labour Party. In a strange way I had arrived!

Under Tony Blair I had no problem with what I saw as the ethos of Labour. The whole direction in which he was taking the Labour Party was towards the centre and away from any question of class. Since the end of Blair's leadership, and increasingly in recent years, I have had difficulty in relating to what again seems like Old Labour, with its left-wing 'us and them' connotations. With the comradeship of the Commons, I felt no problem and the detached atmosphere of the Lords is similar, with some excellent Labour peers from across the political spectrum. That said, with the advent of our now former leader Ed Miliband some declared 'At last we have our party back', and it remains to be seen how far back we go. The constant association with those that have not is commendable and is part of the Labour ethic, but it cannot be a complete way of life. It is counter-productive when constantly used to attack or blame those that have. Hope, aspiration and even a little excitement along the way are part of life, and have their place in, for example, sorting out the serious political problems of the north–south political divide. The so-called dependence on the 'core vote', and the behaviour that goes with it, is not the way to social democracy.

Enoch Powell's famous dictum that every political career ends in failure has enough truth about it to make it stick, but not in my case. My political life has not been perfect, and there is much I continue to try to improve on. However, the way it has all gone leads me to no regrets of any substance. Above all I am happy and I have greatly enjoyed myself, made a few things better and harmed nobody.

Twenty

WHERE AM I NOW, WHERE ARE WE?

The May 2015 General Election was the worst I can remember. The worst personally and the worst in overall quality of exchange. A shallow election fought in the media, amidst little popular excitement or commitment. In the end those who decide these things voted unenthusiastically, but sensibly, in their own best interests. Small wonder the polls were overturned by the electorate the pollsters claim to understand.

Personally it was political agony. The problem with changing parties is that the same depth of loyalty one originally had for the old party does not automatically accompany one to the new. Even if that party has been good to you, you have good friends there and you want to be loyal, this is politics. The country comes first.

No doubt some retain the passion of the convert and can even overstate their new allegiance. For others it's not that easy. The new party changes, but you live in hope that it will change back to your way of thinking: in opposition this is not much of a problem. Then suddenly there comes a General Election, and a concentration of minds, under a leader whom you may have to serve in power, expressing all manner of policies and preferences with which you cannot agree. How much of it can you stand?

Back in 1983, after the Conservatives were returned with a thumping majority, some backbenchers tried to take advantage of the situation by contriving a vote on capital punishment. In accordance with my views of those days I voted in favour and sat in the chamber to hear the result. It was expected to be close. As the minutes passed a feeling of foreboding gradually came over me, getting stronger and stronger. I realised I did not want my side to win the vote, indeed I dreaded it. In came the tellers and the result was announced, with capital punishment roundly rejected. By this time I had resolved never to vote for it again and when the subject duly reappeared in 1988, I spoke and voted against it and went on the *Today* programme into the bargain. It was in effect a confession of past error, and the next morning who should knock on my office door as my redeemer but Michael Foot, who had spoken just before or after me in the debate, to sympathetically congratulate me on my speech. A warm gesture from a great man.

As the election wore on this memory came back to me but this time there was no redeemer in immediate sight. I would be expected to support with votes in the Lords a Labour prime minister whose metropolitan quasi-socialism was just not for me. As I left capital punishment to the wisdom of the House of Commons, so I left this to the wisdom of the electorate. They would decide and in turn I would decide what to do in the light of their decision. They certainly decided and we now have a majority government on the one hand and a Labour Party that has time to work things out, hopefully for the better. Good for the country in both respects, and good for me in that I am again able to live in hope for Labour.

So to Labour. How many chances does the party have to become the progressive centre party alternative that the country needs so desperately? The 'Miliband adventure' has exposed the electoral weaknesses of Labour for all to see. How on earth could such an aberration happen in a party claiming to be intent on power and government? Perhaps the answer is that it is not yet such a party.

The fundamental flaw in the Labour Party lies in its origins, which is that it still cannot decide whether it is a 'Movement' or a 'Party'. It was formed as a factional movement of the working class and as such could have confidently expected to be a formidable third force in British politics, but by nature a movement representing its component sectors of interest. No doubt it would have entered government in coalition, primarily, but not necessarily always, with the Liberals. Suddenly, and before anyone had really thought about it, two Liberal titans, Messrs Asquith and Lloyd George, clashed, with Asquith being deposed by Lloyd George as prime minister in 1916. Thanks in the main to the wounded ego of Mr Asquith, the division was allowed to continue through no less than four General Elections and beyond. From the outset, with Lloyd George as Liberal prime minister in coalition, Asquith retained, and continued to retain, the official leadership of the Liberal Party; he refused to come back into the fold as Lord Chancellor and eventually, as Liberal leader, allowed Labour to form its first government and from there to replace the Liberals as the alternative to the Conservatives. Thus Labour unexpectedly emerged and multiplied, on the back of a factional and working-class vote increasingly supported by Scotland and Wales. Historically this base was too comfortable to last and nobody discovered the effects of changing times more abruptly than Mr Miliband. The public, and particularly the English public, expect Labour to talk to them as a party and not a factional movement. The term 'working people' has become part of the vocabulary of all political parties. But for Miliband to constantly employ it, often in conjunction with references to 'the rich', 'bankers', and so on, made it sound factional and class-based. It did not help to establish the image of Labour as a truly national party. The national challenge for Labour is to get itself into the political centre and its own domestic challenge has to be to establish a working relationship with the unions but with them outside the party. That clears the way to become a progressive social democratic party. Easy to say but difficult to deliver.

Leaders of political parties make an enormous difference. Leaders can change parties, divide parties and can sooner or later fail, and all the time are protected by the tribal loyalty without which no party can succeed. The effects of success or failure are compounded accordingly. As soon as leaders fall an absolute cacophony breaks out, as their erstwhile supporters break cover and vent the frustrations of years of silence. Mrs Thatcher changed the Conservative Party, and the country too, but in the process came near to destroying the historic cohesion of her party. Miliband would most certainly have changed things quite disastrously, Europe or no Europe. Asquith's behaviour seems to have escaped comparison with Edward Heath's 'longest sulk in history', but he certainly managed to play the major role in the diminution of his once great party. Understandably, it withered on the historical vine. It managed to preserve a base but only that. Over the years it steadily became a basket for eccentrics and various degrees of protest vote. Such votes have no roots, are in many cases negative and come and go with glorious abandon. For the present they have well and truly gone. The Liberal Democrats must now build up from scratch, concentrating on their core values, widely shared, and await events. If Labour continues to make a mess of things, their hour could come again sooner than we might think.

The election itself was the worst in quality I can remember, and I have fought ten of them. That said, the redeeming feature was that it was fascinating in the change it embodied and the result it eventually delivered. Winston Churchill once remarked on the subject of election manifestos that they should 'resemble more a lighthouse than a shop window'. This whole election quite exceeded his warning and at times resembled more an oriental bazaar than a serious discussion of the alternatives for the nation's future. There was no great debate. Instead we were treated to a gigantic consumer give-away, which was so expensive, on the back of so little money, that we emerged in a state of bemused disbelief. Not for us to be troubled by Britain's future in Europe or the world, by defence, mass immigration into Southern Europe or, in major party discussion, climate change, international trade competition or even the seriousness of the overall economic background. Instead we witnessed a merry-go-round of set pieces and gimmicks. Not long ago politicians made real speeches to the electorate at large and sometimes got shouted at. Those who sought to govern had style, be it grandly positive or lethally negative. We should remember Prime Minister Harold Macmillan in 1958, referring at the airport, as he was leaving for a Commonwealth tour, to the resignation of his Chancellor of the Exchequer, Peter Thorneycroft, no less, together with his junior ministers, Enoch Powell and Nigel Birch, on an issue of public expenditure. Macmillan paused for effect and with a twinkle in his eye said it had caused him 'a little anxiety' but we should 'settle up these little local difficulties'. Magnificent. Perhaps difficult to get away with nowadays, but still magnificent. And recall too the all-too-clever Harold Wilson in his prime, when belittling, quite undeservedly, his rival Edward Heath over Europe. He compared Heath to a spaniel that rolled over on its back whenever Europe was mentioned. 'Now', he said, 'before I get hundreds of letters of objection from spaniel lovers let me say that I love spaniels too; it's just that I would not put one of them in charge of our negotiations with the Common Market.' Heath hated that one, but negative and even unpleasant as it was, it had style.

Contrast the present, and what do we get? Enter Boris Johnson to assist a boring campaign, accompanying our unenthusiastic prime minister on a visit to yet another infants' school, containing the tiniest possible children, to avoid any risk of spontaneous interrogation. Our heroes arrive at a somewhat bleak backdrop and in they go. The only dialogue to be heard was a soft 'My name's David', and they solemnly joined the class, emerging all too soon brandishing blue hands. The two stars then promptly left, with nobody gathered outside, and were swept away in a large Jaguar car. This epic of modern electioneering was only to be bettered by the leader of the opposition. He suddenly appeared on the news in front of an enormous stone, upon which were inscribed his pledges to us, in seeming perpetuity. This edifice was apparently to be firmly embedded in the pleasant garden at the back of Number 10 so he could be for ever reminded of the immortal words. After that I could hardly stand anything anymore.

This was essentially a technological, media-orientated election. The media were supplied with a constant stream of material which they adapted and used to fill their slots. They did their best with serious interviews, which in general were well worth watching. That said, they did not quite get us there. It took the public to do that, and the debates we had, together with the excellent *Question Time* as a finale, gave them the opportunity. Unfair as television can be, who can forget First Minister Sturgeon bursting upon the scene, and the searing attack on Miliband in the second debate as, with mouth pursed and eyes blazing, she challenged him on his core beliefs: why would he not join her in keeping the Tories out of power? His reply was reduced to irrelevance, and when you couple that with the direct interrogation on *Question Time* about Labour's spending habits in the run-up to the 2008 financial crisis, he was effectively done for. Without those exchanges, where would we be?

Now to the future. The new Conservative MPs represent a significant change. Looking at them duly assembled, I could not but think that only some forty-odd years ago many of them would not have been Conservative MPs. The party then was very different. Here they were representing a cross-section of the aspirant middle class with increasing gender equality and ethnic representation to go with it – much what Tony Blair would have had in mind for the development of New Labour. The Labour Party must stand warned; a repeat internal performance based on class and union power will not do. The Liberal Democrats may be down and out, but the lessons of history are there. If the party prepares itself, the mistakes of others may clear the way. The moral of this rather strange election is how much can change, and how quickly. The so-called 'core vote' can no longer be relied upon, and the old ideologies upon which the concept is based are constantly being diluted. An election dominated by the media and set to serve the media is a fickle thing.

Appendix
CAMBRIDGE
PROFILES

Cambridge Union and Conservative Association (CUCA) profiles 1958–61, and adjacent years.

JOHN BARNES
A particularly brilliant history first from Caius. Cambridge don, author and lecturer in government at the LSE, 1964–2003.

The late LEON BRITTAN
The Rt. Hon. Lord Brittan of Spenithorne; Queen's Counsel; MP for Yorkshire seats, February 1974–1988; Secretary of State; EU Commissioner; Vice-Chairman, UBS Investment Bank.

Most of us of the 1957–61 intake would agree that Leon was, amongst a formidable gallery, the overall star of the show. Scholar, first-class honours, chairman of CUCA, President of the Union and a Fellow of Yale. He accomplished all this with a wisdom, balance and natural warmth that we all appreciated. He acted almost as a father figure to his own contemporaries. It took him time to find a safe seat, but Yorkshire gave him his base, and from there he progressed effortlessly into office, reaching the Cabinet in 1981, at the age of forty-two. He was unexpectedly promoted to Home Secretary after the election in 1983. This was caused by the necessary move of Party Chairman Cecil Parkinson from the Foreign Office, for which he was destined, to Industry, on account of personal circumstances. Geoffrey Howe, destined for the Home Office, as we understood, then became Foreign Secretary and Leon became Home Secretary. He was moved (some say unnecessarily) to Trade and Industry just in time to inherit the impact on that Department of the Westland affair in 1986. Resignation followed and, after a pause, appointment as an EU Commissioner. He had had a glittering domestic career ahead of him but that was not to be. He fulfilled his role as a Member and then Vice-President of the Commission with considerable distinction and a peerage and banking career followed.

The late NICHOLAS BUDGEN
Barrister; MP for Wolverhampton South West, February 1974–97.

A professional and stylish sceptic throughout his life, which sadly and prematurely came to an end in 1998. We may have disagreed on many things but we were at each other's weddings, shared an office when we arrived at the Commons and were friends for life. He succeeded Enoch Powell at Wolverhampton and decided that he would strike an independent, rightish, Euro-sceptic stance with some style, which he increasingly enjoyed. Three weeks after we arrived in the Commons, in our little room in Dean's Yard, I remember him composing his first rebellious speech. He never looked back. The only time I remember him as remotely progressive was at Cambridge, when he spent a Long Vacation in South Africa and, being in touch with a real hard-right racist government, had such a shock that he came back to Cambridge sounding positively moderate on the subject for a term, until he recovered his balance. In 1981 the whips made a valiant attempt to bring him within the tent and he was made an assistant government whip. It was a good try, but he couldn't stand the restrictions on his style and left after a year to resume his colourful political existence, which included amusing us all in the Smoking Room. Among his many talents he was a good point to point jockey as well as a talented barrister who could have gone far in the profession. When all is said and done, my favourite memory of him, as already related, is at Trinity Hall with Harold Macmillan's arm resting on his shoulders. He had asked some irreverent question, we were all laughing, Macmillan was relaxed and everyone was happy. Nick had that effect on people.

KENNETH CLARKE

The Rt. Hon. Kenneth Clarke QC; MP for Rushcliffe since 1970; Secretary of State, Chancellor of the Exchequer, Home Secretary, Justice Secretary and other offices of state.

Ken Clarke arrived at Cambridge in 1959 from Nottingham High School and duly became President of the Union, chairman of CUCA and chairman of the Federation of Conservative Students across all UK universities. My first sight of him was when I was with Norman Fowler discussing CUCA business in the aftermath of an utterly disastrous Union performance on behalf of the government the night before by Hugh Fraser MP. Ken turned up together with Michael Howard to complain and to protest to Norman that we had to do better. After Cambridge he went to the Birmingham Bar, married and lived in Nottingham, where he remains to this day. Adopted early on for the near local seat of Rushcliffe, he entered the House in 1970 and soon became a government whip. In opposition from 1974, he went back to the Bar and barely held on to a junior front bench position. However, once a member of the 1979 government and able to concentrate on his job as an Under-Secretary, there was no stopping him. The rest is history. A delightful and utterly unpretentious man, we all wanted him to come to the Lords, but he firmly told my wife that he would stay in the Commons for as long as he was enjoying it – and so far he still is.

JOHN COCKCROFT

Journalist, company director; MP for Nantwich, February 1974–9.

President of the Union when I arrived in Michaelmas term 1958, he was known as an operator who had mobilised the formidable Union vote of St John's College to become President of the Union the term before Julian Grenfell. A scholar of his college, he went on to the *Financial Times*, industry, the Treasury and then to the *Daily Telegraph*. Into the Commons he came in February 1974, but for personal reasons his political and parliamentary career ended prematurely in 1979.

HUGH DYKES

Lord Dykes; stockbroker; MP for Harrow East, 1970–97, Liberal Democrat peer from 2004.

A talented linguist and prominent in CUCA. Amongst the first to enter the Commons in 1970. An aide to Edward Heath as Leader of the opposition, he remained loyal to Heath throughout his time in the Commons. A left-wing and pro-European Conservative, he became chairman of the European Movement in the UK from 1990 until 1996. He lost his Harrow seat in 1997 and soon after defected to the Liberal Democrats in September 1997. In 2004 he was raised to the peerage and has served as an active Liberal Democratic peer thereafter.

NORMAN FOWLER

The Rt. Hon. Lord Fowler; *Times* journalist; MP for Nottingham South and then Sutton Coldfield, from 1970 until 2001; Secretary of State, Chairman of the Conservative Party, Chairman Midland Independent Newspapers and the Yorkshire Post Group of newspapers and Director of Companies. Life peer.

Chairman of CUCA and Union committee member, he was, at Cambridge and thereafter, forever capable, competent, loyal, wise and a safe pair of hands. Amongst his assets was his ability to always remain entirely normal, affable to all and to handle well any position he was given. At Cambridge his moment of glory came when he hosted the visit of Harold Macmillan to CUCA in November 1960. After Cambridge, via *The Times*, he entered the Commons in 1970 at the age of thirty-two. After a brief spell as a junior Home Affairs Spokesman in opposition he was appointed Shadow Secretary for Health and Social Services, a member of the Shadow Cabinet and facing the formidable Secretary of State, Barbara Castle. He survived with credit and eventually held that office in government for no less than six years. It was an enormous department which was subsequently split into two. He resigned from the Cabinet in 1990 'to see more of his family'. Subsequently brought back by John Major as Chairman of the Party at a very difficult time, he went on to the Lords, writing, chairing major committees on the BBC, communication and latterly HIV/Aids, about which he has published a well-received book.

ROGER GRAHAM

After Cambridge Roger founded a considerable IT business, which he sold in middle age. He retains many interests, including contact with the Conservative Party, and is a supporter and contributor at local and national level. An active committee member at Cambridge, he always made it clear that he was leaving the House of Commons to us and would concentrate on making a commercial success of his life. He has always remained close to us.

JULIAN GRENFELL

3rd Baron Grenfell and Baron Grenfell of Kilvey (life peer), a senior official of the World Bank in Washington DC and in Europe.

President of the Union, Lent term, 1959. Union debates were presided over with an effortless style and adjourned at say 11.05 p.m. 'of the clock'. After a short time in the media, and getting his traditionalist father to become an early patron of the emerging and then somewhat radical Bow Group, he went to the World Bank, where he had a full and distinguished career. He then returned to the Lords, having emerged as a member of the Labour Party. When I arrived at the Lords in 2001 our Cambridge peers and contemporaries gave the traditional dinner of welcome for Norman Fowler and me, the new arrivals, and it is an amusing fact that of the ten present, no fewer than three – Julian, me and David Hacking, another hereditary peer – had all at some time joined the Labour Party. Refugees from Thatcher, you could have called us, and it has never made an iota of difference to our relationships with our old political friends at Cambridge. Julian went on to make a second distinguished career for himself in the Lords, from which he has now retired. A great man and so beautifully English.

JOHN SELWYN GUMMER

The Rt. Hon. Lord Deben; publisher; MP for Lewisham 1970–4 and Eye, later Suffolk Coastal, from 1979 to 2005; Secretary of State; Chairman of Sancroft International Ltd from 1997, life peer.

John arrived at Selwyn in 1958 as an exhibitioner, being the son of a Church of England canon and with strong Church connections. We rose through CUCA together. John's first claim to fame at the Union was to be appointed the 'Lord's Defender' in our termly 'God debate', as we called it. He was perhaps the most fluent Union speaker of any of us and made such a good job of his task that the good Lord would not let him go and he was required to repeat the exercise for the next such debate. This he ably did but having ambitions in the Union he wanted a chance to display his secular skills as well and, by courtesy of the next president, he got his transfer. He went on to become President of the Union and later in 1993 he joined the Roman Catholic Church. In a long ministerial career he distinguished himself as Environment Secretary 1993–7 and remains active in that field today. He is one of three brothers, all of whom have been very successful. At the same time John's son, Ben, sits in the Commons as Conservative Member for Ipswich.

DAVID HACKING
Third Baron Hacking; hereditary peer and member of the Lords until the 1999 Act; barrister, solicitor and International Commercial Arbitrator.

Active in CUCA and the Union throughout his Cambridge years, he was grandson of a former chairman of the Conservative Party, and succeeded his father in the Lords in 1971. A Conservative and then Labour peer, he left the Lords in 1999, after the Peerage Act, and having been a successful City solicitor he returned to the Bar to become an international arbitrator.

MICHAEL HOWARD
The Rt. Hon. Lord Howard of Lympne CH, QC; MP for Folkestone and Hythe, 1983–2010; Secretary of State; leader of the Conservative Party chairman and director of companies.

He arrived at Cambridge from Llanelli Grammar School in 1959, with considerable ambition and a charm that has never left him. I made him my Assistant Secretary of CUCA in the summer term of 1960. I forgot all about it until, years later, in 1999, I spoke from the Labour benches on Ireland and, during one of his rare periods on the backbenches, he followed me from the Conservative side. He was very warm in his reference to me and informed the House that I had given him his first political job, for which he was grateful. This caused a hiatus, and somewhat stunned silence, as everyone wondered what on earth he was talking about. Nobody realised that it was in fact the CUCA position mentioned and on the Labour side a cry went up that 'It is all your fault, Peter.' He was delayed in getting to Westminster by having to wait for his wife-to-be, the former leading model of the 1960s, Sandra Paul, to obtain a divorce. This cleared the way for Conservative selection committees and a safe seat. Meanwhile he consolidated his legal career before he duly entered the Commons in 1983. At Cambridge his political life had been destined to competition with Kenneth Clarke, which has persisted throughout their political lives. At Cambridge they followed and leap-frogged each other in various positions until both achieved the chairmanship of CUCA and the presidency of the Union. At Cambridge he did not have a right-wing reputation at all but he arrived in the Commons with Thatcherism at its height. It did not take him long to embark on a succession of minister-ial jobs but in so doing he steadily moved to the Thatcherite right. This right-wing image developed a momentum of its own and helped to spoil his chances when he faced the British people as leader of the Conservative Party at the 2005 General Election. He did a good job nevertheless, but the ultimate prize then eluded him, as did a real chance to lead the party to victory in 2010.

NORMAN LAMONT
The Rt. Hon. Lord Lamont of Lerwick; merchant banker; MP for Kingston on Thames, May 1972–97; Chancellor of the Exchequer; director of companies.

Arrived in Cambridge from Loretto in 1961, thus linking up with Michael Howard, Ken Clarke and John Gummer. Became chairman of CUCA and President of the Union and entered the Commons via the Conservative Research Department and merchant banking. He was marked out from the beginning as going places, which his considerable ability justified. His active political career came to an abrupt end when, having taken considerable personal flak to protect John Major from the consequences of our ERM exit, he was removed from the Treasury in 1993. Although offered another Cabinet post he declined and went to the backbenches. After a difficult period when his anger was perhaps too visible, he settled down in the Lords and has become a much-valued commentator and writer, mainly on the financial front. When I arrived in the Lords in 2001 it fell to Norman, the first Conservative to speak from the other side of the House after my maiden speech, to congratulate me. His neighbour, not a Commons man, made a hardly charitable comment in urging Norman not to say anything nice about me. He was informed that Norman and I had been friends for years and a generous tribute was paid.

PETER LLOYD

The Rt. Hon. Sir Peter Lloyd; marketing manager; MP for Fareham, 1979–2001; Home Office Minister of State, President, National Council of Independent Monitoring Boards for Prisons 2003–7.

A good and conscientious chairman of CUCA, Michaelmas 1959, with me serving under him in my first officer post as social secretary. He went off into business but emerged to become MP for a safe seat in 1979. He came up through the Whips' Office to become a Home Office minister. He chose to retire in 2001 to help take care of his wife but continued to do useful work for Arab–British relations and pursue his interest in the theatre.

JOHN NOTT

The Rt. Hon. Sir John Nott; MP for St Ives, 1966–83; Secretary of State; merchant banker, Chairman and CEO of Lazard Bros and director of other companies.

A brilliant, acerbic and witty speaker who became President of the Union in 1959. A regular ex-Ghurkha officer, he left the Army, came to Cambridge, married while still there, got called to the Bar but went on to the City, to which he returned after he left the House of Commons in 1983. He was Defence Secretary during the Falklands War but resigned after it and did not seek re-election in 1983. An unhappy end to what had been a successful ministerial career.

The late ROBIN PEDLER

CUCA secretary and history first from Caius. A successful corporate executive.

COLIN RENFREW

Lord Renfrew of Kaimsthorn; Professor of Archaeology at the University of Southampton and then Cambridge; Master of Jesus College, Cambridge.

Colin was on the CUCA Committee and became President of the Union. He had an illustrious academic career ending as Cambridge Professor of Archaeology and Master of Jesus College. This resulted in his elevation to the Lords in 1991, where he sits on the Conservative benches. I was honoured to make the nomination speeches for him each time he successfully stood for the CUCA Committee. I once got a big laugh by saying that his stated interest in foreign affairs was entirely genuine as I had met him on the Champs-Élysées during the Long Vacation. What I did not say was that we had had a great night out together, and after seeing that memorable artist of mime, Marcel Marceau, we ended up at a nightclub called Le Monocle in Montparnasse. What we did not know, in our innocence, was that it was the leading lesbian nightspot in Paris. Greeted by an all-female orchestra, dressed in dinner jackets, grinding out something, and with some regulars resenting our presence, we literally fled.

MICHAEL SPICER

Lord Spicer; economist; MP for South and later West Worcestershire, February 1974–2010; vice-chairman of the party; minister; Chairman of the 1922 Committee of Conservative Backbenchers.

Just too late at Cambridge to be part of our CUCA/Union ensemble he became well known to most of us most of us later on. Made a name for himself at Cambridge by establishing his very own political vehicle known as Pressure for Economic and Social Toryism, aptly known as PEST. Via the Conservative Research Department he went on to establish a successful Economic Advisory Unit before entering Parliament with me, as my agreeable constituency neighbour, in February 1974. He has been a long-standing friend, although our views on Europe are radically different. Once or twice we tried to bring the factions together on this within the party but to no avail as the divisions were too deep. On a personal note he was the long-standing captain of the Commons tennis team and in that capacity did me a great favour by keeping the more right-wing members of his team in place for a morning match, knowing that most of them would be against me in an election, at the same time, for the chairmanship of the British Group, Inter-Parliamentary Union. I won and was grateful.

MARTIN SUTHERS

Solicitor and former Lord Mayor of Nottingham, numerous local interests.

The engine room of CUCA! Martin was always at the centre of activities and a fount of knowledge about the Conservative Party. Committee member and editor of our magazine the *Tory Radical*. The name cost us a lot of thought and says something about how we saw ourselves. Martin did not enter the Commons but remained in Nottingham, where he practised as a solicitor and became prominent in local government. He is close to us all and through the years has been a valued friend and supporter of his fellow Nottingham man, Kenneth Clarke.

The late JOHN TOULMIN

His Honour, John Toulmin CMG, QC.

Scholar, judge and longtime European Bar Council representative and chairman of committees.

CHRISTOPHER TUGENDHAT

MP for the City of London, 1970–6; European Commissioner and chairman and director of companies; life peer as Baron Tugendhat of Widdington. Chairman of Abbey National PLC. Director of Phillips Petroleum, National Westminster bank and other companies.

Christopher was President of the Union in 1960 and via the *Financial Times* he became MP for the City in 1970. In 1974 he joined the opposition front bench as the Shadow Minister of State in charge of European Affairs. In 1976 Mrs Thatcher came to appoint a Conservative Commissioner to Brussels and chose him. He accepted, thereby choosing a different career path and remained there from 1977 until 1985, leaving for a string of commercial appointments and an eventual seat in the Lords.

PETER VIGGERS

Sir Peter Viggers; MP for Gosport, February 1974–2010; minister; solicitor and company director.

A jet pilot during national service, this talent translated into a somewhat dashing way of driving a motor car. As chairman of CUCA, summer 1960, he was responsible for the visits of 'Rab' Butler, our then president, and perhaps more spectacularly the first visit of Sir Oswald Mosley, when he narrowly missed a jelly thrown in the face of his guest, and which landed all too near him. He went to the Northern Ireland Office as a Junior Minister for Industry but he later concentrated on defence matters as a member of the North Atlantic Assembly and on a second career in the City and at Lloyds. He subsequently had an unfortunate experience, as part of the expenses scandal of 2009, over a possible claim for an ornament for his duck pond which was not granted or even pursued, after advice from the finance office, in any event.

INDEX